Everald Compton is an 88-year-old Australian who has for all of his life had a consuming interest in the history and politics of his homeland.

This has been highlighted by the success of his bestselling book *THE MAN ON THE TWENTY DOLLAR NOTES* which tells the inspirational life story of Flynn of the Inland, pioneer of the Royal Flying Doctor Service.

He is well known as the founder of National Seniors Australia, the largest community institution in the nation advocating the needs of older Australians, and as the founder of the Inland Railway project that will link Melbourne and Darwin.

He received the Order of Australia in 1992 for his services to the community and the Centenary Medal for his services to the Transport industry.

He is an Adjunct Professor at the University of Queensland and an Honorary Senior Fellow of the University of the Sunshine Coast.

He has served as an Elder of the Uniting Church for more than six decades and for half a century has been a regular visitor to the Australian Parliament where he has many personal friends among MP's from all political parties.

In *DINNER WITH THE FOUNDING FATHERS*, he has vividly captured the drama and excitement that surrounded the creation of the Commonwealth of Australia in 1901.

He lives in Brisbane with his wife Helen.

Dedicated to Edmund Barton, the first Prime Minister of Australia.

Everald Compton

Dinner with the Founding Fathers

Austin Macauley Publishers™
LONDON • CAMBRIDGE • NEW YORK • SHARJAH

Copyright © Everald Compton (2020)

The right of Everald Compton to be identified as author of this work has been asserted by him in accordance with section 77 and 78 of the Copyright, Designs and Patents Act 1988.

All rights reserved. No part of this publication may be reproduced, stored in a retrieval system, or transmitted in any form or by any means, electronic, mechanical, photocopying, recording, or otherwise, without the prior permission of the publishers.

Any person who commits any unauthorised act in relation to this publication may be liable to criminal prosecution and civil claims for damages.

Austin Macauley is committed to publishing works of quality and integrity. In this spirit, we are proud to offer this book to our readers; however, the story, the experiences, and the words are the author's alone.

A CIP catalogue record for this title is available from the British Library.

ISBN 9781528918428 (Paperback)
ISBN 9781528918787 (ePub e-book)

www.austinmacauley.com

First Published (2020)
Austin Macauley Publishers Ltd
25 Canada Square
Canary Wharf
London
E14 5LQ

Table of Contents

Synopsis	11
Foreword By Tony Windsor	12
Creation, Crisis and Legacy	13
The Call to Federation	14
Book One – The Anniversary Dinner	15
Guests	15
Visitors	16
Eminent Absentees	16
Absent Legends	18
Historic Milestones on the Dinner Agenda	19
Host	20
A Quiet Drink in the Gun Room	22
Powerful Duo	23
Three Musketeers	25
The Huge Shadow of Andrew Clark	26
The 'Also Ran'	26
The Man from Chile	27
A Scottish Coal Miner	27
Agenda	28
The Guests Make an Entrance	30
The Premiers	30
The Believers	33
The Judge and the Reformer	36
The Bushman's Champion	39
The Prime Minister	40
Drinks	41
The Tenterfield Legend	42
Affable Alfred	51

Death of the Aristocrats	55
Minister for Five Days	58

Entrée   *59*
Lucinda Sails into History	60
Author of the Original Constitution	62
The Great Negotiator	63

Main   *65*
New South Wales Votes Twice	65
Free Settlers Have Their Say	67
Radical Federalist	68
Second Colony	68
State of Isolation	69
Kalgoorlie Saves the Day	70
Workers Versus Capitalists	72
Act of God	73
Battle of Westminster	74
Drinks at the Reform Club	75
Capitalising on the Jubilee	76
The Lure of a Republic	77
Taking a Shot at Royalty	77

Half Time   *78*
Passionate Dissenter	78
Aspirants	81
Birth of Murdoch Media	83
The Chief Justice Gets Political	86

Dessert   *87*
Hopeless Hopetoun	88
Who Was Guilty?	90
The Villain Was Affable Alfred	91
Slippery Sam Is Slammed	92
Tasmania Misses Out	93
The Great Day	94
Voters Have Their Say	95
Royals Add Their Blessing	96
Flaws in the Constitution	98

Coffee, Tea, Chocolates, Port, Cigars   *99*
How Successful Was Federation?	99
Suffragettes	101
'The Man in the Street' Takes Over	104
The Convict and the Australian Dream	104

Goodnight	*106*
Elusive Preamble	107
Creating Small States	108
Team Players	108
Cheers for Toby	109
Loner	110
Confession of Slippery Sam	111
How Do We Solve the Problem of the Senate?	113
The Believers Continue the Good Fight	115
Cheers for the Founders	118
White Australia	120
All Whites and All Blacks	124
Forgotten Fijians	127
Relentless Murdoch	127
The Essential Giles	128
Fisher Speaks for the Nation	129
Jeannie	130
Book Two – Ninety Years Later	**132**
Guests	*132*
Visitors	*132*
Towering Presence	133
The Host	*133*
The Importance of Taking Charge	134
Drinks	*135*
Arthur Phillip	136
Chairman Zelman Examines John Kerr	137
Sins of the Senate	142
Creating More States	146
Main	*148*
Sins of the Fathers	148
Indigenous Australia	150
White Australia	152
State Rights	153
The Brits	154
Coffee	*155*
The Former Chief Justice	155
Republic	158
Who Is Eligible to Sit in Parliament?	162
Changing the Constitution	163

The Search for a Preamble	165
Farewell	*166*
The Historian	168
Homeward Bound	*169*
Ponsonby	169
Old Soldiers Never Die	170
Life Was Not Meant to Be Easy	174
The Anonymous Barton	175
Book Three – Epilogue	**177**
The Challenge	*177*
Barton	178
Bird	179
Deakin	180
Fisher	182
Forrest	183
Griffith	184
Kingston	185
Lyne	186
Reid	187
Watson	188
Lucinda	189
Cowen	190
Fraser	190
Whitlam	191
Barwick and Clark	192
Giants of History	193
Book Four – End Notes	**194**
Followers of the Founding Fathers	*194*
Books on the Founding Fathers	196
Chats with the Greats	196
A Great Australian	196
Giant	197
Malcolm's Double	198
Confession	198
Memories	200
Everald's Preamble	201
Constitution	202

Synopsis

Few Australians have any knowledge of how six independent British Colonies joined together to create the Commonwealth of Australia on 1st January, 1901.

It had taken the Founding Fathers of Australia 13 years of constant and difficult negotiations among themselves and with the British Parliament to agree on a constitution for the new nation, hold referendums to approve it and convince Queen Victoria to sign off on it all.

There was high drama involved and much politics, all of which combine to provide a fascinating tale about the incredible people who achieved it all.

I have decided that, to capture the interest of modern Australians, it is best to tell the tale via an historical novel which is loyal to the facts of history and in keeping with the known character traits and political beliefs of those who made it happen.

So, I have assembled ten of the most influential men who made it all happen (alas, no women were allowed to take part in any of the negotiating conventions).

The Founding Fathers meet for dinner at the Melbourne Club on the evening of 1st January, 1911, ten years to the day after Federation occurred.

It is hosted by the first Prime Minister, Edmund Barton. His guests are Samuel Griffith, Andrew Fisher, Alfred Deakin, George Read, William Lyne, Charles Kingston, John Forrest, Chris Watson and Stafford Bird.

Throughout the evening, they review their 13 years as nation builders and how the first decade of Federation had actually worked out. It is a compelling story.

Then, the book moves on another 90 years to when I have Zelman Cowen hosting a lunch in Sydney with Gough Whitlam and Malcolm Fraser on the occasion of the Centenary of Federation. Cowen questions their actions in November 1975 when the coup to remove Whitlam as prime minister almost destroyed the work of the Founding Fathers who would never have approved of what was done that day.

The book concludes with factual accounts of the fascinating lives of the Founding Fathers after Federation so that readers can gain a clearer picture of the lives of these nation builders.

DINNER WITH THE FOUNDING FATHERS reads like a thriller as it tells the tale of one of the great events of world history.

EVERALD COMPTON

Foreword
By Tony Windsor

Australia's political history, together with the lingering impacts of decisions made by previous generations and how they resonate today and shape the current debates about our future, is brought together in Everald Compton's engrossing novel which he has called *DINNER WITH THE FOUNDING FATHERS*. The journey explores the political players and the structures developed to make Australia the modern nation it is today as seen through the eyes of a man who has known every prime minister since Menzies and walked the halls of power for over 60 years.

In the fascinating setting of a fictional dinner ten years after Australia became a federation, Everald has produced an exciting glimpse of the characters involved in forging our unique modern history. He traces the early efforts to unite the states, the debates, the arguments, the personal animosities and friendships formed by common purpose, as well as the all-pervading influence of England in the context of discussions these leaders may well have had at a reunion dinner.

Book One allows the reader to look past the portraits of bearded men and see them as real people with human strengths and frailties, their personal lives as well as their political lives and the extraordinary contribution they made to this nation. Rather than see these men as senior citizens, it highlights the relative youth of some of these 'Fathers' when they embarked on achieving their vision for one Australia rather than individual states.

It demonstrates the compromises that were made to overcome the feared dominance of New South Wales and the tactical skills as well as legal skills required in the writing of our constitution. Agreeing to have an equal number of senators from each state in the parliament, even though the populations were quite different, is a good example of what had to be done to achieve an outcome.

Everald, in Book Two, fast forwards 100 years after Federation to another fictional gathering where Gough Whitlam, Malcolm Fraser and Zelman Cowen, and their guests, look back on the achievements and failings of various governments. It embraces the 1975 Whitlam Dismissal and the crisis it created, while exploring the likely thoughts of the Founding Fathers on the use of the Constitution to dismiss an elected Government. The role of the Senate once again comes into focus with questions asked regarding the original vision of a States House of Review as part of the required compromise to get the states to agree to Federation and the way in which it evolved into a far more partisan entity.

This book celebrates our history in a fashion where those are not normally attracted to historical documents can engage and learn from the past. It also poses some of the unfinished business that still stains our history and our present, the appropriate recognition of the first Australians being one. In the context of the time, it is perhaps understandable that, to achieve an outcome given the political structures of the day, that including Aboriginal Australians in the Constitution may have been a deal breaker, but it is almost unbelievable that, in today's context, our current political fathers have still not rectified this situation through constitutional recognition.

I have known and worked with Everald Compton for 25 years. He is a man of many facets. Having run a successful international fundraising consultancy for forty years, he has since been an important player in the fields of infrastructure and ageing policy and is living proof that progressive thinking and innovation are not the prerogatives of the young.

In his 88th year, I fondly call him Australia's oldest teenager. His love of rural Australia is a reflection of his upbringing and an attachment to those who developed the inland. He has been the driving force behind the Melbourne to Brisbane Inland rail project.

The lesson I take from Everald's contribution to political life is one that both he and the Founding Fathers were able to master – that it is possible to achieve success in developing political policy by dealing with, and being inclusive of, all sides of politics, a capacity that is sadly lacking in today's world, but sorely needed if today's leaders are going to address the big issues of our future.

Everald has had, and still has, the capacity to walk into the offices of Prime Ministers, Premiers, Ministers, Opposition leaders, MPs and engage on key issues. He has successfully defied the left/right tags of convenience that dominate today's political scene and is respected personally and intellectually for his wisdom. A great Australian.

He is a son I am sure the Founding Fathers would have been honoured to have dined with, especially if they were able to read his respectful account of their personal history in Book Three.

Tony Windsor
Former Independent Member of the New South Wales and Australian Parliaments for 25 years

Creation, Crisis and Legacy

You are about to enjoy a political thriller.

It is told in four powerful books in one volume.

The incredible legend of the Founding Fathers of Australia, heroes like no others, is relived in a manner that will stir your national pride.

First is the fascinating tale of their extraordinary Federation achievement which took just twelve years to come to triumphant fruition in 1901.

They drafted a Constitution and then gained the agreement of six state parliaments to hold the successful referendums that approved it.

Then, they took it to London to have laws passed by the Imperial Parliament at Westminster that would give it legal status, as well as gaining the blessing of Queen Victoria in the difficult final years of her pompous reign.

The result was the creation of Australia.

At this moment, it had a population of just three and a half million people who laid the foundations of a nation which would become one of the top twenty in the world in terms of liveability and economic and social stability, accompanied by a fundamentally honest practice of democracy.

Second investigates an almost unbelievable political coup staged by a drunken governor general in 1975 who removed from office a democratically elected Prime Minister who had received a Vote of Confidence from the House of Representatives on the very day of his sacking.

It was a disgraceful misuse of naked power that was never ever envisaged by the Founding Fathers and would have shocked them to the core.

It unleashed upon Australia a long era of political uncertainty and instability driven by an undemocratically elected Senate that has continued an irresponsible rampage of legislative chaos ever since.

The upside is that a door has been opened to an opportunity for significant upgrades to be made to the Constitution which was so carefully prepared by the pioneers of the new nation in a totally different era.

This challenge will bring forth a new breed of Founding Fathers (and Founding Mothers this time) to step forward with the same skill, courage and commitment as those who worked together so splendidly in 1901.

This is a huge call awaiting a brave and visionary response.

Third is an entertaining account of what happened in the remaining years of the lives of the Founding Fathers, plus those who were participants in the drama of 1975, together with those who perpetuate their memory.

It is a legacy that must never be allowed to die.

Fourth contains some pertinent and provocative reminiscences of my own experiences of Australian history gained over 88 years of life as a proud Aussie who grew up in an economically poor family in a tiny timber town where the Methodist Church sought unsuccessfully to be the cornerstone of the society that the Founding Fathers had created.

EVERALD COMPTON
April, 2020

The Call to Federation

"We are a nation for a continent and a continent for a nation."
"One people. One destiny."

Book One
The Anniversary Dinner

At the Melbourne Club on 1st January, 1911, a dinner is held to celebrate the tenth anniversary of the Federation of Australian States.

It is the most prestigious dinner held anywhere in Australia on that New Year's Day which happened to be a Sunday.

Guests

The ten attendees are formidable characters whom you will never forget.

EDMUND BARTON, 61, Barrister

First Prime Minister of Australia. Justice of the High Court of Australia. Former Minister and Speaker of the New South Wales Parliament. Affable host of the dinner.

ALFRED DEAKIN, 54, Barrister

Prime Minister of Australia on three occasions. Former Minister of the Victorian Parliament. The nation's finest orator. Superb negotiator. Renowned spiritualist.

SAMUEL GRIFFITH, 65, Solicitor and Barrister

Chief Justice of the High Court of Australia. Former Chief Justice of the Supreme Court of Queensland. Former Premier of Queensland. Eminent Constitutional Lawyer with a low level of tolerance.

GEORGE REID, 64, Barrister

Former Premier of New South Wales. First Leader of the Opposition in the Australian Parliament. Fourth Prime Minister of Australia. Powerful advocate of Free Trade. Delightful raconteur.

JOHN FORREST, 63, Surveyor

First Premier of Western Australia. Constantly unsuccessful aspirant to be Prime Minister of Australia. Legendary explorer of Inland Australia.

CHARLES KINGSTON, 58, Barrister

Former Premier of South Australia. Minister in the first Australian Parliament. Radical liberal politician. First State Premier to legislate to grant women the right to vote. Infamous philanderer.

WILLIAM LYNE, 66, Farmer

Premier of New South Wales at time of Federation. Long-time failed aspirant to be Prime Minister of Australia. Goulburn farmer, regularly at war with his peers.

ANDREW FISHER, 48, Labourer and Miner

Prime Minister of Australia at the time of the dinner. Former Member of the Queensland Parliament. One-time child labourer in coal mines of Scotland. Self-made man of huge determination.

JOHN WATSON, 43, Dedicated Trade Union Leader.

Third Prime Minister of Australia for a short term of just four months. One of the Founders of the Australian Labor Party who was the first member of their party to become Prime Minister. Indeed, the first Trade Union Prime Minister anywhere in the world.

BOLTON STAFFORD BIRD, 70, Clergyman and Farmer

Long-term member of the Tasmanian Parliament. Former Leader of the Opposition in Tasmania. Tasmanian delegate to the original Federal Council of Australia and the 1891 Federation Constitutional Convention. Distinguished Minister of the Congregational Church.

Visitors

HENRTY BOURNES HIGGINS, Member of First Australian Parliament.

Subsequently appointed Justice of High Court of Australia. Reforming Socialist. Influential public figure.

KEITH MURDOCH, Freelance Journalist from Melbourne.

Gradually acquired a significant portfolio of newspapers. His son, Rupert, built on his achievements to turn it into one of the world's major media empires.

DAVID SYME, Publisher and part owner of the Melbourne Age.

Regarded as the most influential leader of the press in his era. Staunch opponent of Federation. He was concerned that it would lead to the implementation of Free Trade and thus foster the widening of inequality in the new nation. Strong defender of the rights of the working classes and small farmers. He was not a member of the Labor Party, nor a Trade Union.

THOMAS SEDDON, Son of the former Prime Minister of New Zealand, Richard Seddon.

His father was in power when the New Zealand Parliament voted not to participate in the Federation of Australian States, mainly due to the vastly unequal citizenship status of Maoris and Aborigines. The former had voting rights in New Zealand whereas Indigenous Australians had none and, at that point in history, had little hope of gaining them.

GILES, the Butler.

The only fictional character in this book. But, his position as Butler is not fictional. In 1911, no club in the British Empire could operate without its Giles.

Eminent Absentees

Fifteen key figures of Australian history heavily impacted on the dialogue at the dinner.

JOSEPH CHAMBERLAIN, Colonial Secretary of the British Parliament in London.

Masterminded the drafting of the Australian Federation Legislation and managed its successful passage through the Imperial Parliament at Westminster.

ANDREW INGLIS CLARK, Tasmanian Parliamentarian and Lawyer.

Drafted the original Constitution that Sir Samuel Griffith used as the basis for negotiations at the 1891 Federation Convention. Based the wording of it on his experience of travelling to Canada, the United States and Britain to meet constitutional lawyers.

DANIEL DENIEHY, son of an Irish convict.

His brilliant oratory defeated a determined attempt by William Charles Wentworth to establish an aristocracy in New South Wales who would have become foundation members of a local House of Lords. His subsequent life was a tragedy. He died an alcoholic at age 37.

JAMES DICKSON, Premier of Queensland.

Led the Yes Campaign to a narrow victory for his state in the Federation Referendum. Sworn in as a Minister in Barton's first Cabinet, he died several days later. Buried at the Nundah Cemetery in Brisbane.

ROBERT GARRAN, efficient organiser of Federation Constitutional Conventions.

Faithful recorder of historic events and first public servant of the Australian Government.

WILLIAM GROOM, Member for Darling Downs in the First Federal Parliament.

Gave the first speech by a backbencher at the inaugural sitting of the Parliament in May,1901. Selected for this honour because he was the oldest person in the Parliament, he was part of the national folklore, being a former convict who had been sent to Australia after he was found guilty of embezzlement in England. Subsequently gaining his freedom, he quickly fell foul of the law once more, serving a three years' jail sentence for libel. Redeemed himself to become a very successful business man in Toowoomba, including ownership of the Toowoomba Chronicle. Died shortly after making his famous speech. Replaced as MP by his son.

LORD HOPETOUN, First Governor General of Australia.

Member of the British aristocracy, he had formerly served without distinction as Governor of Victoria and was Queen Victoria's surprising choice to be her representative in the new nation. It was yet another indication of her dislike of colonials. Created an embarrassing fiasco over the appointment of Australia's first Prime Minister. Resigned in a rage after a dispute with the Government over his salary and expenses. Few regretted his departure.

ISAAC ISAACS, Barrister

Strongly opposed Federation. Then readily accepted appointment as a Justice of the High Court of Australia despite also opposing its establishment. Became the first Australian-born Governor General in 1931. He was the first person of Jewish descent to receive this honour, but was a noted opponent of the Zionist Movement for an independent Jewish State in the Holy Land.

PETER LALOR, Leader of the rebellion at the Eureka Stockade.

This revolt was the first attempt by Australians to gain independence from England. Lost an arm in that battle. Subsequently won election to Victorian Parliament where he was elected unopposed as Speaker of that Parliament. Inspired the creation of the Republican Movement in Australia.

QUEEN VICTORIA, pompous British Sovereign.

One of the last acts of her long reign was to reluctantly sign the Bill to approve the establishment of the Commonwealth of Australia. She was not impressed with the disrespectful attitude and rough culture of Australians.

JOHN DUNMORE LANG, Presbyterian clergyman.

He chartered three ships (*Fortitude, Chasely* and *Lima*) to carry Protestant Christians from Scotland to Queensland as free settlers, along with himself and his family. Years later, he moved to New South Wales where he became a powerful partner of Henry Parkes in a failed endeavour, prior to Federation, to make New South Wales a Republic.

LOUISE LAWSON, Suffragette.

She lived at Mudgee in New South Wales from where she became a strong backer of Federation. Mother of poet, Henry Lawson. Publisher of a number of influential magazines.

HENRY PARKES,

Five times Premier of New South Wales.

Had the distinction of being declared a bankrupt on three separate occasions. Widely regarded as the Father of Federation, having powerfully inspired the Federation Movement with an historic speech at Tenterfield in northern New South Wales in 1889. Died in 1896, four years before his goal would be achieved. Father of 18 children from three marriages.

JOHN QUICK, MP in Federal Parliament from 1901 to 1913.

Former Member of Victorian Parliament. Leader of the 1893 Corowa Federation Conference which agreed that non-politicians should hold 50% of places at future Conferences and Constitutional Conventions. Vindictive political opponents made sure that he was never appointed to a ministry after Federation. A huge waste of talent.

HELEN SPENCE, Legendary suffragette from South Australia.

Powerful influence in gaining voting rights for women in her home state prior to Federation. Significantly, South Australians were the only women who voted at any Federation Referendum. In the other five states, only males voted. To make matters worse, in some of the states, there was not even universal franchise for males. Voting in some cases was limited only to property owners. Everywhere, voting was voluntary and only about half of all eligible voters ever bothered to vote.

Absent Legends

A prestigious lobby group, a fine ship and an historic building were also prominent subjects of discussion.

AUSTRALIAN NATIVES ASSOCIATION, an all-male movement with huge political clout.

To become a member, you must have been born in Australia, unless you had made the mistake of being born an aboriginal, thereby making you ineligible. They regarded themselves as the prime powerhouse of Federation, constantly seeking independence from 'the mother country'. The association still exists today as a financial cooperative based in Melbourne and operating under the name of Australian Unity (formerly Manchester Unity).

LUCINDA, beautifully appointed ship owned by the Government of Queensland

Barton, Kingston and Griffith sailed on her from Sydney harbour to spend a weekend on the Hawkesbury River in 1891 to work on redrafting Andrew Clark's proposed Constitution. It was a journey that forged a new government for an entire continent, arguably the most famous cruise in the history of the nation.

Lucinda also carried the Duke and Duchess of York into Port Melbourne when they arrived to open the First Australian Parliament in May, 1901. Her prime task at other times was to carry Queensland Premiers on visits to coastal cities.

TENTERFIELD SCHOOL OF ARTS, venue of the Federation Speech.

Henry Parkes gave his great oration there on 24 October, 1889. It is recognised as a national shrine even though few Australians have made a visit to it. Indeed, very few know how Federation actually occurred.

Historic Milestones on the Dinner Agenda

1888 – Federal Council of Australia is established by legislation passed in the Westminster Parliament as a first step towards Federation. New Zealand and Fiji participate. New South Wales declines, thereby rendering the Council to be a disastrous error that stymied any hope of Federation.

1889 – Henry Parkes makes an historic speech on Federation at Tenterfield in Northern New South Wales which reignites the fires of Federation.

1891 – First Constitutional Convention is held in Sydney. Accepts in principle the Constitution drafted on *Lucinda*.

1893 – Corowa Conference on Federation. New Zealand and Fiji withdraw.

1896 – Death of Sir Henry Parkes.

1897 – Second Constitutional Convention held in Adelaide.

1898 – Additional meetings of the Convention held in Melbourne and Sydney to determine extra constitutional clauses put forward by the states.

1899 – Referendums held successfully in all states.

1900 – Westminster Parliament approves Federation after protracted negotiations in London at which Barton, Deakin and Kingston represented Australia.

November, 1900 – Lord Hopetoun arrives in Australia to become Governor General. Ineptly and inappropriately, he invites William Lyne to be the first Prime Minister. Lyne then declines the invitation after an extremely hostile rejection by other Federation leaders.

Christmas Day, 1900 – Edmund Barton appointed Prime Minister and establishes first ministry in seven days without the benefit of a telephone.

1 January, 1901 – Federation declared. Barton Government sworn in. Nationwide celebrations held.

1 March, 1901 – First Federal Election held. Barton's Prime Ministership is confirmed by the voters.

17 May, 1901 – Duke of York, later King George V, opens first sitting of Federal Parliament in Melbourne.

1903 – High Court of Australia is established with Sir Samuel Griffith appointed as First Chief Justice.

1975 – Governor General John Kerr makes a huge misinterpretation of the intentions of the Founding Fathers. He dismisses Gough Whitlam from his democratically elected role as Prime Minister by empowering the Senate to become anarchists. The Australian Constitution is diminished by the event.

Host

Edmund Barton walked from his office at the High Court of Australia to the Melbourne Club at the 'Paris End' of Collins Street in the twilight of a warm New Year's Day that celebrated the arrival of the year 1911 and opened the door to the second decade of the life of the Australian nation.

He had spent the day in the company of his devoted wife, Jeannie, making brief appearances at several functions that celebrated the New Year and which he deemed to be the most important and interesting of the many invitations he had received.

Being a Sunday, he and Jeannie had firstly attended morning worship at St Paul's Anglican Cathedral before moving on to more relaxed activities.

Some of them were the usual New Year picnics at which almost everyone boasted of the visionary and impractical resolutions they vowed to achieve in the year ahead.

Nevertheless, there were some special events that acknowledged the important fact that Australia had been a nation for exactly ten years and Barton had been heavily involved in making this happen. Indeed, without him, it would never have happened. The memory of it all, together with the public recognition of his role, had made it a rather pleasant day.

Friends took Jeannie back to their home thus enabling him to go directly to his office at the High Court. There, he managed to make good use of a spare hour in the late afternoon to take the refreshing nap.

He needed it to revive his ageing frame ready for an important and potentially controversial evening engagement. Then, after a change of clothing suitable to the conservative requirements of the Melbourne Club, he carefully collected a special file of notes he had prepared on matters he planned to discuss at the dinner and purposefully set out towards his destination.

As he strolled along, he was in a happy and contented frame of mind. Unlike the prime ministers of the 21st century, he neither had, nor needed, a police escort.

He looked forward with considerable enthusiasm to hosting an historic dinner with his colleagues who had together provided the leadership that had brought the nation of Australia into being.

Personally, it was also a memorable date in his life as it was the anniversary of the day on which he became the first Prime Minister of Australia, a proud achievement that no one could ever surpass. There could be only one person who was first and he treasured the honour.

It would have intrigued him to know that, over the following century, very few of his successors as prime minister would follow his example and resign their post as a time of their own choosing. They did not have his skill of determining when their time was up. He chose the dignity of the High Court over the indignity of political oblivion.

Of course, his political opponents had happily voted to elevate him to the court so they could then fight over who would succeed him, a battle that Alfred Deakin had won easily.

After just a few minutes, he reached the august building which had been designed to replicate the architecture of the long era of Queen Victoria.

It was exactly 6.00pm.

Pausing for a moment, he took in the conservative look of the building and noted that it really did have an appearance very much in the style of the fine old clubs of London. Then, he pondered the influential role of this grand old club in Australian politics. For the first decade of Federation, the Melbourne Club had proudly and vainly occupied the centre of power for Australian democracy.

The Victorian Parliament, one block away, had been vacated graciously by its MPs so the Federal Parliament could occupy it until such time as it was able to fulfil the constitutional requirement that it find a permanent home in a territory to be allocated by New South Wales, not closer to Sydney than 100 miles.

Right from the first day of the first sitting of Parliament in May, 1901, it became a tradition for honourable members to gather at the Melbourne Club in small groups for breakfast, morning tea, lunch, afternoon tea, drinks, dinner and nightcaps while they discussed and planned legislative compromises that were fundamental to the task of keeping the nation moving forward.

This was quite an undertaking as there had been minority governments for the entire decade that followed, so the effectiveness of the parliament depended on consensus being achieved on every day of every sitting. The sealing of all of those political agreements had been more than just a cosmetic success. The record showed that the new parliament had created an impressive collection of landmark legislation which laid the foundations of a basic structure that enabled Australia to function effectively and move forward as a nation.

In his consideration of all this, it did not occur to Barton that it was in any way odd that such political power had been exercised in the smoke-filled rooms of a club which was a hallowed venue for gatherings of only the upper crust of the nation. That 99% of Australians were not permitted to pass through its doors, was simply a fact of the class distinction that dominated Australia at that time. Nor did he think that it was in any way demeaning that wives of members were not allowed to enter the Club without being accompanied by their husbands or another male designated by him.

Also significant was that no Aborigine could enter. Very few of them would have wanted to go there anyway, an attitude that would prevail into the 21st century, and perhaps beyond.

Alas, these aberrations were the heritage of colonial Australia. In the course of history, they would simply fade slowly away.

Barton had invited his guests to arrive at 6.30pm for drinks prior to dinner which was scheduled for 7.00pm. This meant that he now had a quiet half hour in which he could get his mind into gear as to how he would control the inevitably spirited debates that would occur among the nine strong-willed characters who would join him.

Normally, the Club did not open on Sundays, but it did so on this occasion as many members had wanted to celebrate the arrival of the New Year. Barton had taken advantage of this in arranging the date and venue of his dinner.

He opened the heavy ornate door that guarded the Club.

In keeping with the finest traditions of this very British institution, the butler greeted him warmly and respectfully.

A Quiet Drink in the Gun Room

"Good Evening, Sir Edmund. It is indeed a great privilege for me to greet you and welcome you once more to the finest club in the Empire.

Especially so on the day of such an historic occasion when our nation celebrates its tenth birthday and is rightly honouring those who founded it with well-deserved accolades."

"Thank you, Giles. It certainly is an appropriate moment to celebrate Federation. My fervent expectation is that this will be an evening I will long remember. Thus, I intend to do all in my power to ensure that it will be a grand success and that my guests will enjoy it immensely. With you managing the proceedings for me, it could not possibly be otherwise."

"Thank you for your confidence, Sir Edmund. I have no doubt that it will be a very special night that will exceed your hopes for it, and I am honoured to have a humble role in the careful organisation of it. The manager has had our entire team working diligently on decorating the lounge and the private dining room to perfection and the chef has worked his heart out planning, preparing and cooking a superb menu. You will be impressed with what he has achieved. He has magnificent culinary skills."

"Splendid. I am grateful."

"As you are a little early, Sir, can I prepare a wee dram for you to enjoy while you await your guests? I have a superbly aged Talisker from the Isle of Skye, distilled right at the very spot where Bonnie Prince Charlie hid from the British Army."

"That will be delightful, Giles. Queen Victoria held the same low opinion of the Bonnie Prince as she had of Deakin, Kingston and me when we sought a degree of independence for her colonial subjects who she thought of as being somewhat uncouth.

"Could I suggest that you find me a peaceful corner where I can be alone for a while as I quietly review the manner in which I will conduct the proceedings of the evening?"

"The Gun Room will be just the place, Sir. I will ensure that no one else goes there."

Barton walked up the stairs to the hallowed Gun Room which was devoted to perpetuating memories of the days when all British gentlemen proudly owned and used superb guns. There Giles served him a substantial Talisker, knowing that the great man did not look kindly upon tame drinks.

Fondly known to the nation as 'Toss Pot Toby', Edmund Barton's capacity to enjoy fine food and even finer drinks was legendary, as was his amazing ability to remain sober at all times. His fine legal brain and his formidable negotiating skills were similarly the spice of legend. Without them, the Australian continent would still be governed by six separate fiefdoms fuelled by an unfathomable range of intense parochial attitudes that would have significantly retarded progress.

Edmund, who preferred everyone to call him Toby as it clearly allied him with his reputation, had developed a sentimental attachment to his nickname and joked about it often when in the company of friends. Now, as he pondered his guest list for the evening, he recalled that many of them had nicknames also, a tribute to the fond regard in which the nation held them. This was not surprising as these were the leaders who had made Australia possible.

There were nine invitees on his carefully chosen guest list, inevitably, all male.

It had not occurred to him that it would have been socially and democratically appropriate for one or two women to have been present, given the undeniable statistic that they now accounted for almost 50% of the population even though they had been heavily outnumbered by males in the early years of European settlement. Their absence tonight was predictable. Even so, the Melbourne Club could not fail to acknowledge that Australia had legislated for suffrage for women well ahead of USA and the United Kingdom, neither of whom even had the subject on their political agenda as a possible thought at this point in history.

Be this as it may, Toby got down to serious business.

Powerful Duo

The first two men on his invitation list were the ones whom Barton considered to be the real power brokers who, with him, forged the deal that established the nation.

He was very correct in making this assumption. Most Australians were of the same view.

Samuel Griffith of Queensland and Alfred Deakin of Victoria were revered figures of legend.

As he quietly savoured gentle sips of his wee dram, his thoughts now pondered on their illustrious careers. They were formidable human beings, born leaders with all the personal flaws that are a powerful, perhaps essential, element in the successful exercise of leadership skills.

Barton was very aware that Griffith was recognised nationally as the architect of the constitution, with a God-like status.

Indeed, he had an enormous influence on the original and the final wording, but he was the architect not the originator. This was a fact he had never openly acknowledged. The truth was that he had effectively plagiarised the very thoughtful work of lesser known lawyers who had willingly given their painstaking work to him in what was a considerable act of patriotism.

The prime drafter was Andrew Inglis Clark of Tasmania who had travelled extensively overseas to study other constitutions and undertake research to determine how effective they had been in actual practice. To a lesser extent, John Quick of Victoria had similarly made a significant contribution. In addition, both had laid the foundations for the success of the Corowa People's Convention which effectively revived the cause of Federation after it had slumped into the doldrums.

From his long association with Griffith as a fellow Justice of the High Court of Australia, Toby was conscious of the fact that Griffith was noted for his considerable exercise of ego and his extraordinarily deep-seated jealousy of the achievement of others. This caused him to conveniently disregard Clark and Quick as he saw them as a threat to his stature as the giant of Federation. In fact, he saw Toby as a threat to his place in history.

Additionally, his agile political manoeuvring in his days as Premier of Queensland had earned him the unflattering title of 'Slippery Sam'.

But Barton knew with certainty that, without Griffith's formidable character and his personal stature as an eminently respected judge and barrister, the wording of a constitution would never have been agreed. It was an achievement that earned him the appointment as the first Chief Justice of the High Court of Australia in 1903, a position to which Barton himself had aspired while he was still in office as prime minister. He still harboured this ambition if and when Griffith ever got around to retiring, a thought that did not appear to be in the remotest corners of the mind of the Chief Justice.

Barton had a feeling that tonight's guests would not be averse to the thought of going out of their way to humble Griffith if the opportunity arose. He could not recall any of them ever making a serious effort to develop a friendship with Griffith even though they often sought his advice on legislation that they wanted to get through parliament.

The host's view of Deakin was hugely different to his thoughts about Slippery Sam. He had enormous respect for Deakin as a person, even though they were poles apart politically.

Barton was a quiet Conservative while Deakin was a vocal 'dyed in the wool' Liberal who approached every challenge with enormous personal passion.

Alfred had been almost solely responsible for bringing Victoria into the Federation, despite heavy opposition from influential community groups, particularly among Jewish people led by Sir Isaac Isaacs who wanted a more democratic constitution and the 'Melbourne Age', masterminded compellingly by David Syme, who wanted a society that would eradicate inequality.

Deakin had even overcome the negativity in the minds of voters that was generated by the high degree of suspicion that Victorians had of anything that had its origins in New South Wales, a monumental task indeed.

What fascinated Barton, who himself was a nominally traditional Christian, was that Deakin was an ardent spiritualist. He was a student of all religions and passionately believed that he was guided by a power beyond himself. He had spent many hours trying to identify the source of that power as he had huge difficulty in discovering its source in any of the major religions, especially Christianity. Their God was a lesser one than he envisaged God to be.

Baffling as his dilemma was to many of his friends and enemies, Deakin's spiritual power was a dynamic force in achieving Federation. Once he decided that Federation was the will of 'God', it became a mission that could not be denied, even though he had never in his entire life ever personally discovered the real 'God'. He was empowered by his search for the ground of his being.

In thinking about Deakin, Barton reminded himself that, at this moment in the short history of the nation, Deakin was the only person who had become prime minister three times and he had achieved it within the first ten years of Federation. He was a superb orator, the best Barton had ever heard, and he anticipated that Deakin would eloquently lead many of the debates that would take place at the dinner table tonight. He had an inbuilt mechanism to generate electricity.

He would be pleasant about it too. His nickname was 'Affable Alfred'. But this title was not quite as memorable as 'Toss Pot Toby'. But it was more noble than 'Slippery Sam'.

Three Musketeers

Barton's thoughts moved on to the three great interstate rivals who would be joining him for dinner.

They were George Reid of New South Wales, John Forrest from Western Australia and Charles Kingston who hailed from South Australia.

All of them had been powerful state premiers in the years leading to Federation and each one stoutly defended the rights of his own state in planning how Federation would happen, although Kingston was a profound believer in Federation at all costs. Reid, forever a politician first and a statesman second, had switched sides several times as public enthusiasm about Federation waxed and waned. Forrest was a late starter because Western Australia had become a state only in 1890 and he had to contend with some pessimistic opposition from those in the West who had a profound suspicion of all Easterners. However, all three had emphatically delivered the goods in the end.

The trio also enjoyed the good life as their rotund figures betrayed. Even Barton was a little leaner than any of them despite his unsurpassed love of wining and dining.

Now, Barton recalled the fear that smaller states had of the strong possibility that New South Wales and Victoria would dominate them. This had caused Forrest and Kingston to demand that the senate must have equal numbers from each state, a proposal that had not impressed Reid who had declared that they were behaving like frightened mice. But he gave up the battle when they declared the issue to be non-negotiable. It was one of the few issues of all the constitutional negotiations that had provided no capacity for compromise.

Toby had no doubt that these three would renew that debate tonight, quite vigorously especially as Reid had attained the office of prime minister for a year, while Forrest and Kingston had been denied this honour.

The Huge Shadow of Andrew Clark

Few Tasmanians had caused headlines similar to those generated by Reid and other giants during the tumultuous Federation Referendums.

Except for Andrew Clark.

He had commenced drafting the constitution many years before Griffith ever thought of it. Only his poor health had caused him not to have a more dominant role in its final wording. Then, tragically, he had died in 1904. Barton knew that his presence tonight would have placed a huge restraint on the ego of Griffith. Clark had magnificently earned the right to be present, but, alas, it was not to be.

So, Toby had invited a revered Tasmanian, Bolton Stafford Bird, in his place.

Bird was a thoroughly reliable citizen of the Apple Isle who had represented his state on the short-lived Federal Council, then at the first major Constitution Convention that had approved Griffith's working document in 1891. He had then consistently supported Federation all the way in the Tasmanian Parliament, as well as in the Referendum in which Tasmania had produced the strongest Yes vote of any state.

It was of particular interest to Toby that he was an eminent Congregational clergyman who would set an ethical tone to the meeting, as well as provide a solid example of sobriety. Barton planned to ask him to comment on the importance of the separation of church and state, something that Westminster itself had failed to master when it allowed kings and queens to have the additional title and power of Head of the Church of England.

Toby expected that Griffith would have something to say at this point as his father had been an influential Congregational Minister.

The 'Also Ran'

Reluctantly, Toby gave a thought or two to William Lyne.

Unforgettably, he was a former Premier of New South Wales (and a long-time political rival of George Reid). The founding Governor General, Lord

Hopetoun, had invited Lyne to be the first prime minister, preferring him to Barton.

Thankfully, Hopetoun had been forced to quickly withdraw the commission in favour of Barton when no one of stature, absolutely no one, would join a Lyne Ministry. In particular, Deakin had strenuously opposed it. This meant that Lyne bore no goodwill towards either Deakin or Barton.

However, Toby felt that he had no option but to invite him tonight as he had been the cause of the nation's first major political crisis.

It was appropriate that there should be a frank discussion tonight about how this fiasco had been handled.

The Man from Chile

The next guest was a man whom Toby respected as a genuine political pioneer.

Until 1904, there had been no nation in the world that had elected a Labor Party Prime Minister. John Watson had achieved this honour when he became Australia's third prime minister, following Barton and Deakin. For this reason, he would also be joining tonight's festivities even though he had recently resigned his seat in Parliament, realising that his days of political power were ebbing away.

Watson, who preferred to be called Chris, rather than John, had ruled for only four months before losing a vote of confidence that had been cunningly masterminded by Reid.

In addition to his status as a former prime minister, Barton had especially invited him to dinner because his Labor Party had strongly opposed Federation. Watson and his colleagues had staunchly held the view that Federation was an initiative of the upper classes to create nationwide trading monopolies that would make more money for themselves, doing so at the expense of most Australians especially low-paid workers.

Nevertheless, after voters approved Federation, Watson had loyally accepted the decision in a manner that all profound believers in democracy should do. He then dedicated his parliamentary career to ensuring that the new parliament did not implement what he considered to be unbridled capitalism.

Barton pondered how interesting it would be to hear what he had to say tonight about his powerful battle to stop Federation. He intended to ask him a direct question on the matter, confident that he would get an equally direct answer that would generate a lively discourse.

A Scottish Coal Miner

Finally, Barton had invited the currently reigning prime minister, Andrew Fisher, whose early life in the coal mines of his homeland of Scotland was now part of legend.

Toby was very aware that Fisher had taken no direct part in the constitutional conventions that had been held in the 1890s, but he had been elected to the first

Parliament in 1901 as one of the Queensland MPs, representing a state that had been very reluctant to join a Federation of States and had voted only narrowly to participate.

Fisher, after taking over the leadership from Watson, had in 1910 led the Labor Party to an astounding victory. His government was the first since Federation to have a majority in its own right. He now had the task of leading the fledgling nation into its second decade and Toby wanted to give him the opportunity to give an outline of his plans for the remainder of his term of office.

Agenda

Giles quietly refilled Barton's glass as the chief Founding Father pondered the programme for the evening, thus ensuring that it ceased to be a wee dram. But Toby's personal history revealed that he had never in his life ever been content with just a wee dram.

The agenda had a logical simplicity.

Once drinks were served to his guests and the usual goodwill chatter was over, Toby would call for a toast to Henry Parkes who had ignited the Federation Movement with his famous Tenterfield speech of 1889, but had died before his dream could finally be achieved.

Even though he and Parkes had differed mightily and often down the years over Parkes' wild and reckless decision-making processes, Barton was of the opinion that it would be quite improper to proceed with tonight's dinner without prominent recognition of the old warrior and his undeniable role in the creation of Australia.

With the serving of the entrée, Toby planned that the drafting and negotiating of the constitution at two Federation Constitutional Conventions and several other national conferences would be reviewed critically.

Highlighted amongst all of this would be the momentous weekend of negotiations on the *Lucinda* as it cruised the Hawkesbury River.

What could have been done better during the twelve tumultuous years it had taken to gain agreement to a constitution? Could they have been made it more acceptable and workable for the long term, instead of working to ensure that it would be politically saleable to voters when the vital referendums were held? Had it been a case where they did all that was necessary to achieve the basics of a working federation and hoped then to try to improve it later, coping with all the usual difficulties of doing that. As many a woman will attest, it is not possible to improve a husband after a marriage.

He had it in mind that the main course would be a time to chat about the referendums that each state held to approve Federation.

Barton vividly remembered that it went right down to the wire in both Queensland and Western Australia, while New South Wales had to conduct two votes before getting it through. Only a handful of votes saved the day across the entire continent. Opponents of Federation had claimed that its closeness meant that it was a denial of democracy for Federation to proceed with almost half of those who voted being opposed to it. In addition, one in three of those eligible to vote did not do so. Added to this must be the many thousands of ineligible voters, such as women and all indigenous Australians, who were not asked for their opinion.

This made Toby admit to himself that, in reality, it was fair to say that no more than 25% of Australians had said YES to Federation.

Be this as it may, he had, at the time, decided to ignore the critics.

Small though the winning number of votes may have been, they gave authority for the successful negotiations in London to begin and thus gain approval from Her Majesty and her loyal government to proceed with Federation. He would enjoy a discussion about this as it would bring back many memories of his leadership of the Australian delegation that had spent several months in painstaking negotiations before winning the long battle with Westminster. They had finally agreed that it could be possible for colonials to act as responsible citizens.

His planning provided for a short break before dessert, mainly for a pit stop for the heavy drinkers, but also to allow a few private discussions to take place.

Then, while enjoying the sweet delicacy that the chef had delectably prepared, there would be a time to remember how they organised the grand celebrations of 1901 and the historic elections that followed.

Governor General Hopetoun had given Toby only seven days between Christmas and New Year to contact, invite and get approval from the five people he chose to form the initial Federal Ministry, an especially stressful task as all of the potential appointees were spread across the nation and difficult to contact quickly. But all of them had been anticipating a message from him so he had met the deadline exactly on New Year's Eve. This enabled him to organise his ministry to work efficiently as a team in their temporary role of an executive government until Australia's first national election could be organised and held in March of that year.

From that election day onwards, the practice of politics took over from negativity of parochialism in an emphatic manner even before the first parliament could meet in Melbourne in May.

They were mighty days, filled with the unexpected, but immensely fascinating, particularly as the new government was perilously short of operating funds as they had no taxing powers until the new parliament could meet to legislate them.

As port and cigars were enjoyed, he would lead them in a political review of what had been achieved, and had not been achieved, in the first decade of nationhood, with no holds barred. It was vital that they should face up to their errors and work out what to do about them while they still had the power to achieve the right results.

He was very certain that his guests would raise additional matters that each felt were important. He would allow a debate on them all as this would ensure that it was a vintage evening. He reaffirmed to himself his view that he would forever be proud to have attended this gathering and never ever forget it.

With a spring in his stride, and despite his heavyweight frame, he bounded down the steps from the Gun Room to the Private Member's Lounge.

He would be ready and waiting to greet his guests as they arrived and provide each of them with a top-quality drink of their choosing. He reckoned that every one of them had earned the best that he could offer them. They probably thought so too, but most were sufficiently modest and wise to keep such a thought to themselves.

The Guests Make an Entrance

While the host had been savouring his pleasant drink in the Gun Room, his guests were making their way to the club.

In a similar mood to their host, they had a sense of anticipation in an evening of quality, together with a determination to say things that they had bottled up for twenty years from 1890 until now, during which they had put the cause of Federation ahead of the accumulated political wounds they had suffered.

Momentum was building.

The Premiers

John Forrest had made the long journey from Western Australia by boat, just as he had done several times a year for two decades. The transcontinental railway had not yet been built.

It was a slow experience that always put him out of contact with political crises when his colleagues could reach him only via Morse code messages to the ship's captain. It highlighted a problem that every Western Australian has, then and now, constantly faced in struggling to become fully involved in national affairs.

As was his usual practice, he had taken a comfortable suite at the historic Hotel Windsor where he would be certain to meet many political powerbrokers who could bring him up to date with the hot topics of the day. For many who were not members of the Melbourne Club, this grand hotel served as a fashionable alternative to the club as a centre for political intrigue at the highest levels. For the ladies of Melbourne, it was a socially respectable place where they could gather without having to be accompanied by their husbands.

After scouting around all the bars and restaurants in the hotel, Forrest discovered that George Reid of New South Wales and Charles Kingston from South Australia were staying at the Windsor also. He made personal contact with them and arranged that they would assemble in the foyer of the hotel and walk together to the club which was only a few blocks away, along Spring Street, past the Parliament and into Collins Street.

Like Toby Barton had done earlier, they enjoyed their pleasant evening stroll. Forrest decided to use the time profitably by posing a question.

"How many people are there in our nation who instinctively think of themselves primarily as Australians, with a greater sense of honour than they do as Queenslanders or Tasmanians or whatever?"

"My people," said Kingston, "will always think of themselves as South Australians, but they are gradually growing in pride with the thought of being Australians. I find this steady change of attitude to be really quite heartening."

Reid, having infamously wavered in his support for Federation from time to time over a decade, was now an affirmed nationalist, but also a happy stirrer. He formed the view that it was appropriate to stir the pot just a trifle at this moment by adding a little dark humour.

"My sense of the current situation is that New South Welshmen are clearly and firmly the most committed Australians. This is because we think, quite correctly, that we are running the show totally. Some of us have it firmly in our minds that it is an undeniable truth that Australia was established only when the five other states begged to be allowed to join New South Wales and we decided magnanimously and graciously to tolerate all of you as part of our nation. It's probably wise for you chaps to let us continue with this delusion. In the final analysis, Australia wins."

Kingston, proud of his South Australian heritage which was created by an Act of the British Parliament that declared it to be a colony of free settlers with no convicts, felt a call to irreverently respond.

"What person, in rightful possession of their full mental faculties, would ever want to be a New South Welshman. 90% of you are descended from convicts, and the worst ones at that."

"And proud of it," said George. "A touch of criminality is a fine cornerstone on which to build a switched-on society. The vivid imagination of the criminal class always leads to the expansion of a prosperous economy."

Forrest changed the course of the conversation away from Reid's banter. In a somewhat sombre tone added his own view of the cohesion of Australia. "I must confess to you both that there is a growing feeling in Western Australia that we made a huge mistake in joining the Federation. We are located a long way from the action and have few ways of controlling that action or even meaningfully participating in it. The Nullarbor Plain is as huge a natural barrier as you can find anywhere in the world and it decisively divides our nation. I know it well because I rode a horse across it in my days as an explorer. It is now my job to curb the growing influence of the anti-nationalists in my state. I am trying to create a genuine Australian culture that acknowledges our isolation in a positive manner and seeks new ways that will bring the nation closer together. It's hard going, but necessary."

Kingston offered a further thought, a much more positive one. "To keep Western Australia happily involved in our Federation, we must give priority to building the proposed railway across the Nullarbor that will cut travel time and provide a vital trade link. We should raise the issue tonight with Andrew Fisher. I know from my discussions with Western Australian MPs and Senators at Parliament that all is not well with them. I am somewhat troubled that they have grave concerns about their future within the Commonwealth. We should not let it fester for too much longer or it will become an incurable sore."

"I don't think that, by itself, the railway will solve the Western Australian problem, laudable though the project is," opined Reid. "The cost of the West trading with the East is huge, a tyranny caused by distance. Eventually, our Federal Government will have to face the necessity of providing some sort of freight subsidy that will foster trade across the Nullarbor. For a fervent Free Trader like me to say this is nothing short of blasphemy on a huge scale, but it could be that this is the one time when my colleagues and I will have to be pragmatic and try to curb our economic ideology just for a moment."

"This is the first smart thing I have ever heard you say in your political career, George," was Forrest's surprised retort.

Reid took advantage of this backhanded compliment. "If we can pull it off, you will owe me quite a few drinks, John, as I will lose a lot of conservative friends. From our regular skirmishes in Parliament, you will be aware that the generous ideological concession I have just made is causing me great pain, physically and mentally."

"While you fellows are debating the crucial issue of who will be paying for the drinks," said Kingston. "I want to take the opportunity to plead the case for railways that South Australia needs. Can I remind you both that a written commitment was made to South Australia, as a condition of signing up to Federation, that a railway would be built from Adelaide to Darwin via Alice Springs? At that time, as you know, the Northern Territory was under the control of the South Australian Parliament. We passed it over to the new Federal Government with this nation building obligation being clearly acknowledged in no uncertain terms. Not the slightest effort has been made to honour this promise over the past decade. It is an appalling breach of faith.

"And while I am at it, can I say that we desperately need a railway running directly from Adelaide to Sydney. Right now, we are blotted out of the Sydney market because we have to send our freight via Melbourne at a huge cost that can be avoided by a direct track."

"Good heavens," implored Reid. "I made an incredibly bad mistake walking to the club with you two fellows. Australia is about to go bankrupt as it strives to pay for your railways and I will cop the blame, as usual, because I was benevolent enough to offer to help you."

"Well, if we are going to go bust, let's do it for a glamourous and noble reason. We, the citizens of New South Wales, will insist that a grand bridge be built across Sydney Harbour that will be the envy of the world."

"We will praise you mightily for that awesome vision, George," said Forrest. "So long as you pay for it solely with New South Wales money. You have a constant and growing surplus of it as the result of your quite unfair, and often monopolistic, trading with the rest of us."

Reid was saved by their arrival at the club.

Giles proudly escorted them in.

He was in awe of their political power. These famous parliamentarians were genuine leaders.

The Believers

At that moment, Alfred Deakin was travelling from his home in South Yarra by the horse-drawn carriage that was available for use by the Leader of the Opposition in the Federal Parliament. He detested the role and title. Having been prime minister three times, and not likely to be appointed for a fourth, being in the political doldrums was a genuine let down that he was not enjoying. It lacked the essential trappings of power that enabled a leader to achieve results.

He had arranged with Bolton Stafford Bird to meet him at the Congregational Church that was located nearby Deakin's home. For his visit to Melbourne, the distinguished Tasmanian clergyman was the guest of the local Congregational Minister, a religious denomination he had loyally served all his life.

Travelling together to the club was a splendid opportunity for Deakin to talk about his favourite subject, religion. He knew that Bird, as one of Australia's better-known Christian leaders, would be more than interested to take part in a lively discussion that enabled him to express his thoughts on the relationship of faith and politics.

It was some time since they had last met. Deakin recalled that it had been at the funeral of Bird's Tasmanian colleague, Andrew Clark, in 1904.

After exchanging warm greetings, words of praise for Clark's role in Federation, and regret that he was no longer with them, Deakin raised the subject that had been on his mind when he had sent a note to Bird offering to provide him with transport.

"Bolton, you and I have known one another for more than twenty years now and you are well aware that I am a spiritualist who enjoys studying every one of the major religions in my lifelong search to find the ultimate source of spiritual power.

"My unshakeable conviction is that there is a power beyond myself, and beyond the current thinking of all religions, and this belief has been an important factor in my passionate certainty about the absolute rightness of Federation. I have no doubt that it was the will of God to do what we did. It is my intention to express this conviction at the dinner tonight, just as I have done consistently over two decades, at interstate Federation negotiations, as well as throughout my service in two Parliaments, firstly Victoria, then Federal."

The response from Bird was a carefully considered one. "I have not a shadow of a doubt that you hold the passionate beliefs that you do, Alfred, and that you will express them strongly tonight. As a Christian, I am convinced that my God always seeks to unite His people no matter what their circumstances. Thus, the whole exercise of Federation has been, in my view, a pathway that God wants his Australian people to follow. A door was opened to us that gave us the opportunity to create a genuine community of people from many ethnic and religious backgrounds and then to make it a successfully progressive one in every respect. I believe that we are on the right pathway, but we must fill the gaps that cry out for enlightened action."

"Well, Bolton, we will be in a minority at the dinner, but we can stir the debate throughout the evening by affirming that Australia clearly needs a core of ethical values and basic social beliefs to be framed into its constitution as it steps into the future. I am certain that George Reid will have a happy slap at us. This will give us a splendid opportunity to take matters further."

Deakin's comment struck a chord with Bird.

"At the initial Federal Council meeting that I attended as Tasmania's representative over twenty years ago, when we had our first formal discussion about the possibility of a Federation of States, I suggested that a statement of national beliefs had to be the basis of a preamble to any constitution that we created, but my observation fell completely flat. I raised it again at the 1891 Constitutional Convention, but there was very little interest in it or support for it, so my proposal did not make it on to the Agenda for the 1897 Convention. It is highly possible that I did not express the case in the most appropriate manner or as convincingly as I should have or perhaps, I simply did not have enough political clout or do sufficiently effective lobbying. Whatever the reason, gaining even a discussion about it was as difficult a task as growing a rose out in the desert. With heartfelt regret, I must openly acknowledge that I have failed lamentably."

Deakin expressed the view that a majority of delegates to the conventions saw such a preamble as an attempt to embed the church into the constitution and they were determined that there must be a clear separation of church and state.

Bird's response was that it was a pity that they held this view. Nevertheless, he knew that they had been concerned that Queen Victoria held two positions, Head of State and Leader of the Church of England. Clearly, they did not want such an anomaly repeated in Australia. That, in fact, was a legal matter which, he felt, should be considered separately from any statement of the faith and ethics of the people.

He added, "If we want Australia to continue to be a nation of high-principled people, the vast majority of whom believe that Christianity is their way of life, then that conviction should be expressed somewhere in the constitution. It is important that migrants who come here to live should be aware that they are taking up life in a Christian nation. At the very least, they must undertake to respect this fact without being required to adhere to any Christian beliefs. I am certain that this can best be achieved by having a powerful preamble to the constitution approved at a referendum expressly called for that specific purpose. It can then be included in an Oath of Citizenship."

"Your comments are valid," replied Deakin. "Getting this accepted is a huge task still before us, but we must not shirk from it. Let us try to get some traction on the subject tonight. Then, we can again talk about it on our homeward journey."

Bird agreed, then added, "We can also endeavour to have a time table set for action or it will drag on for years."

"I have an uneasy feeling that it may go on for a century," was Deakin's sad observance. "But a start must be made on it sometime, so it may as well be now."

They crossed Princes Bridge, passing by St Paul's Anglican Cathedral and turning right from Swanston Street into Collins Street at the City Hall. This took them past Scots Presbyterian Church and St Michaels, the congregational bastion, then along towards the Melbourne Club whose Christian members spent more money there every year than they ever thought of giving to their churches and felt not a single pain of guilt about it.

"Our religious beliefs are highlighted by some fine Churches in this city," commented Bird. "At some point in its history, Melbournians must have felt that Christianity was an important part of their lives, sufficiently important enough to spend huge sums of money building magnificent churches. It is splendid that the Christian tradition is not dying. I note that at the three fine churches we have just passed, people are starting to gather for Sunday Evening Services."

This caused Deakin to reaffirm his low opinion of churches. "Their congregations irresponsibly waste their potential to influence public opinion on Christian matters. They spend countless hours arguing constantly, in the most "holier than thou" fashion, about their widely divergent and pious versions of theology and morals, few of which are of any interest whatsoever to most of the people of Melbourne, indeed Australia."

Bird, knowing this to be true, added a diagnosis, "We can blame that all on the Reformation that so tremendously impacted on our world four centuries ago. Until then, the popes did not tolerate any such debates about religious beliefs," was Bird's sad response. "They made statements of doctrine which were unchallengeable. In fact, a handful of them were claimed to be infallible. None of their devout followers were brave enough to dispute one word of it."

Deakin observed that this raised an important issue.

"A significant part of your disappointment in not getting a statement of beliefs into a preamble to the constitution is the indisputable fact that we would never have been able to get Catholics and Protestants to agree on what the wording should be. There would have been a bitter fight that would have become very personal and would have, in all probability, ripped the nation apart. I venture to say that, at the end of it all, their self-righteous war would have led us to a point where we would still have had no preamble to our constitution."

"Be this as it may, we can make sure that a debate about it does not get personal tonight. There has to be a rational way to achieve our aim."

"If the conversation tonight does get personal, it won't be over religion. It will be about political power or economic ideology or disappointed egos or the quality of the wine."

The club came into view and the sight of it caused Bird to say a word of praise for their host.

"You know, Alfred, it really has been an extraordinary organising effort by Edmund Barton to get such an impressive gathering to assemble here tonight and I am most honoured that he invited me to represent Tasmania at what will be an historic dinner. To arrange for ten busy people to attend during the holiday season, with some travelling such long distances, is tremendous. It will have been a tiring journey for John Forrest to come from Bunbury to here."

Alfred was not at all surprised that it was happening.

"Toby is one of the world's great organisers and influencers. Not only did he arrange the birth of a nation here on our continent, you should have seen him in action when we spent months in London in 1900 arranging for the British Parliament to authorise Federation. In his pleasantly reserved manner, he charmed and cajoled the lords and ladies in a way that had to be seen to be believed. In the end, they ceased to regard him as a crude colonial and accepted him as one of their own in a fashion that was not in any way patronising."

Bird agreed. "I stand in absolute awe of what he achieved."

"Well, here we are our privileged destination. The Melbourne Club," added Deakin.

"It is a place for feasting and drinking of such high quality that even the British aristocracy find to be acceptable to their acute sense of pompous grandeur. But, may I hasten to say that it is not a Temple of the Lord. It is a bastion of the rich and powerful of this fine city. Its honourable members only think about God when they want to blame Him for the presence on earth of rascals with whom they have done bad business deals. And they freely blame God for the droughts that ravage their vast pastoral estates with increasing regularity, plus any economic recessions that occur from time to time, as well as anything else that may annoy them. He must be delighted that He is not ignored by the horde of mercenaries who are members here."

Bird found that comment interesting.

"We have an opportunity to add a positive thought to your comments on the profound theology of the Melbourne Club, Alfred. In reality, what their God-blaming theology means is that the members of this club are exposed to God in a constant manner. This gives us a very real evangelistic platform from which we can get them to take Him seriously. But, I doubt that the Almighty will be overly sympathetic to their problems."

Giles greeted them warmly. He was a huge fan of Deakin. After all, the great man had been prime minister three times.

The Judge and the Reformer

Samuel Griffith travelled likewise. As Chief Justice of the High Court of Australia, he too was entitled to a carriage and had invited Chris Watson to travel with him to the club.

They were not fellow travellers politically, or social partners for that matter, but Griffith had watched and admired Watson's tenacity and strength of purpose during his four short months as prime minister. His political opponents had been especially uncooperative and relentlessly merciless.

Many Australians experienced enormous difficulty coming to terms with the fact that a representative of common labourers could be placed in charge of a nation. They regarded it as a mini version of the French Revolution that must be repelled before a Melbourne version of the storming of the Bastille could become a possibility.

In truth, the Colonial Secretary in London had placed Australia on his high-alert list with considerable foreboding.

Griffith had decided that this short journey represented an opportunity to continue his enjoyable and irresistible practice of stirring the political pot from the sidelines even though High Court judges are required to observe protocol and remain above the fray, quite clearly and impeccably, at all times.

"I hope Mr Watson that you will not be restricted in your comments tonight by the fact that you were prime minister for a far lesser term than any of Barton, Deakin, Reid and Fisher. Nor should you be restrained by your recent decision to leave Parliament, entirely at a time of your own choosing."

"Thank you, Chief Justice, for suggesting this. I am of the strong conviction that Federation should have brought with it a succession of enlightened governments that embraced a far greater social involvement of even the humblest of people. However, the MPs who have been elected so far seem to hold on to the ancient belief that life always has been and always will be based on the survival of the fittest in a restricted society where the rich have the exclusive right of owning and controlling the marketplace. I intend to express this view strongly tonight if Toby Barton gives me the opportunity as there can be no doubt that class distinction in Australia is widening. If it continues, Australia will go backwards, both socially and economically."

Griffith responded quickly. "Andrew Fisher, as the current leader of the party that you brought to national prominence, is clearly moving in the direction of the greater equality that you espouse. I will be surprised if he does not support you strongly in whatever comments you choose to make this evening."

"He is a strong ally, having grown up in poverty in the coal mines of Scotland, so he has personal experience of where the battle lines have been drawn. It is the conservative factions of our Parliament who promote and enhance the great divide of humanity. The upstairs and downstairs element of British society is ingrained in their bones. George Reid, John Forrest and William Lyne are staunch unbending flag bearers for unrestrained market capitalism. They hold the strong conviction that no restraints can be placed on the rich and powerful that will curb their constant strivings for the creation of more monopolies without which they do not believe that modern economics can survive. They are intelligent people, but their view of the world is extraordinarily narrow and unrealistic."

"Deakin should be on your side. He is as close to a socialist as we have in Parliament, more so than anyone I know in your Labor Party."

Watson agreed. "He is clearly to the left politically and economically, but he has a low opinion of my beloved Australian Labor Party. He feels that we are owned body and soul by trade unions and that those unions are run by thuggish people who are not intellectually bright. He thinks that we are totally incapable of participating in any enlightened debate with capitalists and, therefore, are a dead weight in his saddle bags."

Griffith added some optimism. "It is an obsession that many bright people share. Deakin has a very sharp mind, but he is not pompous. I think that you should seek to engage him in a lively debate tonight. I will chime in whenever I can get an opportunity to broaden the discussion."

"My thanks once more, Chief Justice, for your helpful suggestion. I will do my best to pick the right moment to take him on."

Griffith held the view that it was long overdue for Deakin to meet his match in debate. The man was altogether too confident. In Sam's view, it was his aura of intellectual superiority that was the root cause of Deakin being deposed as prime minister three times. Many of the 'run of the mill' politicians spent a lot of time trying to bring him down to size, with few achieving much success. Their motivation had not been generated by his arrogance because he actually wasn't arrogant. He was just too smart for his own good.

He posed a personal question to Watson.

"I note that since leaving Parliament just a few short months ago, you have become highly active once more in the Trade Union Movement. Do you think you could create a situation where socialists like Deakin, who will never ever consider becoming members of a Trade Union, can find a secure political home within your party?"

This was a question that had personal importance for Watson. "I am working on this quite vital issue, but it will take a long time to get a satisfactory result as the divide is huge. Most Unions believe that the Labor Party is their vehicle and theirs alone. They see intellectuals as being part of the privileged classes, a pompous elite who have never gotten their hands dirty and are not really true believers in the cause of removing the scourge of inequality."

Griffith took it further. "Can I express the view that the time will come when the political survival of the Labor Party will depend on Unions moderating their isolationist views and developing a much broader political base than unionists will ever have the potential to do? I see it as an unavoidable change."

"Agreed. My intention with my own life is to create a dual career by becoming active in business while maintaining and strengthening my Trade Union links so I may be able to use this twin connection to create a different attitude within my party."

"I wish you well with that. It seems to me to be essential that, one day, capital and labour must come to a consensus about how they can work together to determine the future of Australia. This will be essential if we aspire to become the economic and social powerhouse of the Southern Hemisphere."

"This admirable goal will be achieved only when capitalists accept that pride of achievement will bring people much greater satisfaction than just having money in the bank."

"Equally, it will depend on workers accepting that not all wealthy men are evil, nor can all intellectuals be described as elitist."

"I have no personal issues whatsoever with your viewpoint. Even so, it remains a monumental task to convince the workers of Australia that wealthy fellows are good blokes and vice versa. Even so, it is clearly worth a try. Indeed, it would be irresponsible not to make it a priority."

Giles was waiting on the footpath to assist them from their carriage. He was enormously respectful of the Chief Justice. However, he was instinctively aware that Chris Watson did not really fit the scene among the bluebloods of the club.

After all, he was a commoner. Nevertheless, he received him with respectful courtesy. After all, he had once been the prime minister.

The Bushman's Champion

William Lyne walked alone, something that he quite liked doing. He was a house guest of friends who lived nearby St Patrick's Cathedral in North Melbourne, the spiritual centre of the city's growing Catholic population. It was only a short walk south from there to the club. This gave him a chance to admire the quite massive cathedral that had been built by devoted followers of the faith only a decade and a half earlier, right on Parliament Square.

He was not in a hurry as did not think for a single moment that any of his fellow diners would be concerned if he was late, nor would they greet him with warm brotherly love. Their negative attitude did not bother him so long as they treated him with courtesy. These were the fellows who had publicly deserted him in 1901 when he had received the accolade of a lifetime in being offered the Prime Ministership of Australia by the Governor General. He had deliberately made no attempt to cultivate their friendship thereafter. But, tonight, he would humble them by forcing them to account for the very partisan and personal politics they had subjected him to at that hurtful and humiliating time.

His prime goal in life was quite clear in his mind as he strolled leisurely into Collins Street.

"One day, I will become prime minister and, as one of my first tasks, I will settle a few scores with quiet satisfaction. Then, I will fundamentally change some ill-advised policies that are taking the nation in the wrong direction. I will return Australia to the rural roots that were the foundation of its economy from the time the First Fleet arrived. I will not allow the rapid growth of capital cities to continue in the utterly aimless manner that they are now doing. Huge populations must not be allowed to gather there where they are simply consumers, not producers. We will no longer be waging a battle called 'Sydney or the Bush.' It will end with a decisive victory for the Bush. Cities will become hugely dependent upon the wealth generated by Rural Australia and I will never let them forget it."

Furthermore, as he approached the club, he affirmed his entitlement to be there. He was one of the 'landed gentry'. In truth, he was in its top echelons.

Quite intentionally, Giles was not at the door of the club to meet him. Nevertheless, Lyne had quietly found his own way into the hallowed premises and soon located Toby Barton who welcomed him civilly with a warm handshake that conveyed a desire to make peace at last.

He was blithely unaware that Giles had regarded it as quite caddish behaviour for Lyne to have tried to steal the Prime Ministership of Australia from his hero, Toby, a decade previously. Therefore, he was of the opinion that Lyne did not measure up to the quality of person who should be allowed into the club.

Had Lyne known this, he would have been utterly unconcerned and regarded it as an accolade of honour. Actually, it would have been a reassuring acknowledgement that he stood quite apart from the rest.

The Prime Minister

Andrew Fisher journeyed to the club alone in the prime minister's carriage that bore the seal of the Federal Government on its doors. Pedestrians in Collins Street applauded as he stepped out of his carriage on arrival at the club and he responded with warm dignity as Giles proudly led him in with an air of understated triumph.

Fisher had been somewhat surprised when Barton had invited him to attend tonight as he had not been elected to attend any of the Constitutional Conventions of the 1890's that had led the progress towards Federation and, therefore, could not claim legitimately to be one of the Founding Fathers. This non-involvement was not a personal decision. He had simply not been invited by the Queensland Government to represent it in any Federation negotiations and, at the time, had not pressed for a position of influence.

This was a stroke of good fortune as there had been important work to be done in his home State. Queenslanders had a deeply ingrained suspicion of the predatory motives of New South Wales and Victoria.

This had sparked a controversy that had raged about the possibility that a Federal Government would ban the Kanaka slaves used extensively by Queensland farmers on their cane fields in the deep north and return them to their island homes out in the Pacific. This had made Queensland politicians very reluctant to come to the table and they had done so only at the eleventh hour, despite all the goodwill they had shown to Henry Parkes when he had visited them to raise the matter a decade earlier.

So, Fisher had diligently and purposefully gone to work on the issue and he had concentrated his efforts into the final year before Federation when he had done his utmost to make sure that Queensland finally voted Yes. An undeniable personal factor in all of it was that his passionate advocacy of Federation proved to be the culmination of his purposeful strategy to ensure that he would have a significant political career. It was his first major step towards achieving his goal of becoming prime minister.

When that referendum victory had been achieved, he had no hesitation in deciding to leave Queensland politics and contest the seat of Wide Bay in the elections for the first Federal Parliament. Thankfully, he won it, had held it ever since and was now in his second term as Prime Minister, his first having been terminated by an unexpected coup on the floor of Parliament that has been astutely organised by Deakin. This still rankled even though he had gained his revenge a year later.

But, as far as tonight's dinner was concerned, he supposed that Barton felt that it would add to the importance of the occasion if the Prime Minister attended and talked about where Australia was heading. He would be quite happy to do this, if invited, as he would welcome whatever advice his fellow diners may offer him in return as their combined experience of politics and government was massive.

Whatever were Barton's thoughts, Fisher was anticipating that the constant rivalry which existed among the main players would add up to a dramatic occasion that would teach him how to survive in a parliament that changed its leaders quickly. This would ensure that he was not wasting his time by coming to the club tonight.

Besides, he had a few difficult issues on his mind that related to the path along which Australia was heading and he hoped that his fellow diners might raise these matters without any prompting so it would not look as though he was anxious about any of them. He was still, at heart, a canny Scot. In addition, he was a teetotaller. He would not run up a huge bill at the bar for Toby to pay.

Drinks

"Greetings and salutations, my friends."

Barton was a picture of goodwill as he walked into the room to greet his elite group of fellow nation builders.

They responded with warmth and good humour as he shook hands all round.

Now that Barton was a Justice of the High Court and not a member of Parliament, he was no longer a political rival of any of them. They greeted him as such. Some fondly regarded him as an old adversary who had now seen the error of his ways and become respectable in his senior years.

The warmest greeting came from his boss, Samuel Griffith, the Chief Justice. This somewhat surprised Toby, but he responded appropriately.

He and Griffith had experienced an inbuilt career rivalry, but they worked together at the Court quite well and had established a solid professional relationship. It reflected the way in which they had worked together towards a shared goal during the many tense battles that paved the way to Federation. Often, they had disagreed with considerable passion, but generally contrived a means of finding common ground.

Toby was delighted that 15 minutes of pleasant chatter followed, mainly featuring their families and general well-being as his guests greeted one another. They managed to mix this pleasant informality with revelations about the latest political gossip.

Finally, it was time for business so Barton tapped his glass to call them to order. He invited them to take a seat in one of the fine leather chairs that are a fundamental asset and privilege of every gentleman's club throughout the realm of good Queen Victoria.

"You are aware of the agenda I have in mind for tonight's grand reunion from my prior discussions with you and I know that you have prepared your thoughts on each matter. So, let us draw our chairs into a circle and begin our reminiscences of history while we wait for entrees to be served. We will be talking about what I believe has been the most important event in our own lives and the lives of ALL those who live on this continent. I have asked our butler, Giles, to keep your glasses filled so that none of you run out of the fuel that will power our debates."

They quickly settled and re-charged their glasses as Barton set the discussion underway.

"Appropriately, we will begin with toasts to eminent pioneers of Federation who have passed on, but are not forgotten."

The Tenterfield Legend

"Henry Parkes is first. It is fair for me to say that he was the greatest nation builder of his era. Sadly, he died four years before we finally won the Federation battle.

"George Reid, you were one of his foremost adversaries in the New South Wales Parliament. Indeed, you were one of the reasons why he was premier five times. You enjoyed knocking him off with impressive regularity, forcing him to keep making dramatic comebacks. May I invite you to propose a toast in his honour?"

"Delighted, Toby. I will begin with a few comments about his legendary Tenterfield speech. Without doubt, this was the launch platform for the final movement to achieve Federation and, the significant thing to be noted about it was that it was soundly based on our need to have one army, not six."

Reid's opening line locked minds into gear as his listeners endeavoured to recall the contents of that famous oration. Most could remember only the highlights of it. Had they enjoyed the privilege of perfect memory, they would have recalled the Sydney Morning Herald's front-page coverage of the full text of it almost a quarter of a century ago.

That powerful newspaper recorded it this way, noting as it did that Parkes was both Premier of New South Wales and Member for Tenterfield, even though he did not live in that prosperous rural community. They had elected him without him ever visiting them until the day of the great speech.

The headline summed up the precise goal.

A GOVERNMENT FOR THE WHOLE OF AUSTRALIA

Then, Parkes made the formation of an Australian Army the core of his argument.

The Imperial General who recently inspected the troops of the colonies has recommended that the whole of the forces of Australia should be united into one army. It would be pleasing if we could rely on being safe without taking military precautions at all, but this is impossible. We must take measures to defend ourselves. The knowledge of the fact that we are in this condition of security will spread all over the world and make us additionally secure.

There are two very important questions towards which I ought to draw your attention.

You must have heard something of the Federal Council in which New South Wales has not yet taken a place. If we are to carry out the recommendations of General Edwards, it is absolutely necessary for us to have something more than the Federal Council. We need one central executive authority which is able to bring all the forces of the different colonies into one national army.

Some colonial statesmen have said that this might be done by means of the Federal Council, but this Federal Council has no authority to do anything of the sort. It has no executive function, and, moreover, is not an elected body, but merely a body appointed by the governments of the various colonies. It does not therefore carry with it the support of the people. It is constitutionally weak, and, under the Imperial Act which created it, no such tremendous power was given as that which the exigencies of Australia might demand.

It has been suggested that the Imperial Parliament in London should be asked to pass a measure authorising the troops of the colonies to unite in one federal army.

But, even if this were done, there would be an absence of the necessary central executive government. Each of the colonies would object to the army being under the control of the Imperial Government, and no one of the colonies could direct it.

The great question which we have to consider is whether the time has now come for the creation on this continent of an Australian Government as distinct from the local governments now in existence.

Here, the *Sydney Morning Herald* recorded that there was prolonged applause.

The people of Tenterfield were proud to live on a great island continent. A state called New South Wales was irrelevant to them.

Fired up by this generous response to his opening words, Parkes raised the tempo a notch.

In other words, to make myself as plain as possible, Australia now has a population of three and a half millions, and the American people numbered only between three and four million when they formed the great Commonwealth of the United States. The numbers are about the same, and surely what the Americans did by war, the Australians can bring about in peace – without breaking the ties that hold us to the mother country.

The crowd was now cheering. They had no doubt that Australia was a better place than the United States of America and they wanted to prove this beyond doubt.

Believing as I do that it is essential to preserve the security and integrity of these colonies that the whole of our forces should be amalgamated into one great federal army, whenever necessary – feeling this, and seeing no other means of attaining that end – it seems to me that the time is close at hand when we ought to set about creating this great national government for all Australia.

This subject brings us face to face with another subject. We now have from South Australia to Queensland a stretch of about 2000 miles of railway, and if the four colonies can only combine to adopt a uniform gauge, it will be of immense advantage in the movement of troops, as well as the operations of commerce and the various pursuits of society. These are the two great questions that I want to lay before you.

This rang a bell with the locals who could not work out the nonsense of having to change trains at the Queensland border just because parochial governments had chosen to have different rail gauges. They applauded mightily, absolutely unaware that a century later there would still be three rail gauges.

I have just returned from Brisbane, and the object of my visit was not to force my advice on the authorities there but to discuss with them these matters.

Unfortunately, owing to the illness of the head of the ministry there, my communications were rather more of a private character than otherwise, but without disclosing any confidences, I think that I can state I understand both sides in politics sympathise warmly and closely with the views I expressed.

These words were not exactly accurate. Queenslanders were not really inclined to be in a Federation with New South Wales, but this did not deter Parkes. He got right to the core of the matter.

As to the steps which should be taken to bring this about, a conference of governments has been pointed to, but we must take broader views in the initiation of the movement than has been taken hitherto. We must appoint a convention of leading men from all the colonies – delegates appointed by the authority of parliaments, who would truly represent the opinion of the different parliaments of the colonies. This convention will have to advise the constitution that would be necessary to bring into existence a Federal Government with a Federal Parliament for the conduct of national business.

More sustained applause. Parkes was sounding like a common-sense bloke who knew how to create a nation.

The only argument which could be advanced in opposition to the views I have put forward is that the time has not yet come, and we must remain isolated colonies just in the same way as we are now. I believe, however, that the time has come.

In the words of Brunton Stephens, I would ask –

'Not yet her day. How long 'not yet'. There comes the flush of violet! And heavenward faces, all aflame. With sanguine imminence of morn. Wait but the sun-kiss to proclaim. The day of the dominion born.'

I believe that the time has come, and if two governments set an example, the others must soon of necessity follow, and we will have an uprising in this fair land of a goodly fabric of free government. And all great national questions of magnitude affecting the welfare of the colonies will be disposed of by a fully authorised constitutional authority, which will be the only one which can give satisfaction to the people it represents. This means a distinct executive, and a distinct parliamentary power, a government for the whole of Australia.

And it means a parliament of two houses, a house of commons and a senate, which will legislate on all great subjects.

The Government and Parliament of New South Wales will be just as effective as now in all local matters, as will be the Government and Parliament of Queensland. All great questions will be dealt with in a broad light and with a view to the interests of the whole country.

The *Sydney Morning* noted in a subsequent editorial that Parkes was playing colonial politics. He planned to merge New South Wales and Queensland, then force the other states to join one at a time. This strategy was soon replaced with a broader picture. Nevertheless, it formed a basis to start.

I, therefore, take advantage of this opportunity which has arisen for the consideration of this great subject, for I believe that the time is at hand when this thing will be done.

One great thing to be accomplished is the massing together of our military forces, whenever necessary, and this cannot be effected by any other power than one representing all of the colonies.

In conclusion, I thank you for the kindness you have shown me. I have no fear but the Federal Parliament will rise to a just conception to the necessities of the wider sphere of political existence. This great thing will have to be done, and to put it off will only tend to make the difficulties which stand in the way greater,

In the meantime, there is this substantial work of defence to be carried out, which we cannot do by any other means – which cannot be done by any existing machinery.

At that moment in Tenterfield in 1888, there was a standing ovation for Sir Henry which lasted for several minutes. Champagne corks popped as they toasted the vision of a new nation.

Parkes had lit a fire that would not be extinguished. However, right at this moment, the diners at the Melbourne Club were relying on George Reid's memory of the great speech to reignite their ability to comment on it.

George was the largest person in the room and his presence was even more formidable. He operated on the assumption that the Good Lord had intended that he should dominate every occasion. Clearing his throat, he continued with his intent to honour Parkes as a man whom he respected for his political skills, but disliked intensely as a person.

"Throughout his long career in public life as a newspaper editor and politician, Parkes wanted to separate the Colony of New South Wales from its English masters. You will recall that Parkes childhood in England was such that his family lived in poor circumstances. He was determined that the English version of poverty for the lower classes would not spread to Australia.

"So, forty years before Federation, Parkes tried to make New South Wales a Republic and he had the powerful support of John Dunmore Lang, one of the most influential clergymen Australia has ever had and most likely ever will have. Between them, they built up a tremendous personal following among those who resented their colonial status. Nevertheless, the Parliament at Westminster would not have a bar of it because the Americans had wounded them badly by winning the War of Independence. They would not allow another set of rebels to rock their treasured colonial boat.

"So, Henry decided that the first step to freedom was to gradually unite the six colonies into one and then go on to change its structure into that of a republic as a vital second step. He was way ahead of his time with this agenda and he did not ever retreat from it, even though he kept inventing new scenarios to achieve it."

Chris Watson intervened, "May I interpose George?"

Reid nodded his assent. "The Labor Party was totally behind Parkes as far as his republican sentiments were concerned, even though his speech at Tenterfield emphasised the retaining of close ties with our mother country. Those royalist comments of his were just vote getting tactics at the time. He did not realise just how domineering the Imperial Government in London would be in maintaining control over the Empire. I can see no reason why Australia should be controlled from England on any matters whatsoever. For instance, it is quite wrong for Britain to control our infant Navy in the way that it does now. An absolute outrage. They are deliberately dwarfing its development in order to maintain their supremacy."

"Now, Chris, while I agree that your comment has a reasonable degree of accuracy about it, you should know better than to interrupt Reid in full flight."

"I do, George. I have incurred your wrath on a number of memorable parliamentary occasions.

"Be this as it may, and before you continue to propose your toast to Parkes, can I remind you that Peter Lalor was our first Republican, not Parkes. Lalor's revolt at the Eureka Stockade was intended to destroy the credibility of the Victorian Colonial Government in Melbourne and set the colony free from its incompetent imperial masters. His brave initiative was doomed to failure at the time because it was an amateur initiative that had too few followers, not enough guns and bullets, and little time to get them organised, trained and disciplined.

"Nevertheless, it was a valiant failure that created a long-term impact. The spirit of Eureka has never died and never will. We must ensure that it has the same place of honour in our national history as does the fine speech by Parkes at Tenterfield."

"Quite true, Chris, but remember that Lalor was an Irishman and that explains everything about his impetuous rebellion against his colonial masters. I can say this without fear of retribution as we don't have any pure-blooded Irishmen in this room tonight."

Reid launched forth once more with his Parkes toast.

"First of all, we should never forget that Henry was a superb self-publicist. He had given a copy of his intended oration to the *Sydney Morning Herald* before he left Sydney and got an undertaking from the editor to put it on the front page on the day that he delivered it in Tenterfield. He was determined to foster an instant public debate about its prime recommendations. He probably said a lot more that day than was reported in the version he gave to the *Herald*, But, this was Henry's style of politics.

"He was even confident enough to predict that the Queenslanders would be supportive of Federation even though he wrote the speech at his Sydney home before he went to see them in Brisbane on his way to Tenterfield. They were suitably courteous to him, but were actually non-committal about Federation. Even so, it is quite clear that the doors were left open for further talks.

"History records that the Herald carried out its promise enthusiastically. They ran with follow up stories for days and fuelled a huge public debate about it. This enabled Henry to put Federation on the map in a big way. Had he not forged a partnership with that influential newspaper, his speech may never have been reported in such a public fashion. Tenterfield is a very long way from Sydney, culturally, politically and geographically.

"Secondly, we should not forget that Parkes advocacy of Federation at Tenterfield was primarily based on frightening the voters about our lack of a defence capability. He said Australia needed one army to defend itself against potential invaders such as Japan, China and Russia, remembering that Mother England was a long way away. Most of us agreed that we needed to organise an adequate means of defending the continent.

"However, he largely ignored the economic advantages of Federation. These came to be of far greater consequence in the long term. The rest of us had to make it a prime issue over the following decade. Nevertheless, Parkes was an extraordinary character. You just could not ignore him, even if you despised him as I did.

"Such was his personal power, he was elected as member for Tenterfield in the New South Wales Parliament at a time when I don't think he actually knew where it was located.

"It all happened because he had, in a huge electoral upset, lost his long-held seat in Parliament at a General Election. He needed to find a new one in a hurry and Tenterfield conveniently became vacant at the same time. He approached the locals by letter, humbly suggesting that they elect him to represent them. The locals thought it was a great idea to have a man of his fame and prestige to be their spokesman in Parliament.

"This was why his arrival in town that day was such an historic event. Most of the citizens never ever believed that one day they would actually set eyes on him.

"Let me move on to his personal history. As a prime example of his exceptional life, let us all remember that he had three wives and eighteen children, three of them out of wedlock. He was also bankrupted three times, following the example of his father who was a bankrupt in England. Let me hasten to say that none of his bankruptcies were ever caused by corruption. He just had an unfortunate talent for investing in dud business ventures.

"Eighteen children would have bankrupted most of us, but he recovered from every one of his personal debacles to rise again and again. That he became Premier of New South Wales five times was a phenomenal achievement. It is a significant record that will surely stand as a record forever in any parliament. When we look at his life in totality, we must all acknowledge that it is a huge tragedy that he did not live to see Federation achieved.

"May I add, Toby, that, without in any way wanting to deflate your enjoyment of this evening, had Parkes managed to stay alive, he would have insisted on being the first prime minister and you would have missed out. If necessary, he would have challenged you to a duel over the prize and, knowing his ability to survive, the bookmakers would have given us all some very good odds on the probability that he would have won."

"I reckon it was the 18 children that killed him, not tough politics," quipped John Forrest who enjoyed a childless marriage.

"No, John, you have got it all wrong again, just like all of those far away 'Sand Gropers' over in Western Australia. Surely some salacious public scandals get reported in your newspapers over there. The facts, old chap, are that it was the wives who died first. They had a rough time. The record shows that he neglected them, although not intentionally. He just didn't leave himself sufficient time to think about them. He had to spend an enormous number of days on his never-ending struggle to stay afloat financially. Creditors followed him around everywhere. I can't honestly remember any time when he was not stony broke.

"I think it was ingrained in his soul that he had been destined to live in a parlous financial state. May I reemphasise a fact that I made earlier. As a small boy of only eight years, he was forced to commence working on the roads in England as a rock breaker because his father was penniless. He came a long way from that awful start in life and was fortunate to live to 81 years despite the way that his young body had been cruelly punished."

George paused.

Another voice took advantage of the silence. "I am certain that most of us have neglected our wives in our quest for political power. We are what we are because of their love, tolerance and loyalty. I shed a tear for Henry's wives. Indeed, I have enormous admiration and respect for them." Thus, spoke Prime Minister Andrew Fisher.

"All too true, Andrew," acknowledged Reid, "But, with genuine appreciation that he deserves the accolade, let's drink a toast to the extraordinary old rascal. Without him, there is a high probability that we may not be enjoying this dinner tonight."

"Hear, Hear. To Henry Parkes. Cheers."

"If it is possible," added Reid, "may he rest in peace."

Barton endeavoured to have the last word on Parkes. "George, I agree with your view that Henry would have aggressively claimed the office of prime minister ahead of me but, thankfully for my political career," the Lord intervened.

"Can I ask you a question? Despite the fact that it was a New South Wales Premier who lit the fire that led to Federation, it took two referendums in our state to gain assent to join the Commonwealth. It's an academic question now, but a large part of the problem was that you and others had such considerable political animosity towards Parkes. This clash of personalities and opinions created power politics of such a volatile extent that it severely hindered the cause of Federation. The grand vision was caught in unrelated political crossfire in the New South Wales Parliament that had the potential to destroy the entire movement."

Reid knew that he must make an eloquent response to this potentially embarrassing question.

"As you know from personal experience, Toby, Parkes was a very difficult old bugger to handle even on his best days. But, it is true that our disruptive local politics did play a delaying role in the march towards Federation and I must bear some personal responsibility for this. My team was doing its best to bring him down as Premier of New South Wales as often as possible and Federation got burnt quite regularly in the skirmishes. However, and more importantly, many people in New South Wales took exception to the constant accusation by other states that New South Wales was a great ogre which was trying to gobble them up, both economically and politically. I will admit that there were many occasions when I wanted to tell them all to go to hell. Fortunately, saner heads prevailed as the clock ticked steadily towards midnight."

This was too much for Deakin. His Victorian nostrils began to flare.

"George, with all the love that it is possible for any politician to muster, may I say that the real issue at stake at the time was not that the smaller states distrusted New South Wales. Your citizens, fuelled by political antics, held the view that Victoria was in fact calling the shots re Federation. You wanted to pull us into order and put us firmly and finally in our place. By this you meant that we should acknowledge publicly that we were number 2 in the pecking order. You created a crisis that had no basis in the facts of the matter."

"Quite close to the truth, Alfred. But, let me make a slight correction. In the popularity stakes, I have always put Victoria stone cold last and I have it in my mind to continue to do so until the end of my days. After all, hardworking statesmen need some form of pleasure, perverse though it may be. My life would be utterly boring if I could not thump a Victorian on regular occasions in order to stir you all out of the huge inferiority complex that you have."

Barton moved to intervene, but William Lyne beat him to it.

"As a fellow member with Parkes in the New South Wales Parliament, I can still remember the outrage created by the manner in which he addressed the Parliament in our Centenary Year of 1888. It provoked our bestselling weekly newspaper *The Bulletin* to take him on over his plan to take control of Federation by proposing to change, legally and constitutionally, the name of New South Wales to Australia in that very year. He then planned to offer the other states the privilege of joining Australia at their leisure, preferably being absorbed one at a time, with New South Wales calling the shots on every occasion. Queensland was chosen as the first one to receive a benevolent invitation. This was why he travelled to Brisbane so soon after our Centenary celebrations, then journeyed back home via Tenterfield. The editor of *The Bulletin* was so outraged that he declared that Parkes ambition was to be appointed King of Australia and change the name of the nation to 'INSOLVIA', a rather cheap shot at Parkes constant financial woes.

"I am somewhat embarrassed to report that several of us clubbed in together to buy the editor of *The Bulletin* a large bottle of high-class champagne in appreciation of the manner in which his journalism had stopped Parkes in his tracks.

"Having confessed to this, can I also affirm George Reid's assertion that Henry's oration at Tenterfield was a distinctive turning point in our national history. Without it, the Federation movement would have died at that time and it would have taken a few decades to revive it. At that point in my life, I would have helped it to die. In fact, it is a miracle that it did not die but, as the result of the Miracle of Tenterfield, we are together tonight."

Andrew Fisher added a word. "I recently met a man who had been present in Tenterfield on that historic day. He told me that Parkes had sent clear instructions ahead of him, informing the local mayor that he would be making a dramatic speech on Federation that day. He said that he had arranged for the speech to be prominently reported in the *Sydney Morning Herald* and then sent on to other major newspapers across the continent, thereby making Tenterfield the most famous rural town in Australia. It would be revered in history as the birthplace of Federation. He requested that significant local support be mustered to turn the occasion into a grand event. Some reports reveal that his message to the mayor discreetly inferred that his career in local politics may turn out to be at an inglorious end if the celebrations were not the greatest ever.

"The mayor obviously took it all seriously as, by that stage of his life, Parkes was an absolute legend. Everyone in town was given a half day holiday and the streets were lined with flags and bunting. The local band marched ahead of Parkes when he arrived. They played patriotic songs.

"The Henry Parkes Dinner was held in the largest hall in town, the School of Arts, but it could seat only 80 people so the mayor made attendance at it an issue of social stature. Those who missed out got the clear message that they were not in the top ranks of Tenterfield society. I yearn for the day when I can visit a town where the locals will greet me with similar fervour. It hasn't happened yet, but I live in constant hope."

George Reid could not believe what he was hearing. "Goodness me, Andrew, surely a leader of your stature can find a town full of Scotsmen somewhere in Australia who will turn out in their kilts and play their bagpipes for you. Now I come to think of it, the most likely place would be Glen Innes. It's not far from Tenterfield. On the only occasion I visited the town, their Scottish brogue was so bad, I thought they were speaking Gaelic."

Fisher was equal to the occasion. "Now, really and Truly George, whenever you speak in Parliament you are so incomprehensible that we all presume that you are making a hash of trying to speak Gaelic."

Affable Alfred

Before Reid could respond, Kingston waved his arms and made sure that he would get a word in before Toby could bring the Parkes tribute to a conclusion.

"Toby, can I say that I genuinely believe that Parkes speech at Tenterfield was not the greatest speech in the making of Federation. It was just the most highly publicised. It certainly gave new life to the Federation Movement that had previously faltered a number of times due to the economic recession of that era, the huge drought, sheer parochialism and irresponsible apathy mixed with some bloody-minded politics.

"May I say that, in my view, it was a dynamic speech by our fellow diner, Alfred Deakin, to the Australian Natives Association Convention at the Shamrock Hotel in Bendigo a decade later in March, 1898, that turned the tide against the virulent opposition to Federation from the media and other vested interests. This speech created an unstoppable final surge towards the creation of an Australian nation at the precise time that the referendums were underway."

"Thank you, Charles," responded 'Affable Alfred'. "With all the humility that I can struggle to muster, I happen to think that it was the best speech of my life, but I would not put it in the class that you have just suggested, much as I would be delighted if it were."

"You underrate yourself, Alfred. As you well remember, your speech was entitled, 'The Greater the Odds the Greater the Honour'.

"Responsible people who attended have told me that it was a corker. All the previous speakers that night had said that Federation would drag Victoria down to the level of New South Wales and would put Sydney's free trading capitalists in control of the Australian economy, while thousands of workers would be further downtrodden.

"You totally changed the tone of the entire convention, not by addressing their nonsense, but by outlining a vision of a great nation powered by fine people. The delegates went back to their local communities all over Australia absolutely fired up and became the leaders of the Yes vote in referendums. Can I say that every time I read that great speech of yours, I am inspired?"

"My gratitude once more, Charles, but the real drama of that occasion occurred the previous day.

"David Syme, publisher of *The Age* summoned me to his office and, with a high degree of anger, demanded that I not go to Bendigo to advocate Federation. He said that the people attending the Australian Natives Association Dinner were powerful leaders from all over Australia. Syme rightly felt that there was a great danger that an influential speaker could influence them to could go back to their local communities and heavily influence people to vote Yes, whereas, in his view, a NO vote was in the best interests of Victoria.

"He vented his anger to me in front of a room full of his own journalists and in their full hearing. He told me that he would withdraw henceforth all editorial support from my entire political career if I went to Bendigo. This being so, he emphasised, my life in politics would be over, never to be revived. I would be politically dead and buried. He could not believe that I could be so irrational as to create a situation whereby this would inevitably happen.

"I had never before been in a room where there was so much hostility directed towards me. Yet, their intense venom motivated me to go and make my speech. It was not an act of either bravery or defiance on my part. I must say that my thoughts on the journey to Bendigo were that it was possible that I was about to carry out an act of gross stupidity. Thus, having made a political decision that I would have to live with, I had no real option but to go through with it.

"Before Syme had issued his ultimatum, I had been concerned that my speech would not be reported at all. So, I reckoned that if he attacked me for what I said, everyone across the continent would actually get to hear my words and could decide for themselves who was right, me or Syme.

"Luckily for me, he scathingly assaulted me on his front pages for several days after the speech and he syndicated it to every newspaper he could think of. I was beside myself with delight. I could breathe again. I could not have bought that publicity even if I had spent thousands of pounds that I did not have."

This drew a caustic comment from Charles Kingston, "Syme is a pompous loudmouth and a blackmailer. He had no hesitation in publicly withdrawing his support of you on what he attended to be a permanent basis."

"He did just that, Charles. And HE did so for a considerable period of time, but not permanently. He ridiculed me about everything I said about anything at all, political or not, even if he agreed with my comments. However, he is not a fool and, eventually, realised that he was on the losing side and his readers were no longer listening to him. In fact, his circulation figures began to drop. This was a humbling experience for him. He had always believed that he was the conscience and voice of Victoria, indeed Australia, who must be obeyed without question. He had to admit to himself that perhaps he wasn't."

That brought Chris Watson into the fray once more. "My experience of life, political and otherwise, is that too many newspaper publishers think they are God. I do hope that, in the years ahead, quite a few more of them have humbling experiences like the one that Syme inflicted on himself. It will vastly improve the profession of journalism in Australia."

Barton intervened, "Let me propose a toast to you, Alfred. It was a great speech that hit the right mark at the right time. Bravo."

They drank heartily and applauded mightily. Even Lyne joined the accolade without actually smiling.

Deakin, who had a photographic memory, silently recalled his speech and the stony silence with which he was initially greeted in Bendigo.

THE GREATER THE ODDS, THE GREATER THE HONOUR

Members of the Australian Natives Association, we have heard much tonight of politicians and a good deal from them. We have also heard something of the Federal Convention and addresses from some of my fellow members, but it is in neither capacity that I propose to speak, because I recognise that the united Australia yet to be can only come to be with the consent of and by the efforts of the Australian born. I propose to speak to Australians simply as an Australian.

You are entitled to reckon among the greatest of your achievements the Federal Convention just closing. The idea of such a convention may be said to have sprung up among you, and it is by your efforts that it must be brought to fruition.

This was received with some slight sounds of encouragement. They were warming to his positive attitude. He was recognising their status and influence.

We should find no difficulty in apprehending the somewhat dubious mood of many of our critics. A Federal Constitution is the last and final product of political intellect and constructive ingenuity. It represents the highest development of the possibilities of self-government among peoples scattered over a large area. To frame such a constitution is a great task for any body of men. Yet I venture to submit that among all the federal constitutions of the world you will look in vain for one as broad as its popular base, as liberal in its working principles, as generous in its aim as this measure. As far as I am concerned, that suffices me. Like my friends, I would if I could have secured something nearer to my own ideals.

But for the present, as we must choose, let us gladly accept it.

Hear, Hear, was the response from a growing number.

I fail to share the optimistic views of those to whom the early adoption of union is a matter of indifference. Our work is not that of an individual artist aiming at his life's achievement, which he would rather destroy than accept while it seemed imperfect. What we have to ask ourselves is whether we can afford indefinite delay. Do we lose nothing by a continuance of a separation between state and state? Do not every year and every month exact from us the toll of severance? Do not we find ourselves hampered in commerce, restricted in influence, weakened in prestige, because we are jarring atoms instead of a united organism? Is it because we are so supremely satisfied with our local constitutions and present powers of development that we hesitate to make any change? The governments from which we take the powers with which the Federation is to be endowed are without exception less liberal than government provided in this constitution. We are not to fall into the hands of foreigners. It is not to tyrannical rulers that we propose to remit federal authority. Those to whom we propose to entrust the sole creation and control of the new government are the Australian people.

Warm applause. Frowns were disappearing.

At a time like the present, this Association cannot forget its watchword – Federation – or its character, which has never been provincial. It has never been a Victorian, but always an Australian Association. Its hour has now come. Still recognising the quarter from which attacks have already begun, and other quarters from which they are threatening, we must admit that the prospects of union are gloomier now in Victoria than for years past. The number actually against us is probably greater than ever; the timorous and passive will be induced to fall away; the forces against us are arrayed under capable chiefs. But few as we may be, and weak by comparison, it will be the greater glory, whether we succeed or fail. These are the times that try men's souls. The classes may resist us; the masses may be inert; politicians may falter; our leaders may sound the retreat. But it is not a time to surrender. Let us nail our standard to the mast. Let us stand shoulder to shoulder in defence of the enlightened liberalism of the constitution. Let us recognise that we live in an unstable era, and that, if we fail in the hour of crisis, we may never be able to recall our lost national opportunities. At no period in the past hundred years has the situation of the great empire to which we belong been more serious. From the far east and the far west alike we behold menaces and antagonisms. We cannot evade, we must meet them. Hyper criticism cannot help us to outface the future, nor can we hope to if we remain disunited. Happily, your voice is for immediate and absolute union.

Now, the tempo of the gathering was stirring. There was electricity in the air.

One word more. This after all is only the beginning of our labours. The 150 delegates who leave this conference, returning to their homes in all parts of this colony to report its proceedings, will, I trust, go back each of them filled with zeal and bearing the fiery cross of Federation, every branch should be stimulated into action, until, without resorting to any but legitimate means, without any attempt at intimidation, without taking advantage of sectionalism, but in the broadest spirit of Australian unity, all your members unite to awaken this colony to its duty. You must realise that upon you, and perhaps upon you alone, will rest the responsibility of organising and carrying on this campaign.

The greater the odds, the greater the honour. This cause dignifies every one of its servants and all efforts that are made on its behalf. The contest on which you are about to engage is one in which it is a privilege to be enrolled. It lifts your labours to the loftiest political levels, where they may be inspired with the purest patriotic passion for national life and being.

Prolonged applause now. A few rose from their chairs to convey their enthusiasm.

Remember the stirring appeal of the young poet of genius, so recently lost to us in Bendigo, William Gay, and whose grave is not yet green in your midst. His dying lips warned us of our present need and future duty, and pointed us to the true Australian goal – 'Our garment, with hands unfilial we have basely rent,

*with petty variance our souls are spent, and ancient kinship under foot is trod,
O let us rise – united – penitent – and be new people – mighty, serving God!'*

They rose as one and cheered. It took several minutes for order to be restored.

For Affable Alfred, that heady evening in Bendigo just seemed like yesterday. He had savoured the wild applause and then the pleasure of shaking hands with about a hundred or so delegates who surged forward to assure him personally that they were going home to campaign strongly for a YES vote. They fulfilled their promises mightily and delivered the votes he needed for an emphatic victory.

For now, his agile brain clicked back to connect again with the proceedings of tonight's dinner at the Melbourne Club where his fellow founders had so unexpectedly and generously honoured him. He felt that there was a genuine warmth of gratitude around the table.

Death of the Aristocrats

Barton was endeavouring to move on, but, before he could continue, Chris Watson intervened, courteously, yet again.

"There is another fine champion of greater democracy for British colonies whom we should honour with a toast.

"His name is almost unknown to most Australians. Nevertheless, almost sixty years ago, he electrified a huge, mostly male, audience at the Victoria Theatre in Sydney in August, 1853, at an Independence Rally organised by his mentors, Henry Parkes and John Dunmore Lang, around the time that New South Wales was seriously considering ways and means of putting to an end the indignity of being governed directly from London and when Parkes and Lang were advocating a Republic.

"He was Daniel Deniehy, son of an Irish convict and a brilliant young lawyer. Deniehy was a much sought-after public speaker of outstanding eloquence who became an outspoken political opponent of the redoubtable monarchist William Charles Wentworth. It was Wentworth who had openly opposed a Union of Australian Colonies that was first promoted at that time.

"Infamously, Wentworth had also petitioned the Queen to create and legally establish an Aristocracy in Australia (of which he and carefully selected friends would be the first to be elevated as lords) so that New South Wales would forever be linked to the British Crown. He had suggested to Her Majesty that she should create a House of Lords in a New South Wales Parliament with strong powers of veto over a Lower House. After his proposed House of Lords was created, he planned also to arrange that only aristocrats and property owners would be allowed to vote in elections for the Lower House, no commoners. It was a pompously arrogant attempt to permanently embed the British system of class distinction in Australia.

"Being a proud Irishman, Deniehy was appalled by everything that Wentworth stood for, so he gave his speech the delightful title of 'The Bunyip

Aristocracy'. It stopped Wentworth in his tracks. Can I read to you the final paragraphs of this splendid oration?

"I am sure that Alfred will agree that this man was in his elite league as an orator. However, I must sadly report that, a few short years after he delivered it, Deniehy became a hopeless alcoholic and a severe sufferer of depression, dying tragically at age 37. Having drawn huge crowds to his speeches wherever he went, only five people attended his funeral in Bathurst.

"This misfortune does not in any way detract from the quality of the fine Victoria Theatre speech I am about to quote from. You can hear for yourselves what a patriot he was. His words were directed both to the legislators in London and to the people of New South Wales. History records that, despite herculean efforts by Wentworth to revive his proposal after Deniehy's assault, he failed to become an Australian aristocrat. His proposed title of Lord Wentworth of Vaucluse was never bestowed upon him.

"Fifty years later, the Australian States created a Federation despite the efforts of people like me and the Labor Party for reasons quite different to those of Wentworth. Thanks to Deniehy, it was done without having to create any British style aristocrats.

"Let me hasten to remind you that, unlike Wentworth, when I was opposing Federation, I was representing the cause of workers, not bluebloods." Anyway, these are the last words of a spellbinding speech.

A HERITAGE BEFITTING THE DIGNITY OF FREE MEN

Colonial governments must prepare to open their arms to receive fugitives from England, Ireland, Wales and Scotland who would hasten to the security and competence they are denied in their own land. The interest of those countless thousands must be involved in their decision to grant us self-government. These migrants are entitled to look for a heritage that is befitting of free men.

Bring them not here with fleeting visions and false hopes. Let them not find a new-fangled aristocracy swarming and darkening these fair free shores. They must be offered a land where man is bountifully rewarded for his labour and where just laws no longer recognise the supremacy of a class than it does the dominance of a creed.

Watson paused.

"It is important to note here that Deniehy was challenging the very basis of British society, i.e., an upper class being necessary to keep the peasants under control."

But, fellow citizens, there is an aristocracy worthy of our respect and of our admiration. Wherever human skill and brainpower are eminent, wherever glorious manhood asserts its elevation, there is an aristocracy that confers eternal honour upon the land that possesses it. That is God's aristocracy, Gentlemen, that is an aristocracy that will bloom and expand under free institutions, and forever bless the clime where it takes root. I hope that you will take into consideration the hitherto barren condition of our continent. I myself am a native of the soil and I am proud of my birthplace. It is true that its past was not hallowed in history by the achievements of men whose names reflected a light upon the times in which they lived. We have not a long line of poets or statesmen or warriors; in this country Art has done nothing but Nature everything. It is ours, then, alone to inaugurate the future. In no country has the attempt ever been made to successfully manufacture an aristocracy pro re nata. It cannot be done; we might as well expect honour to be paid to the dusky nobles of King Kamehamaka, or to the ebony earls of the Emperor Souloque of Hayti.

The stately aristocracy of England was founded on the sword. The men who came over with the conquering Normans were the masters of the Saxons, and so became the aristocracy.

The followers of Oliver Cromwell were the masters of the Irish and so became their aristocracy.

"We should note," said Watson, "that Deniehy was well aware that the Lords and Ladies of England were not revered by the majority of the residents of the Great South Land, most of whom had fled from their oppression. The audience was on his side. Had I been there, I would have been cheering."

But I would enquire by what process Wentworth and his satellites have conquered the people of New South Wales, except by the artful dodgery of cooking up a franchise Bill. If we are to be blessed with an Australian aristocracy, I should prefer it to resemble, not that of William the Bastard, but of Jack the Strapper. But I trespass too long on your time, and would in conclusion only seek to record two things.

First, my indignant denunciation of any tampering with the freedom of purity of the elective principle, the only basis upon which sound government can be built.

Secondly, I wish you to regard well the future destinies of our country.

Let us, with prophetic eye, behold the troops of weary pilgrims from foreign despotism which would ere long be flocking to these shores in search of a more congenial home, and let us now give our earnest and determined assurance that the domineering clique which make up the Wentworth Party are not, and never shall be, regarded as the representatives of the manliness, the spirit, and the intelligence of the freemen of New South Wales.

"That really was a cracker of a speech. It magnificently taught William Charles Wentworth and his fellow would-be aristocrats to work out which country they belonged to, England or Australia. The tragedy is that some of Wentworth's admirers still have not made the choice.

"The happy ending of it all is that their pompous plan for a blueblood Australia founded on social decadence died a natural death."

After several more of his guests had voiced their approval of Daniel Deniehy, Barton finally regained his planned course of the proceedings.

Minister for Five Days

"It's time to move on from our wholehearted recognition of the skills of Henry and Alfred and Daniel so we can toast the former Premier of Queensland, James Dickson.

"It was a tragedy that he died a few days after he was sworn in as a Minister of our first Cabinet and before he could be democratically elected as a member of our First Parliament.

"As has been pointed out by Andrew, Queensland was perilously late in entering into negotiations for Federation, but it was largely Dickson's efforts, alongside the strong public advocacy of Andrew Fisher and the discreet intervention of Samuel Griffith that finally got them to the table at the eleventh hour. This was surprising to Alfred, Charles and me. We had prepared for the worst, but it was a very welcome result. Indeed, it was the deal breaker that ensured Federation would happen.

"You will recall that James Dickson was with us in London for the negotiations that were necessary to have our Federation Bill pass through the British Parliament. He went there as an observer for the Queensland Government, not an official delegate.

"He worried constantly that we were offending the Crown and was convinced that we were wrong in stoutly defending important sections of the Constitution that the British were not happy with. We had to constantly remind him that the Constitution had been approved by referendums which we would have to hold again if we made substantial changes. His understanding of the Empire was that imperial protocol required that we should give ground to our 'superiors' in London and this caused us to often exchange harsh words of disagreement with him in order to supress his negativity. Thus, it came as a complete surprise to us that he came home to fight hard for Federation when we were expecting him to do the opposite. I think that this was a revelation to you too, Sam."

"It was absolutely amazing. He had cabled me from London several times seeking my advice about his concerns. I was Chief Justice of Queensland at the time and he regarded me as his legal adviser. His anxiety was so profound that he also contacted me by the slow process of letters by which he could bare his soul in great detail, as well as his regular cables, during the many months you were all in London.

"We mainly discussed the rights and wrongs of Australians having the legal right of appealing to the Privy Council in London as the final Court to which Australians could have access. I told him that I thought London would insist on retaining the right and he took the whole matter seriously, believing that it would be fatal for us to offend Westminster in any way. I noted that he returned from London a changed man, mainly relieved that the access to the Privy Council had been retained. When he died soon after helping to achieve Federation, I wondered whether, on his return home, he had suddenly become aware that his health was fragile and decided to die a hero rather than a spoiler."

"I think that you have nailed it in one, Sam," responded Andrew Fisher. "I served with him in the Queensland Parliament and it was clearly obvious that he was always lukewarm towards Federation right up until the eleventh hour. But, this change of heart was the most important hour of his life. It meant that he will be recorded in history as a Minister in the first Australian Government. Had he lived, he would have given the Ministry his very best shot."

There was one matter that Fisher did not convey it to his fellow diners.

Just prior to his death, Dickson had courteously advised Fisher that he intended to run against him for the seat of Wide Bay in Queensland in the Federal Election which was scheduled for 1 March that year. Had that happened, Dickson may well have won as he was a popular premier at the time. This would have had a lethal impact on Fisher's political career and he would not now be Prime Minister. Such is life. It was not dissimilar to Parkes dying and paving the way for Edmund Barton.

Fisher decided that there was nothing to be gained by raising this tonight.

Reid could not resist a shot at Deakin and his spiritual beliefs.

"Alfred, my good friend, may I ask of you an important religious question. No doubt you believe that God intervened and thoroughly scared the hell out of Dickson to the extent that he joined the Federation team in fear and trembling of the wrath of the Almighty."

"It is highly possible that He did. But, the Good Lord may have made a mistake by focusing on Dickson. He is not noted for making errors of judgement but He may have been better employed by putting a bolt of lightning into your soul instead."

"Well, He may be working on me right now. This splendid Scotch is revving up my soul to an extraordinary extent. I am ready to believe that God was the creator of fine whisky and gave His considerable blessing to its use."

The Deakin-Reid verbal duel ended with a genuinely warm response to this remembrance of Dickson as the first of the Founding Fathers to fall.

Barton decided to move on from the toasts.

"I will call a halt at this point. Giles has just indicated that the entrée is ready, so we should head for the dining room. I am certain that the difficulties of having Federation approved in all six states will raise its head again during the evening."

They proceeded forth to the dinner table as Barton had suggested and did so with a positive spring in their step. The lively debate over drinks had created hope that the chatter was destined to grow much more interesting and enjoyable as the proceedings progressed through a delightfully long evening.

Entrée

"You will note, with pleasure I am sure, that our entrée is crayfish. I plan that, while we are enjoying it, we will discuss the momentous weekend of March, 1893, when our esteemed Chief Justice, Sam Griffith, cruised around the Hawkesbury River with Charles Kingston and myself on *Lucinda*. The

Queensland Government had made this fine ship available to us because Sam was at that time Premier of Queensland and had sailed on her to reach Sydney for the Federation Convention of that year. Happily based on such a superb craft, there was nothing but magnificent river and mountain scenery to divert our attention from preparing a quality draft of the Constitution of a new nation in conditions of total peace and quiet.

"We finally left the boat with a substantial document in our hands ready for debate in the halls of parliamentary power, and across the continent among those who would eventually vote for or against it in Referendums. I am now going to invite Sam to review what happened over that weekend.

"Before I give the floor to the Chief Justice, can I bring to your attention that a member of the Melbourne Club has generously donated the crayfish we are about to enjoy. As you know, the price of crayfish at the Melbourne markets is so outrageous that only the Mafia can afford to buy them. Our benefactor sails out regularly to King Island in Bass Strait to buy crayfish from the local fisherman and makes a feature of serving them to his friends here at the club.

"Cheers to this generous Australian who admirably wishes to remain anonymous as he wants none of us to believe that he is trying to buy either political or judicial favours. As we all know, not many venerable members of this club practice such a noble discipline.

Over to you, Sam."

Lucinda Sails into History

Sir Samuel Griffith always spoke in the finest legal tones so that all listeners would be utterly aware that he was the Chief Justice of Australia without him ever having to remind them of his position of eminence.

It hadn't always been that way. In his two terms of office as a powerful and controversial Premier of Queensland, he had been a consummate politician in that role, ruthlessly destroying some former political friends along his way to the top.

He had earned the nick name of 'Slippery Sam'. It described him well as it was justly earned in achieving deals around the hallowed halls of the Queensland Parliament.

Such was his reputation, it surprised no one that many of the Honourable Members had actively and persistently contrived to get rid of him, finally succeeding in having him appointed as Chief Justice of Queensland so as to get him out of the way in a most respectable fashion. Little did they know that he had been deftly aspiring to hold that position for a long time.

In reality, he believed that his destiny was to be appointed to the House of Lords in London and be appointed as one of the Law Lords.

He had been in the Slippery Sam tradition on the *Lucinda* that weekend when history was created. The draft of the Constitution that he had taken on board had been drawn up by Andrew Inglis Clark of Tasmania who was to have been a fellow guest for the weekend had he not taken very ill with pneumonia. Sadly, he had to be left behind in a Sydney hospital in a quite serious condition.

After the public learnt of the spectacular drafting achievements on *Lucinda*, the myth grew that it was Griffith who was the constitutional mastermind when his actual role was that of improving on the work of Clark, the original mastermind behind its quality drafting. While the subsequent upgrading did require a significant legal mind of the quality of Griffith, Clark's initial work was quietly ignored and Griffith had done nothing to put the record straight.

Now, as he launched forth on the *Lucinda* story, his fellow diners fully expected him to perpetuate this distorted and unfair recording of history.

"Those of us who were at the Federation Conference in Sydney in 1893 will recall that there were many divergent opinions as to what should be contained in the Australian Constitution. Thus, it was obvious that we would never be able to reach a consensus if the debate continued on the floor of a large meeting. So, we managed to have a resolution passed that gave all delegates a long weekend off work while I got together with Charles and Toby to do some serious re-drafting so that we could have a document that could have a genuine chance of being approved when we reconvened on the following Tuesday.

"Fortunately, I had travelled to Sydney on *Lucinda* so we sailed away on her out of Sydney Harbour, past the leafy North Shore suburbs and on up into the Hawkesbury River for three nights and two days from Friday afternoon to Monday morning.

"The Hawkesbury provided a delightful background. This splendid river has some of the finest scenery in the world and it typified the spectacular landscape that can be found in many parts of our fine nation whose future we were planning. We anchored in a delightfully peaceful spot on the river called Refuge Bay and it proved to be a great place to take refuge from the Convention. There, we locked ourselves into the Gentleman's Smoking Room on the Upper Foredeck and spent hour upon hour crafting words that we felt would be appropriate in our quest to achieve unanimity across a new nation.

"Our task was made easier by the fortunate fact that a great son of Tasmania, Andrew Clark, had given me some detailed documents on how the Westminster system of government could be married with the American and Canadian Constitutions to create a unique constitutional framework for Australia. These papers included a preliminary draft of a constitution.

"Clark had, in fact, deliberately visited all three of those nations for the specific purpose of having prolonged discussions with their constitutional lawyers on this matter. His commitment to our common cause was that of a patriot."

Griffith appeared to be more than a trifle uneasy as he made this surprising confession. It was almost as though he made a slip of the tongue that he was now regretting.

Barton smiled approvingly as the truth of Clark's role was finally being acknowledged with a quite reasonable degree of grace, even if only to an audience of nine.

Kingston looked somewhat stunned, indeed astonished.

Seemingly unaware of the drama he was creating, Griffith ventured on. "Somehow, we waded through all of Clark's bountiful research and planning by adding and subtracting words. Finally, we reckoned that we had the right model for a sound constitution for a new nation. We could not have completed the task in one weekend if we had started with blank sheets of paper or had the benefit of a book of speeches that had been made about Federation in past years.

"History reveals that when the Convention resumed on Tuesday, after we had some time to briefly review our work with Andrew Clark who had sufficiently recovered from his illness by Monday to spend a couple of hours with us on Sydney Harbour, we managed to have it approved in principle by the Convention in a matter of days. This was only made possible because we agreed to some amendments that did not crucially alter it. It enabled a few egos to be stroked while reaching the point of it being ready for much wider debate involving thousands of people far beyond our meeting.

"Even the Conferences that followed over the next 5 years, as well as the 1898 Constitutional Convention altered it little, except for a small number of controversial issues relating to the powers of the senate and the rights of the states. Many attempts were made to gut it totally, but, eventually, after long and passionate debates, the delegates would return to its basic democratic intent.

"Now, with the benefit of hindsight, I can see ways in which it can be improved, and it could be that the Australian people will hold many referendums in the years ahead in order to do so, but I think it will largely stand the test of time. I regard its adoption as the finest achievement of my life."

Author of the Original Constitution

As Slippery Sam paused to sample another taste of superb crayfish, Bolton Stafford Bird sought and gained Barton's permission to speak.

As a Minister of the Faith, who had heard many confessions in his time, he had noted Griffith's partial confession, and decided that it was opportune for him to seek full redemption for the great man.

"Could I express my gratitude to the Chief Justice for his graceful and gracious acknowledgement of the role of my fellow Tasmanian, Andrew Clark, and may I be so bold as to propose a toast to Clark. Without in any way disparaging or diminishing the great work that was done on *Lucinda* by Sam, Charles and Toby, most Tasmanians believe that, but for the tragedy of his poor health on that historic weekend, Andrew would now be enshrined in history as the author of the Australian Constitution.

"As we are all sadly aware, he died in 1904 just three years after achieving his dream of an Australian nation. But for that tragic event, he would be here tonight at this dinner in my place as I am not fit to stand in his shadow. While I represented Tasmania as a member of the ill-fated Federal Council, as well as at the first Federation Convention, few noticed that I was there, but they were all very aware of Clark.

"I honour him with this toast that not just acknowledges his superb work on the framing of the Constitution. It also recognises his eminent service to

Australia in making the uniting of the nation work so successfully in the First Parliament. Despite his rapidly failing health, he worked ceaselessly at this practical and necessary task of making sure that Federation actually worked after it was achieved in 1901 until he left us in 1904."

Somewhat tardily Samuel Griffith raised his glass, but Kingston and Barton did not hesitate. They knew that Clark's papers rarely left their hands during the entire weekend of verbal toil on the Hawkesbury River.

Prime Minister Andrew Fisher had a smile on his face. Back in those heady days in Queensland politics prior to Federation, he and Griffith had been political foes. He enjoyed watching him squirm just a little this evening, but gave him credit for having mentioned Clarke quite voluntarily during his comments on the miracle of the *Lucinda*. It was an act of grace. Sir Samuel had just graduated into the world of humility, even if only for one evening. He waved his hand to Griffith as a symbol of his approval.

The Great Negotiator

Toby turned to Charles Kingston, the formidable political giant from South Australia who was the third draughtsman on *Lucinda*.

"Charles, your thoughts about the historic weekend will be of considerable interest to us."

Kingston endorsed Griffith's comments on Clark and his delight that Bird has proposed such an appropriate toast. He then mentioned the rigour with which they had done their work. Each day consumed thirteen hours of concentrated debate. He then highlighted the issues that would turn out to be the kernel of the constitutional debates for five years after the weekend on the Hawkesbury.

"As Sam has indicated, we laboured long and hard over several crucial matters. Little did we know that despite all of our good work that weekend, these vital issues would be remorselessly debated over and over again at public forums across the nation for which there seemed to be no end.

"The first was to decide how the powers of Government would be divided between the Commonwealth and the states, a thorny issue that remains with us to this day. We can expect that it will continue to be the issue about which most proposed changes to the Constitution will be based for decades to come.

"Secondly, there was the hotly debatable matter of how each arm of government would collect their revenue, whether it be from taxes or levies or tariffs or fines. Once we agreed on practical financial solutions that we thought all states would buy in solving those delicate matters, the drafting of the appropriate words came relatively easily."

Then, there was the issue of the establishment of an appropriate Upper House of Parliament. Did we really need a senate, what powers would it have, how many senators would there be, how would they be elected and what should be the exact relationship should be between senate and the House of Representatives. To this day, I am not sure that we agreed upon the right solutions. In fact, I have fear in my soul that history will decide that we got it quite wrong."

He closed by pointedly praising Barton and omitting any special reference to Griffith.

"Can I add, Toby, that a major reason why, in the end, we achieved a valid draft Constitution was your ability to settle the disputes that occupied us hour after hour. You would suggest words that enabled the three of us to feel that we had some sort of a victory on each occasion."

Barton silently noted the slight to Griffith, but thanked Kingston for the praise that he felt he did not fully deserve and then added his own views.

"You will recall, Charles, that we also had to consider the possible attitude that London would take to every clause we drafted. We knew that they would want powers that would enable them to regain control of us if Federation ever collapsed. We were especially aware that many parochial citizens in positions of influence across our continent were already writing letters to London to tell them that Federation was doomed to fail. But, overall, we had to take care that we did not include any words that would cause us to be defeated in the subsequent referendums. It was enormously difficult, but incredibly fascinating and, finally, most satisfying.

"May I add that, at the conclusion of each tiring day on the *Lucinda*, I was eternally grateful to Sam for his commendable foresight in placing on to the boat a plentiful quantity of superb single malt Scotch Whisky from some of the finest distilleries in the Highlands, supplied benevolently from the coffers of the Government of Queensland. It was my sincere belief that the taxpayers of Queensland would not begrudge us the pleasure of several wee drams each evening."

Griffith was content to keep his peace and remain silent. An expectation of being the least popular bloke in the room was ingrained in his persona. He was acutely aware that, on the *Lucinda*, he had often driven Barton and Kingston to the point of total exasperation with his pedantic insistence on infinite detail. Nevertheless, he knew that the world would keep going around only if someone looked after the necessary details.

Watson summed it up, "I hope that Queensland preserves *Lucinda* as a significant monument of our national heritage. She accommodated a momentous event that created a fundamental turning point in the history of our continent. Three men, and the spirit of an absent fourth, sat on her decks and wisely produced an incredible document that has survived years of debate and will continue to be debated for many more. I confidently predict that most of its content will remain intact. The product of their hard work and expertise became our respected Constitution. May I toast the *Lucinda* and all who sailed on her on a weekend that will be long remembered in Australian folklore? May the creative spirit that it represents never die."

"Hear, Hear." They rose as one, drained their glasses, then broke into applause.

As they resumed their seats, Andrew Fisher posed a question, "I find it astonishing that a Victorian was not onboard *Lucinda*. The drafting team comprised a Queenslander, a New South Welshman and a South Australian. But for illness, there would have been a Tasmanian there. As Western Australia had become a state only in the previous year of 1890, they were not yet ready to play a part. Alfred, why did you not insist on being onboard to represent Victoria."

This evoked a sombre response from Deakin.

"Firstly, the Convention did not elect me on to the drafting committee. Secondly, I was personally delighted that Toby was elected because of his huge skills in legal drafting. Lastly, there is an old saying that too many cooks spoil the broth. Three people could do the job in a weekend. Any more would have added to the difficulty of making decisions. Could I add that there is a humility about Victorians that may be a trifle lacking in our northern neighbours."

That heavily parochial New South Welshman, George Reid, straightened in his chair, ready to return serve, but decided that he would let it go. Deakin had responded humbly to Fisher's question. Every so often, it made sense to let Victorians have a tiny victory.

Giles appeared. He was delighted with the way the whole evening was proceeding. He and his team cleared away the entrée plates, recharged glasses and served the main course with flourish.

Main

Toby got them quickly down to business again. "Now is the time to consider the Referendums that were held to approve or disapprove Federation.

"The background is well known to you all. We needed all six states to vote Yes. We had reached a crucial point in our nationalistic crusade where the Federation Movement would collapse if there was one negative state. It was essential that we send a totally positive message to the British Parliament that all states were requesting them to pass empowering legislation that would enable those states to come together to form the nation of Australia. It would have been intolerable if one state had opted to go it alone and become a separate nation.

"The prime beef we are about to enjoy comes from the lovely highlands around Bowral, thanks to good arrangements made by William, the grazier in our midst. Our thanks William.

"Now, while we enjoy it, I will invite a speaker from each state to recall the story of how they achieved a positive vote despite highly effective opposition and a surprisingly considerable depth of apathy among our voters. We will go by size of population. New South Wales will have the floor first."

New South Wales Votes Twice

George Reid decided to enjoy himself a little more. "Ah, Toby, not only does New South Wales have the largest population in Australia, our people are of the highest quality and no Victorian could produce beef like this."

A low groan emanated from Deakin.

Toby intervened, "William Lyne, as you were Premier of New South Wales at the time of Federation, may I suggest that you speak on behalf of our state. Will you refresh our minds as to why, other than for the fact that many people were not admirers of the politics of Henry Parkes, New South Wales required two referendums to be held before deciding to join the Federation when all the other States needed only one."

Barton waved his hand in the direction of the man who had gone within a whisker of becoming Australia's first Prime Minister. Lyne looked surprised. He had expected that Reid would be called to speak on behalf of New South Wales and was more than a trifle baffled as to why the garrulous George had not insisted upon it, having been Australia's fourth Prime Minister.

Be this as it may, Lyne was delighted to be given this opportunity to speak his mind.

"As George indicated to us earlier, there were many factors in play throughout the era when the two Federation Referendums were held in New South Wales. A major issue for us was the unseemly hatred that other states had hysterically generated about New South Wales being a grizzly bear that would consume them. It became a huge factor in creating negativity amongst our voters. Hatred is most probably not the correct word to describe the unfortunate situation. It was almost an irrational jealousy.

"We hold the view that New South Wales has the loveliest portion of land in the whole continent and is able to prosper mightily without any help from the other states. So, why on earth would we want to go into a Federation. To be truthful, many of our people feared, not entirely incorrectly, that some of the other states were economic duds who would drag us down to a lower standard of living. After all, the great bank crashes of 1893 originated in Melbourne, not Sydney, and we recovered from the subsequent general recession much more quickly. Those pathetic parochial attitudes towards us really were childish in the extreme.

"In addition, Free Traders and Protectionists were staging never ending battles in our State Parliament and both sides feared that Federation could bring too many of the other side into the political arena. Assurances had to be sought from colleagues in other states that this contest of economic ideology could continue to be fought on a level playing field once Federation occurred.

"We also had a strong Women's Suffrage Movement that seriously diverted our attention combined with a still powerful push for a Republic of New South Wales even though its prime champions, Henry Parkes and John Dunmore Lang, had passed on. Those supporting that republican view felt that a merger with other states would weaken our chances of totally freeing up the chains that tied New South Wales to Westminster.

"In an attempt to get everyone onside, we passed legislation requiring that a minimum vote, well above 50%, was needed to approve Federation. No other state had set the bar this high. The figure that our Parliament had settled on was a minimum of 80,000 votes in favour of Federation, something that no other state had done. This threshold caused a narrow loss for Federation in the first vote and a narrow win in the second. We have to acknowledge that Australia became a nation only by the slimmest of margins in its largest state. We were just as big a threat to Federation as were the very insular Governments in Queensland and Western Australia."

George Reid always had difficulty in staying out of discussions. He succumbed once more to this enjoyable weakness and stirred the pot with a provocative comment.

"William, you are being far too gentle with our friends who have gathered here tonight in the fervent hope of enjoying our company. We must be frank with them and fully confess to our sins.

"We know that if any state had an achievable vision of staying out of Federation and becoming a separate nation, it was New South Wales. You and I both know that deep in our hearts there was a powerful desire to go it alone. We really were not a genuine part of the Federation Movement until the last minute. The reality is that, if Toby had not been around as a relentless architect and advocate of Federation, we would have pulled out. His persistence kept our isolationist tendencies in check."

Silence reigned.

Reid's words vividly reminded them all that Federation really was a miracle. The gods had smiled upon them.

Barton moved on. He gave the nod to Deakin who was much more a nationalist than he was a Victorian.

Free Settlers Have Their Say

'Affable Alfred' was widely acknowledged as the finest exponent of debating skill in the Parliament, if not the entire nation. It was a well-deserved honour that few disputed. He wore the accolade with both humility and pride.

"I have no difficulty in agreeing with William's diagnosis of the political, social and economic conditions that prevailed in New South Wales throughout the decade of 1890, even though I think that their Parliament could have handled the parochial politics much better than they did in the referendum campaigns. Too many MPs sat on the fence and gave no leadership.

"But, as William has identified, the failed first vote in New South Wales, followed by a narrow winning vote, simply mirrored the perilously close results in Queensland and Western Australia for totally different parochial reasons. Federation really was a close-run thing. It could easily have gone the other way.

"Nevertheless, there was a strong vote for Yes in Victoria, despite the strenuous efforts of David Syme and his Age newspaper. The ties to old England are still very strong in our state due to our local history of being founded by free settlers more so than convicts. Most Victorians believed that the future dominance of England in the Pacific Ocean was important and this would require our continent to be one strong nation with stout defences and economic strength. I still subscribe to this belief, whether it be for us alone, or whether the British remain as our partners, but preferably the former.

"As William and George have said, there is a strong anti-New South Wales attitude in Victoria. Many of our Yes voters were people who had one goal in mind. They wanted to let New South Wales know that Victorians were providing the leadership of Federation and that Victoria would become the powerhouse of the nation in the fullness of time.

"I can fully understand why William and George were offended by all these attitudes and I regret that the parochialism that is prevalent in my home State is still so pronounced."

George stirred once more.

"Ah," he responded, "at last we have a small display of compassion from the brotherhood of Victoria. May God be praised for moving their hearts of stone."

Alfred was affable.

Radical Federalist

Next came the always overpowering Charles Kingston of South Australia. Whereas Deakin was a persuader, Kingston was an arm twister.

He was the unshakeable strongman of the Federation Movement, who had never once wavered in his determination to make it happen. Had he been called upon to walk over dead bodies to ensure the right result, then he would have done so. Notably, his tolerance level was quite low.

"The vote in South Australia was never in doubt and was made more inevitable by the strength of the women's vote. As I have constantly reminded you all a thousand times over, South Australia was the only state that was brave enough and wise enough to give women that right.

"Our women had a strong sense of independence in their souls and, for them, this meant a self-governing nation with as much freedom from London as was possible, and preferably one that was not dominated by men. This was a big issue for them as the Brits were treating their suffragettes with extreme brutality and for no valid reasons. Women in South Australia were appalled at what was happening to their sisters in Britain and they wanted the Parliament at Westminster to carefully take note that the women of South Australia had powerfully exercised their right to influence the fate of a new nation.

"But, over and above all that, South Australians believed that our continent should have a powerful central government. So, we threw our weight behind it mightily and produced a solid majority for the YES vote. Unlike our more-timid friends in Queensland and Western Australia, we made sure that those who wanted to vote No were denied any oxygen."

Second Colony

Bird raised his hand to claim the next spot on the speaking agenda even though Tasmania was the smallest state by far.

"As Tasmania was the second colony to be founded in Australia, I want to cheekily claim precedence over Western Australia and Queensland in this discussion. I am confident that my friends from those states will forgive me for this transgression."

Fisher, Griffith and Forrest nodded their approval.

"A YES vote was never in doubt in Tasmania. I have no need to remind you that we are a small struggling society without a sound economic base. Therefore, we had everything to gain and nothing to lose by becoming part of a strong nation.

"Furthermore, we had pride in the great work that had been done by our favourite son, Andrew Clark, in creating a sound basis for a solid constitution to be written, was a strong factor in comprehensively defeating the NO voters. Many of us promoted the romantic view that it was, in genuine reality, our constitution and that we in Tasmania were the nation builders.

"We would have been devastated if Federation had not gone ahead. Thankfully, even though it was a close-run thing in some states, common sense prevailed across the entire continent and all of Tasmania applauded.

"I warmly thank all of you for your outstanding leadership in bringing Federation to reality. There are very few places in the world where a Federation such as ours has been achieved is such a peaceful manner."

State of Isolation

Barton now called on 'Slippery Sam' Griffith.

"Sam, please recall for us the reasons why our Queensland friends nearly didn't make it."

"It certainly was touch and go. There always is a huge parochial vote in Queensland about anything and everything. The animosity to Federation was simply a reflection of normal attitudes.

"With apologies for any implied offence to William and George, Queenslanders have an enormous suspicion of all that New South Wales does, and we do so to a far greater extent than Victoria. We are certain that New South Welshman will always do us harm. Our folk actually believe that you enjoy treating us as poor relations.

"With goodwill to Alfred, may I say also that many of our Queensland voters hold the firm view that Melbourne is just a suburb of London, a little like Mayfair, a lot of toffs who would never survive for more than five minutes up in the tropics.

"Actually, I am not really sure that we yet accept that any other states have a right to exist. The issue relating to the fate of the Kanaka labourers in the sugar cane fields of North Queensland was a hugely divisive issue. Our canefarmers in the North were afraid that an Australian Parliament would send the Kanakas home to New Caledonia, New Hebrides, Fiji and Papua from where we had pirated them as slaves very much against their will, just as America had done with Africans.

"They were right to hold that view as you fellows quickly voted to do exactly that as part of an essential promotion of a White Australia. On the other hand, a significant number of Queenslanders, especially those residing in Brisbane, rightly joined you in feeling that keeping Kanakas as slaves was utterly immoral and wanted the new nation to affirm their outrage at Queensland being part of the shameful slave.

"Eventually, we won a very narrow victory, even closer than that in New South Wales. Upon reflection, I am sure that defence was the core issue that finally got Queensland over the line in favour of Federation. Many Queenslanders were worried that the Chinese or Japanese or both would invade us sometime in the near future as they sought land for their growing population. They wanted a national army and navy to defend the massive coastline of Queensland which covers over three thousand miles, much of which is unpopulated."

Barton asked Fisher if he would like to add a comment.

"Thank you, Toby. I am pleased to endorse what Sam has said. He has concisely described the situation in my home state. Perhaps I can add one comment. I am prepared to forecast that, a century from now, Queenslanders will still bear a deep suspicion of New South Welshmen. It's in our blood."

Kalgoorlie Saves the Day

John Forrest knew that he would be called upon to be the last speaker so he waded right in without waiting for a call from Barton.

"Every one of us should be grateful to the voters out in the Goldfields of Kalgoorlie. They carried the day for the Federation cause in Western Australia.

"Perth voted No. This further incensed the miners as they believed they were carrying the entire economy of Western Australia on their backs and wanted a new state with Kalgoorlie as its capital, free from Perth whose residents they regarded as privileged freeloaders.

"They believed that, by achieving Federation, they would have a better chance of carrying out a breakaway from Perth as the constitution of the new nation provided for the creation of new states. They were determined that the Goldfields would be the first new state to be created.

"We would not be sitting here today were it not for them. People over in the East ignored the fact that Western Australia only became a state in 1890. We had a lot to learn about governing ourselves and uniting our people when Federation was almost immediately thrust upon us. Our sense of identity was very fragile. We had an embarrassing inferiority complex which you found to be obvious in your discussions with us. But, thanks to Kalgoorlie, we made the right decision about joining with you.

"As a result, one day, Western Australia will be the dominant State of Australia. None of us will live to see it, but it will happen, just as sure as the sun will rise tomorrow morning. It is our undeniable destiny. Just remember that you were the first Australians to hear this great news right here in this eminent club tonight."

Barton had more speakers in mind, but George Reid was feeling yet another enormous need to be loquacious. He felt a call from the Almighty to humble just a trifle what he perceived to be a bit of arrogance from Forrest.

So, he intervened, "Why have you not yet founded a new state based on Kalgoorlie, John. As I see it, the locals over there are demanding that their passion for a separate state should be realised. As you have said, it was their sole reason for voting for Federation and must be honoured. It is a long overdue debt that cannot be written off, especially as there is now no legal impediment to their statehood. As you know, it can be achieved quite easily, so why are you delaying the matter."

A need for honesty consumed Forrest at this moment. With a humility that was absolutely out of character, he responded, "You well know, George, that Perth, for financial reasons, cannot afford to let the Goldfields go. Without them, we are financially unviable. Separation from them just can't be allowed to happen. But, let me deftly change the debate and ask Chris Watson a significant question."

George could not be dispensed with quite so quickly.

"Just hold on for a moment old chap before you verbally assault my left-wing, but honourable, colleague, Chris.

"This Goldfields matter must be fixed right now. It seems to me that they have been let down by outrageous negligence. I will travel with you to the Goldfields and we will tour the whole region, including places like Esperance for the purpose of promising them the new state to which they are entitled. It is a disgrace that they were conned. It gives politics a bad name. They must think that our Federal Government is composed of bushrangers."

Rubbing his massive gut, which was a regular habit, Reid added, "If I am wrong, John, in my staunch advocacy of this, then may I be damned."

Forrest also rubbed his substantial gut and then responded amiably, "Well, George, if I am there with you in Kalgoorlie, the fat will well and truly be in the fire."

Then Forrest went on to deliver a king hit.

"Okay, George. I take up your offer. You and I will go together to the Goldfields at the earliest date we can arrange. But with one proviso. You must promise me that you will travel with me to the Riverina and New England in your home state. There, we will promise each of those prosperous regions that they will henceforth be new states. Both regions have never ever wanted to be part of New South Wales. They are sick to death of being bled dry by Sydney. You know it, but you ignore it."

Willian Lyne joined the fray with unexpected fervour that seemed to be almost out of character.

"I will strongly back any movement to give Riverina the right to be a new state. I own a large property down there. Invite me to the meetings and I will lead the charge. We will get a huge vote in favour of the privilege of saying goodbye to Sydney."

"Now, now, gentlemen! Let peace and calm return to our brotherly ranks," intervened Barton.

"I am sure, George and John, that we can safely leave it to you both to organise visits to the Goldfields, Riverina and New England but, in the meantime, please go ahead, John, and ask Chris the interesting question you mentioned a little earlier before George became carried away by his obvious love of the Goldfields."

Workers Versus Capitalists

Anxious to avoid any further discussion about Kalgoorlie, Forrest quickly took up the invitation.

"Chris, can you remind us all why the Labor Party opposed Federation and do so in such a very aggressive manner?"

Watson was equally pleased to get this opportunity to clear the air about what had been a huge controversy at the time.

"We honestly felt that Federation was a plaything of capitalists rather than a visionary exercise in nation building. Our strong view was that the prime aim of the wealthy was to make more money by eliminating interstate tariffs. This would make it much easier for them to expand beyond state markets into large national monopolies while destroying local competition, particularly among small business people. I continue to hold this view and I am saddened that it still remains the prime goal of capitalism. Its clear intent is to crush the battlers of the nation. Why would anyone with any sense of humanity want this to happen?

"But, having said this, I acknowledge that we are now a sovereign nation, legally established by a democratic vote of the people. I can find no valid reason why anyone, especially my party, should now try to turn the clock back. We took the view that, as responsible people, we should make the best possible use of our new national government to enhance the basic rights of workers and small business men. I tried and failed to achieve this as prime minister in 1904, but, now that our fellow Labor Party member, Andrew Fisher, is prime minister, we are taking up this battle again in a much more organised manner that will bring measurable results sooner rather than later.

"The past decade has shown us that Australia has begun its national political history with a fierce battle between Free Traders and Protectionists. With the advent of Andrew as PM, this is being changed to a struggle between capitalists and workers. One day, the latter will win the class war. At the very least, we want 'Jack to have a fair chance to earn equality with his master'. We are much more determined about this than you are in making Western Australia the most powerful state in the nation."

This gave Andrew Fisher an opportunity he was looking for.

"While agreeing with the sentiments that Chris has expressed, may I say that I would prefer not to describe the implementation of our current political strategies as a struggle. It is quite simply a social movement which has as its vision the goal that, one day, money will not dominate the market place. The skills of the people will become the prime economic force there. We will not be beholden to a few wealthy people as is the tragedy right now. Millions of ordinary people yearn to secure their rightful place in the sun.

"May I add belatedly a further comment. It is in reference to the reluctance of Queenslanders to join Federation. There has always been a mistaken belief in my home state of Queensland that Sydney and Melbourne were the sole centres of money power and that we had missed out consistently. Queenslanders felt that Federation would make this injustice worse. They still do think this way. It's an issue that we have to work on as a nation because Tasmania, South Australia and

Western Australia hold similar views. We must strive to have a nation of six strong states that work together to complement one another. A nation that has its economic and political power overly concentrated in Sydney and Melbourne is not an enlightened country, nor will it ever be a strong one."

George Reid stirred ominously, but Barton cut him off.

Act of God

"Let me sum this up so we can move on. What we have all acknowledged is that it was somewhat of a miracle that Federation actually occurred here in Australia. My friend Alfred is certain that it was an Act of God. I respect his sincerity on this matter, but I doubt that it actually was. Nevertheless, history will at very least record it as an extraordinary event that united an entire continent as one nation and converted most of its people from the negativity of parochialism to a vision of national pride."

Deakin could not remain silent.

"I would not have voted Yes to Federation, if I had not been absolutely certain that it was the will of God. It was quite miraculous that Federation actually happened. Does any one of us here tonight actually think that we are unique miracle makers just because we think that we are great leaders who are totally self-sufficient? I think not. There is quite clearly a spiritual power beyond us all. It provides us with a personal fire power which enables us to achieve special goals."

This statement caused silence to descend upon the dinner.

No one wanted to take on Deakin on this matter. It was a subject from which they knew he would never retreat. In addition, they rarely gave it sufficiently prolonged thought that would enable them to competently debate it with him. At that moment, they were united in the view that it would be wise to act as though they belonged to an order of monks who had taken vows of silence

George Reid shared the view that the conversation needed to be diverted away from religion, but not before he took a final shot at Deakin. He partook of a couple of large gulps of Barossa Red and exclaimed, "Why have we not mentioned our long battle with the British Government to get the Commonwealth of Australia Act through the Parliament at Westminster in 1900. If ever there was a miracle that came out of the heavens it was our final victory there. The Colonial Secretary, Joseph Chamberlain, was a pompously stubborn old buzzard who regarded our delegation as wild colonial boys who were not showing due respect for the British Crown. He did not ever stop spanking us. God must have got to Chamberlain at the end of it all for him to have finally said Yes. You were there, Alfred. Surely you must have fervently called upon the Lord to scare the daylights out of Chamberlain."

"I did and He did," was the immediate and sharp retort from Deakin.

Reid was wise enough to take it no further.

Battle of Westminster

Barton had not needed any prompting from Reid to begin a discussion about the British Parliament. He already had it on his agenda as one of the prime items on the agenda for the evening and suggested that, as the leader of the delegation to Westminster, he should open the batting with a few pertinent comments on the memorable saga that was played out in gaining legal approval of Federation from London.

"I still can't understand why a parliamentary debate about the Commonwealth of Australia Act had to last for several months. This was far longer than we ever anticipated and really had been an astonishing lesson for us in the ingrained culture of colonial superiority that pervaded Britain.

"The stark reality is that they could not get over the fact that the descendants of their worst convicts had returned to make demands of them.

"Shortly, I will ask Charles and Alfred, my fellow travellers on this tough journey, to add their opinions, but let me set the scene.

"Charles and Alfred did the tough negotiating work with the mandarins at Whitehall while I concentrated on carefully cultivating the goodwill of the high and the mighty. My task was not easy. Neither was theirs. Queen Victoria was not amused. She did not like the word Commonwealth. Actually, it was 'Common' that she didn't like. She gave us the indelible impression that anything common was just a wee bit below her."

As could be expected, Reid happily butted in, "You didn't act like a commoner, did you, Toby? Or use any common language in her presence. You surely didn't use words like 'Fair Dinkum', 'Stone the Crows', 'Starve the Lizards' or 'Bloody Galahs'. Worse still, did you call her a Pom and ask if you could use the Dunny. I always wondered why the negotiations took so long. Are we now belatedly discovering the real facts of the matter?

"After all these years, we are now to find out that you may well be to blame for those interminable delays. Victoria must have thought you were a bush whacker. Did you give her the clear impression that you may be a wee bit sordid for the lords and ladies to cope with. You should have known that she would convey to you the fatal words, 'We are not amused'.

"An even worse concern for us, Toby, is the horrendous thought that your staunch advocacy of basic Australian culture disturbed her to such an extent that she decided to give up on her long reign and seemingly endless life. We can't discount the fact that she died three weeks after we celebrated Federation. Can we be assured that you were not responsible for hastening her overdue demise?"

"George, may I commend you for your observations which are not all that far from the truth. I was tempted on far too many occasions to be outlandishly Australian, but I concentrated solely on convincing Her Majesty of the noble intentions to which we, her loyal servants, humbly aspired. I said that our goal was to be a nation of common wealth, a land where there was no upstairs and downstairs. She wasn't at all sure that the House of Lords would be happy about such a lowering of the noble social standards that had been observed for centuries. It may well be that she worried herself to death over the coming demise of her Empire.

"Actually, she was quite correct in making a presumption about the attitude of the Lords. But, we quietly hinted to them that on this matter and several others, we could be tempted to act in similar fashion to that which George Washington had boldly and decisively conveyed to the British Crown a century or so earlier. This seemed to generate a more moderate understanding in their minds of our strange colonial ways. They simply could not be humiliated once more in front of the whole world by losing yet another large colony. The French and Germans and Russians would have laughed mightily and happily for years and years and years The Brits would have descended into some form of eternal purgatory if Australia had unilaterally declared itself to be a Republic."

Alfred took up the dialogue.

"It took a long time for us to come to terms with how pedantic the British proved to be in settling on the wording of our Constitution and relating it to the Bill they had to get through their Parliament at Westminster so as to give our new nation its fundamental legal stature. They wanted to retain as much control as possible, the exact same error they had made with the American Colonies.

"We were thunderstruck when Chamberlain presented us with a long list of changes to the Constitution that they required us to accept or our Federation would not be approved by his Parliament. We told him that any substantial changes would require us to hold six more referendums which could quite easily be lost. He was aghast that the colonies in Australia thought they could instruct the British Parliament as to what it should do.

"We stood our ground and took heavy abuse. But, after a while, Chamberlain got the message that he was close to being publicly humiliated by colonials and contrived to beat a gallant retreat, backing off on almost all their demands.

"As we all know, there was one notable exception. They insisted on the Privy Council, as their supreme law-making entity retaining its powers as the final Court of Appeal so that any loyal British subjects who were convicted by courts in Australia could appeal to loftier minds in London. They could not tolerate the thought that the final fate of an English gentleman could be determined by a kangaroo court that had been appointed by illiterate Australian squatters who had few social graces. This demand was nothing more than absolute arrogance, but, after battling against it for many weeks, we went along with it so we could achieve our prime goal of Federation.

"We contrived vague words into their legislation which would not require us to hold referendums on the matter. The agreed wording conveyed that we could reopen the Privy Council battle at an appropriate time after our Parliament was established and operating and we had established our own High Court. Chamberlain asked us not to raise it again until after he was dead. We agreed."

Drinks at the Reform Club

Charles Kingston, a thoroughly radical revolutionary, had found the pompous traditions of Old England to be unbearably elitist, utterly obnoxious, outrageously obscene and hopelessly decadent. He was certain that the entire British Empire was in dire need of a comprehensive clean-up in the same manner as the French had done so thoroughly in their great revolution a century earlier.

"The extraordinary feature of our deliberations over there was a very strange ritual that they unbelievably followed which was absurdly childish.

"We would negotiate constitutional issues with parliamentarians and bureaucrats all day at Whitehall and Westminster, but we would not get a firm commitment on anything until after we had explained it once more that same evening to pompous groups of old aristocrats who were all honourable members of the Reform Club. This would take place in the bar of that revered club, over Gin and Tonic followed by Port and cigars. There were lots of grand old fogeys who would spend all day, every day, at the club drinking Stout, followed later by Sherry which would then lead them to upgrade to Port in order to attain an enlightenment which would enable them to determine our fate in an appropriate manner.

"Astonishingly, they firmly believed that nothing could ever be put through Parliament without them giving it a prior nod. We finally came to the view that they were not misguided in that outlandish belief in their privileged power. Incredible though this nonsense appears to be, it actually existed. They were an accepted cog in the wheel of the functioning of the British Establishment.

"Forrest commented that it really was quite insulting that Australian delegations had to make two long boat trips to London and back before the British were finally convinced that they could and should approve the quite logical aspiration that six of their own colonies, occupying the same continent, should choose to unite.

"It wasn't actually two negotiating journeys," explained Kingston.

Capitalising on the Jubilee

"The first one that I attended was in 1897 to represent South Australia at Queen Victoria's Jubilee Celebrations. Likewise, every other state had an official representative in attendance. While we were there, we took advantage of the ceremonial requirements of our visit to do the rounds of Westminster and Whitehall, in order to meet with the great and the mighty. Our intent was to brief them on the significant progress we were making towards achieving Federation by the turn of the century.

"While doing this, we made arrangements to send a formal negotiating team to meet them in a couple of years, as soon as possible after all states had voted to approve a constitution. We invited them to do some prior homework by preparing initial drafts of legislation for us to consider from the moment that we arrived on our second journey.

"Those preliminary meetings proved to be a benefit to us. We gained some knowledge of the strange ways in which the British Government worked. An interesting issue that arose in 1897 conversations was that Her Majesty's Private Secretary told us that she, and the ministers of her Government, regarded the six Australian Colonies as Counties of England, just like Cornwall and Kent, and could not fathom why we would want to cease to be Counties of Old England. She would consider granting each colony some seats in the House of Commons and the Lords.

"There was a thought that we could also play County Cricket. There would have been the logistical problem of getting our teams there and back by three months' boat trips but Her Majesty did not worry about matters of trivia.

"At least, the receipt of this gracious advice gave us a couple of years notice of how we could plan to let her down gently."

The Lure of a Republic

Forrest wasn't satisfied with that.

"Can I comment as one who has formally sworn his allegiance to the British Crown and its people on many occasions. I am of the view that, had the Brits dropped their pomposity and been reasonable, it all could have been achieved in weeks, not the many months you had to stay there.

"I am convinced that we really should have followed the American example. History may prove eventually that it was a ghastly mistake that we did not declare our independence in a peaceful and civilised manner without seeking their approval. We have been unreasonably humiliated by the pompous colonial attitude of Britain for far for too long."

"Absolutely," roared George Reid, "we should have sent them a letter that declared immediate unilateral independence and invited them to come all the way out here to sort out the paper work at our timing and convenience. Could have all been done over cigars and port here at the Melbourne Club. This is a far more imperial club than anything they have in London. After all, every one of our members here is a top-quality commoner who is loyal to the nation.

"There was even one famous member, Robert O'Hara Bourke, who died of thirst out in the middle of the desert trying to spread the tentacles of the British Empire. Now I come to make mention of it, he was most probably the only member of this fine club ever to die of thirst."

Thus, began the decline of the British Empire.

Taking a Shot at Royalty

Bird felt the need to add a somewhat more sensitive element into the debate.

"We must not underrate the fact that the British had harboured some deep suspicions about us for a long time. The mutiny at the Eureka Stockade at Ballarat a half century earlier had shaken them more than they were ever willing to admit, as had the attempted assassination of Prince Alfred at Clontarf in Sydney in 1849 on the first ever Royal Visit to our land. Fortunately, he did not die from the gunshot wound and the would-be assassin was proven to be mentally ill.

"Then, we had the revolutionary saga of Parkes and Lang trying to bring into being a Republic in New South Wales right after William Charles Wentworth had been defeated in his attempt to establish an Australian aristocracy who would have presided over our affairs of state from a local House of Lords.

"When we put all of this together, it is obvious that we had a little ground to make up with the Royals, but I must say that the three of you did it magnificently with an astute exhibition of courage and dignity."

Deakin saw a glorious opportunity to give Reid a strong serve.

"Luckily for us all, the assassination attempt against the Prince happened in New South Wales where no one can shoot straight. Had it occurred anywhere else on the continent, he would have died instantly and Her Majesty would have been so outraged that she would have been forced to send out a fleet of gun boats to bring us down. She would have despatched the guilty ones to establish a new penal settlement out at Lake Eyre. Of course, this poses the question of whether or not she had ever heard of Lake Eyre."

"Please don't make me laugh too much, Alfred," said George Reid, acknowledging Deakin's piercing wit. "I will be forced to go to the lavatory. I have a terrible fear that it will be full of Victorians. You really can't trust any of them anywhere."

Chris Watson decided to end the sparring match with a dash of pragmatism.

"We could have shown our desire to totally cooperate with Her Gracious Majesty, Queen Victoria, by helpfully suggesting that her navy would be in its best strategic position if they invaded us by travelling to Sydney Harbour via the Great Barrier Reef. Most of them would not have made it through the coral as their knowledge of Australia is so poor they would not have known it even existed. We really should start using our natural resources more creatively than we now do in the service of the nation."

George Reid felt that a compliment was necessary.

"We really made a terrible blunder, Chris, when we only let you serve as prime minister for four miserable months. You really deserved a couple of extra weeks."

Half Time

Wisely, Barton aptly discerned that this generous comment from Reid was the cue to announce it was time to take a well-earned break.

Much vintage alcohol had been happily consumed by his guests, and himself. It now needed to be despatched. There also was a clear call for some exercise after very healthy servings of splendid fare from the Chef.

"We will resume in fifteen minutes."

Passionate Dissenter

After their necessary pit stop, the Prime Minister accompanied by four former Prime Ministers, went for a stroll around the club saying hello to the many members who were wining and dining. They did much hand shaking and back slapping in the bar, club dining room and lounges. Politicians in every era have never ever stopped campaigning, so why refrain tonight?

All of them, Fisher, Barton, Watson, Deakin and Reid were greeted warmly. After all, how often are five prime ministers ever seen together in the one place. It could not have happened before in Australia. The nation had been electing its prime ministers for just a decade, with the fifth one having only recently been sworn in. Most presumed that such a gathering of eminence was not likely to happen ever again.

As they entered the dining room to check on whether any good friends were enjoying the club's up-market New Year dinner, two famous faces beckoned them to their table. The Prime Ministerial team happily accepted their invitation and were soon shaking hands with two men who had been eminent participants in the battle for Federation.

David Syme, Publisher of *The Age*, which was arguably the nation's foremost newspaper and its most controversial opinion maker, was dining with Justice Henry Bournes Higgins of the High Court of Australia, not to be confused with Professor Henry Higgins from George Bernard Shaw's Pygmalion.

Higgins in his earlier life had been a prestigious barrister of eminence far beyond his home state of Victoria who exercised a huge influence on the final wording of the Constitution as a constructive armchair critic.

For a considerable period of time, Syme was a formidable opponent of Federation, declaring that it would pave the way for unbridled capitalism, while the poor would become poorer. He and Watson shared similar philosophies on this matter, but Syme was more radical, very much so. His ferocious attack on Deakin had not been an isolated one. The fiery literary barbs that flew from his pen had hit many others, sometimes inflicting mortal political wounds.

A butler helpfully arranged five more chairs around their table and Syme offered to buy them all a drink. Wisely, Fisher exercised his power as the current prime minister by declaring that they had already imbibed generously at the Barton dinner and needed to stay sober enough to be coherent for the remainder of the evening. He tactfully suggested that they should get their conversation underway as they had exactly eight minutes left to talk before they had to return to continue their dinner and its increasingly interesting debate.

Predictably, George Reid decided once more to be somewhat playful and provocative as he was not a fan of Syme.

"David, have you ever resumed speaking to my friend Alfred and even gone so far as to buy him a drink. My understanding is that, a decade ago, you announced in your newspaper that, because of his strong advocacy of Federation, you had banned him totally from the Victorian Establishment. In addition, you had purposefully sought to have him despatched to the hottest parts of the Sahara Desert as a thoroughly undesirable character who deserved the ultimate punishment. We are all very aware that he upset you mightily when he made a wonderful speech to a large gathering of your friends who were members of the Australian Natives Association and had assembled for their Bendigo Convention. He did this in defiance of you and your all-powerful newspaper, the headlines of which we all await in fear and trembling daily?"

Syme kept his renowned temper in check. Coldly and carefully he chose his words, looking solely at Read.

"For once in your life you are absolutely correct, George. My warmest congratulations to you for your extraordinary effort in crossing the line between innuendo and fact. It has been a long time coming.

"Yes, I did banish Alfred, except that I had in mind the Tundras of Siberia in preference to the Sahara. My concern at the time was that Victoria had been moving steadily and purposefully towards establishing a genuine democracy. It was gradually becoming a society in which lowly paid people would gradually receive adequate remuneration for their work and have a genuine chance to remain in work as they made their way up the ladder of life. New South Wales had a polar opposite view of fairness, rapidly installing rampant free market capitalism. This meant that Victoria, at the moment of Federation, faced the clear possibility that it could lose the benefits of all of its social advances by joining with New South Wales. I felt that Alfred was so committed to the principle of getting six states together, he was overlooking the real possibility that his own State of Victoria could go backwards, socially and economically, if and when Federation occurred. In my mind, he was in bed naively with sinners, and you, George, ranked highly among these unfortunate souls."

Watson, to the surprise of no one, backed Syme's political and economic philosophies without sanctioning his appalling treatment of Deakin.

"At that time just before Federation, I held the same view as David on the many issues relating to inequality. As did the Labor Party. Just as you did Henry. The stark difference is that I did not regard Alfred as a sinner. Now, I must acknowledge that Federation did not turn out anywhere near as badly as we thought it might, mainly due to ten years of steady, progressive, responsible government provided by the political friends that surround me right now, especially Alfred whom you unfairly and unreasonably hit."

This blunt comment from Watson caused Syme to make an astute assessment of where this conversation was going. It made eminent good sense to make a gallant comment, a posture he was not used to, nor comfortable with.

"I was eventually proved wrong and made my peace with Alfred. Even so, I hold the unshakeable view that we have made slower social progress by entering Federation than we would have if we had remained an Independent State of Victoria. Getting together with New South Wales at that moment in history was not a plus for Victoria."

This was the time for Deakin to act with a gracious response.

"And I received your overtures of reconciliation with goodwill David. Furthermore, I believe that my record in Federal Parliament shows that I have fought persistently for a liberal social democracy to the extent that its cause is progressing, not retreating. You must not allow yourself to become overly gloomy on this subject."

Henry Bournes Higgins, speaking as one who had been a Member of the First Federal Parliament before being elevated to the High Court, was moved to enter the conversation.

"As soon as we could do so in the new Parliament, we established an Arbitration Commission which has begun a process of advancing the rights and remuneration of workers. It is a start, and it was not too soon. Workers all over the world are now in revolt. Sometime in the next decade, Socialist revolutions will begin in Europe and spread from there. We should thank David for identifying and forecasting this potential upheaval right from the time he began his newspaper."

The Prime Minister added, "Given that a people's rebellion has been steadily brewing against the Czar in Russia since the atrocity of Bloody Sunday in 1905, I think that the Russians will, within a decade, become the world's first major Socialist Republic. It will spread from there.

"In addition, a worker's revolt against major corporations is beginning in a relatively peaceful manner in my homeland of Scotland, particularly in the coal mines where I worked decades ago. It will spread from there. We can be proud that, here in Australia, we have anticipated this and have taken some significant steps that will turn the rights of workers into a humanitarian positive for the whole nation and especially for them. Our economic and social transition will be peaceful. It may not prove to be so in Russia."

Barton had been the only one not to speak thus far, so he put forward his thoughts.

"We made our move to Federation just in time, indeed at the very right moment in history. Most Australians are prospering as a direct result of it. Because we are a new nation that is positively planning for its future, we are able to stay ahead of the upheavals that are about to become an unpleasant reality in older civilisations around the world. Our challenge is to make sure that we stay on the front foot by keeping our ears to the ground at every level of society and acting appropriately with sound government policy. I have no doubt that we can and will do it."

"Time to go," said Fisher.

"May peace be with you," he said, shaking hands with Higgins and Syme, knowing full well that Syme would never be at peace for as long as he lived.

There were genuine expressions of goodwill all around. A good end, after a shaky start.

Watson led the way back to the Private Dining Room. He did not really belong in this bastion of capitalism, but he was enjoying it. Maybe, one day, he could win over the hearts and minds of its members, miraculously encouraging them to reach out to the peasants and vice versa.

Aspirants

Meanwhile, back in the club's elegant and spacious washroom, Lyne, Kingston and Forrest were somehow left behind, not that they were in any way aggrieved by this.

Here they were. Three eminent elder statesmen gathered together in in a common cause. Fervently, even desperately, each of them wanted to attain election as Prime Minister of Australia, but had not quite made the grade as yet.

What was very clear to everyone who knew them was that they were not about to give up the chase. Each believed they had the ability and the stature to do the job and do it well. They had no doubt that they had earned the honour and felt that they were being unjustly denied it as the result of the votes of several small, undesirable political factions who would sell their souls by courting favours from those in power.

Forrest, the most frustrated aspirant of them all, was loud and passionate in his denunciation of their undeserved plight.

"Until Fisher rose from Queensland politics to his current position of dominance as prime minister, New South Wales and Victoria had shared the prime ministership. It's time for their dominance to come to an end. Even Fisher, coming as he does from the gold mines of Gympie, is an Eastern Mainlander too. They have locked out the South and the West because they reckon we have too few voters to cause any threat to their power and they feel no need to please any of us. We won't be a genuine nation until every state has provided a prime minister, just to prove that we have created a legitimate Federation.

"Every time there has been a change of prime minister, I have put my hand up and campaigned strongly for the job, yet they have told me that they can't choose a Western Australian because it takes too long to get to and from Perth by boat. Ridiculously, they claim that this will cause problems if ever there is a national emergency that requires instant decisions. Absolute garbage. Abraham Lincoln's home was a long way from Washington."

"They told me the same thing about me being a resident of Adelaide," retorted Kingston. "It was absolutely crazy that, at the final Constitutional Convention, we were given no option but to agree to locate the national capital somewhere in New South Wales. You will recall William that we had to make that concession otherwise you fellows would have voted No.

"I had previously put forward Port Augusta as the ideal site. It is about half way between Sydney and Perth and will one day be the origin of a road and rail link going north to Darwin, making it the transport hub of the continent. But, the only one to vote for this great idea of mine was me. Most fellows at the Convention thought that going to Port Augusta would be the equivalent of joining the French Foreign Legion or being sent to Devil's Island. One of them even asked me if there was a pub there."

"Correct," admitted Lyne. "New South Wales would have voted No, emphatically, if we had not obtained agreement for New South Wales to host Australia's capital city. This is utterly unchangeable, so let us not waste time on it. However, coming back to the issue of who should be prime minister, the current selection process has got a lot of city snobbishness about it. You and I are country boys, John, and they believe that this means we are not educated enough to be a prime minister. Yet, Australia rose to greatness from its lowly status as a convict settlement solely because of the agricultural industries that were created beyond the Blue Mountains. People in Sydney and Melbourne rode on the sheep's back for a century and now have their noses up in the air about it. I find it to be massively offensive."

"Well," said Forrest, "it's time for all the nonsense to stop. We just have to work out when is the best time to strike at the rotten heart of it all. I am angry enough to start a revolution."

In a state of high dudgeon, he led them back in the direction of the Private Dining Room.

As they strolled along, Lyne asked, "Does your anger stem from the steady rise of the Secession Movement in Western Australia, John? Is it strong enough to be a genuine threat to the continuance of Western Australia in Federation? If your state leaves then that is the stone-cold end of your chances of becoming prime minister?"

"The Movement isn't yet strong enough, William, but it will gradually become so if the rest of Australia does not invest some time and effort into the development of my state and taking seriously our right to be heard in the corridors of national power."

"As Premier of New South Wales, I was not a Federation fan for a wide range of reasons, but now that the deed is done, it would not be wise to make any effort to turn it backwards. What must we do right now to stop Western Australia from seceding?"

"Make me prime minister."

Birth of Murdoch Media

There were two orphaned remnants of the diners.

One was the high profile and often-political Chief Justice of the High Court and the other was the sincerely religious, Bird, a proud son of the smallest state in the nation. They had somehow been forgotten by their fellow diners and so they elected to return to their dinner venue for a quiet chat.

Their solitude lasted less than a minute.

An aspiring young journalist, Keith Murdoch, son of the influential Minister of the Camberwell Presbyterian Church, entered the room without having been invited and introduced himself. He looked to be in his mid-twenties and was.

"Chief Justice and Reverend Bird, my apologies for intruding unannounced. My name is Keith Murdoch. I am a freelance journalist, more often than not writing for *The Age*, and I am also privileged to be one of the young members of this club. I learnt of your august gathering here tonight while dining with friends in the Club Room. I am wondering if I may be so bold as to take a minute or so of your time to ask if any significant plans for the future of our nation have been set in train as the result of your deliberations here this evening?"

Bird looked to the Chief Justice to respond.

Griffith was not noted for holding journalists in high regard. He was of the firm opinion that they did not have orderly minds capable of effectively arguing an issue and clearly conveying it with any eloquence to their readers. This meant that his response had little warmth.

"Mr Murdoch, I do not welcome your uninvited presence in our private dining room but I am able to make this brief comment to you.

"I can confirm that ten Founders of the Commonwealth of Australia have dined together here at the club this evening for the purpose of celebrating a decade of Federation. We have extensively reviewed our long battle to achieve Federation and critically assessed how we may have done it better. We are about to assess the way we have governed the nation since. This means that, in a few minutes, over dessert and coffee, and among other things, we will talk about how Australia could best achieve its finest future as a nation from the starting point that we have created for it. I am certain that, by the time we all make our way home at the end of the evening, we will have made some carefully considered recommendations to the Prime Minister. If you can waylay Andrew Fisher on his way out of the club in an hour or so, you may find that he is willing to comment."

Looking both frustrated and disappointed, Murdoch looked to Bird for a more informative response, unaware that this man of faith was also an old hand at handling the media, both as a parliamentarian and a preacher whose sermons were often quoted and criticised in newspapers.

"I will be most interested, Mr Murdoch, to read in *The Age* an article of quality journalism that tells us your personal thoughts, as an objective outsider of the legislative processes, on what pathway Australia should follow in the years ahead. You will not need our help with this. Can I suggest that you do this sooner rather than later as we will all welcome your guidance? You may sow seeds in the minds of many parliamentarians far beyond those attending tonight's gathering."

"I was hoping to hear a genuine account of history making plans for national expansion directly from you. Your dinner tonight has brought together a most powerful group of Australians who are legends of our national history. Such an assembly is not likely to happen again. It is vital that they issue a statement to the nation."

"What would you hope we may have discussed?"

"Well, now you have put me on the spot, may I say that Australia has an urgent need for powerful and disciplined political parties. Currently, we have a mixture of small parties, none of whom have a genuine power base of members or followers in the community. Those sad parties change their names with great rapidity to suit political convenience and then run around forming strange alliances, most of which have proven to be ridiculously and dangerously unstable."

The Chief Justice responded sharply, "What, Mr Murdoch, could possibly be wrong with a parliament filled with small parties? It is fair to say that the Federal Parliaments elected since 1901 have provided sound and productive government. Good legislation has been passed regularly and will continue to do so because those parties are operating with a bipartisan attitude. My experience of life is that if something is not broken, you don't try to fix it. This parliament is an efficiently operating entity."

"With courtesy, Chief Justice, may I remind you that Australia has had five prime ministers in just one decade and, within those five, Deakin has held the job three times. Australians yearn for the stability provided by long-term leadership."

"Down in my home State of Tasmania," said Bird, "no one has so far complained personally to me about a lack of national leadership. There is a general feeling that democracy is working in a productive way in our Federal Parliament."

Murdoch became much more vehement. They were playing games with him and it annoyed and offended him.

"I am of the firm belief that we are entitled to have a stable government, led by a strong political party, that has a clear majority in its own right and can govern without challenge for a full term of three years. With such a sense of solidarity, we will achieve much more."

Samuel Griffith would not have a bar of this monopolistic theory of good government.

"Wherever it is practiced around the world, the history of democracy has shown that majority governments inevitably become arrogant. This leads them to pass legislation that has not been clearly thought through because they have no genuine opposition that forces them to do the detailed homework that quality legislation requires. When a government has to negotiate with others every day in order to get legislation passed, much better legislation is achieved as a result because you have had to listen to other viewpoints and are able to improve on what you originally planned.

"When I was in politics in Queensland, and particularly when I was Premier, I achieved much more when I had to fight for votes for the successful passage of every piece of legislation I put forward. In fact, I was in coalition with a strong political opponent by the name of McIllwraith who did not like me and I detested him. Despite this, we tolerated one another sufficiently to enable us to achieve so much together that newspapers eventually called us Griffillwraith."

Bird agreed. "As an old Minister of Religion, can I say that Jesus of Nazareth himself was a superb negotiator. He fraternised on a daily basis with tax gatherers, thieves, prostitutes and rich men who used their money badly. His negotiating skills were such that he kept them in the same tent. He is a good role model for us to follow in welding society together by the generation of consensus between the high and the mighty and the lowly and the weak."

Murdoch was growing more agitated. His tolerance level was about as low as Griffith's.

He was unimpressed with their view of what constituted good government. He regarded their attitude as pompously patronising. Why would anyone with half a brain want the job of running a country without having the clear authority to do so?

"I really am surprised that men of your stature and experience approve of what is clearly an unstable situation in our Federal Parliament. No matter what virtues the delicate art of democracy may be construed to have the fact is that if there is no power, only chaos can result."

Griffith had the last word.

"If you study my personal political history in the Queensland Parliament as its Premier, before I became Chief Justice of Queensland and then came to occupy a similar role at the High Court, you will find that they nicknamed me 'Slippery Sam'. I gained this honourable title because of my ability to change my mind many times over in order to gain workable agreements on legislation. I regarded this title as an accolade and I enjoyed all the political battles in which I participated. History shows that I achieved some notable results.

"Now, can I suggest politely that you take your leave as Reverend Bird and I were commencing an important conversation when you interrupted us and we are now running out of time before our fellow guests return."

"My apologies for wasting your time."

"You have not wasted our time. We look forward to reading a hard-hitting, but thoughtful, article from you in *The Age* on the sins of minority governments," was Bird's friendly farewell.

Murdoch departed with as much grace as he could muster in the circumstances. He detested people who did not regard his opinions as profound.

One day, he thought, *I will control a powerful newspaper empire. These arrogant and egotistical fools will come grovelling to me for editorial support of their agendas. I will make them crawl on their hands and knees and force them to beg to me before I write one pleasant line about any of them.*

His thoughts were prophetic, but not with regard to the Founding Fathers.

It was their successors would progressively become incurable media tarts. Those in power in 1910 were relatively straight forward men who followed a loftier path to fame. They achieved goals that they set for themselves by sorting out all the obstacles on the floor of Parliament. Rarely did they feel the need to respond instantly to newspaper commentary or criticism.

The Chief Justice Gets Political

Now they were alone, Griffith made a wry comment.

"Murdoch annoys me but I have a feeling that he will go far. He possesses an aggression that will gain him more victories than defeats. Let us put minority governments out of our minds for a moment.

"As a Tasmanian, Bolton, are you at peace with the way in which the Federal Parliament is gradually and deliberately taking over matters that the states emphatically declared were theirs when they signed up for Federation?"

"I am. I always had it in the back of my mind that Federation would be marked by an erosion of State Rights as we understood them to be. In truth, I probably saw it as an inevitability as one day, Australia may be a nation of many small states that provide community services on behalf of a Federal Government that funds them. I am certain that Launceston would be delighted to be separated from Hobart, so would Devonport."

"This," said the Chief Justice, "will mean that there will be no local governments as the new states will take over the current functions of local governments. The Constitution already provides for this and I advocate it because I am a staunch defender of State Rights as my record of judgements in the High Court clearly shows."

"Well now," said Bird, "let's raise this thought later in the evening and see what response we evoke. If we can break up Victoria and New South Wales into smaller states, it will blunt their annoying rivalry."

Their fellow diners returned to the room, ready for action.

"Ah," commented Reid, "for you two to have remained here alone, it must mean that you have been plotting to disturb our peaceful talk-fest in some delightfully sinister manner. You surely have not acted like cads and bounders and slyly spiked our drinks, have you?"

"George," quipped Sam, "even if I spiked your drink sufficiently enough to lay you out on the floor of this splendid club, you would still manage to create an argument and most probably win it."

"I am delighted that you know me so well, Sam, and have such a finely attuned appreciation of my modest talents. I am enormously flattered. We must dine more often."

Dessert

It was time for some dedicated indulgence into the realm of sweet things, a state of joy that did not happen often in politics, but this was a special night.

The Chef, yet another admirer of the American Revolution, had chosen Apple Pie and Cream, stolen from a Confederate recipe and using top quality apples from Tasmania. Bolton Stafford Bird had arranged for the very best to be carefully chosen and picked from the Huon Valley and shipped directly to the club for this evening's sole use. Reid had contacted a dairy farming friend at Bega and prevailed upon him to prepare a very special cream from his prime cows and ship it to Melbourne packed in a mountain of ice. The Chef had added a delicate dose of Cinnamon to it. Even good Queen Victoria would not have turned up her nose at it. She would have been quite genuinely amused.

The ten Founding Fathers, having shown great discipline by arriving back at the dinner table on time, now showed an element of indiscipline by tucking enthusiastically into the figure-destroying pie which the chef had served in generous quantities on large plates.

They were ready for more lively reminiscences.

With a loud clearing of his throat, Barton invited the gathering to take part in a chat about the Day of Federation that had been celebrated on 1 January, 1901. This would open the way for reminisces of the subsequent General Election on 1 March that year which determined who would be Australia's first MPs and senators. Then, they planned to talk about the Grand Opening of the First Parliament on 1 May by the Duke of York (later King George V). These events were the three momentous consequences of the achievement of Federation.

Hopeless Hopetoun

Toby called on William Lyne, clearly aware that some electricity was about to circulate around the table.

This was the conversation they eagerly anticipated to be the high point of drama for the evening even though they had all suffered from displays of Lyne's anger on this delicate subject, usually on a one on one basis, on many occasions previously. This would be the first collective venting of wrath. Most wanted to express an opinion about the dramatic politics of the months prior to Federation and the hugely significant consequences.

"William, as we all vividly recall and will never forget, the newly appointed Governor General of Australia, Lord Hopetoun, called upon you, not me, in December 1900, to be the first Prime Minister of Australia. You were not formally sworn in as prime minister, but Hopetoun did give you a written invitation to form a government and you immediately began the task of doing so. His highly controversial action proved to be a painful experience, not only for you, but for every one of us as well, especially me. I was massively offended by his decision as it failed to recognise a decade of arduous toil for the cause of Federation by several people in this room, of whom you were not one. I had, with some degree of vanity, expected that Hopetoun would send for me. Would you like to talk about his extraordinary blunder from your personal viewpoint?"

Lyne was clearly stirred by the question. In his view, Toby had framed his invitation to speak about this controversy in a highly personal and provocative way. He decided to respond similarly.

"The thought of those dark and dismal days is still personally painful, but the clock can't be turned back. It is all over, even though the pain of humiliation still lingers in my whole being and will do so forever.

"Hopetoun was British to his boot heels. He always followed strict protocol which meant that he felt compelled to invite the premier of the largest state to be the first prime minister. I was Premier of New South Wales at that precise moment of history, so I got the call from him. Nevertheless, not one of you would back my appointment, nor even consider joining my ministry. Your quite vocal rejection of his choice insulted Hopetoun enormously, causing him great public embarrassment. I was greatly aggrieved by your negative response as I had not sought a Commission from the Governor General. He called me of his own volition."

The evening was steadily becoming too emotional for George Reid even though he was pleasantly sedated by the excellent red wine from South Australia that he was enjoying. The club had made this splendid vintage available in plenteous quantities, based on the clearly biased advice of Charles Kingston who, no matter where he travelled, constantly promoted the virtues of the wines of the Barossa Valley.

He felt compelled to interrupt yet again. "William, you brought this tragedy upon yourself. Hopetoun acted with technical correctness in inviting the premier of the largest state to be the first prime minister. At this juncture, may I confess that when Hopetoun asked my advice on the matter, I told him that the prime minister must come from New South Wales but I did not suggest that it should be the premier. Even so, you should have declined politely at the very instant that Hopetoun invited you and firmly advised him to invite Toby immediately.

"You had been, at best, very lukewarm towards every aspect of Federation from the day that you were first elected to the New South Wales Parliament and you sat on the fence throughout both referendums while clearly leaning towards NO. I only sat on the fence for the first one. Barton and I were the two advocates who finally got Federation over the line in New South Wales and Hopetoun should have been intensely aware that common sense required him to ask one of us. He reluctantly chose Toby as his second choice. I was more than a bit peeved about this because Toby had never been Premier of New South Wales while I had that honour for six years prior to 1898. But, I must wholeheartedly acknowledge that Toby had been superb in his persistent negotiation of every aspect of Federation and had thoroughly deserved the honour which, belatedly, was awarded to him.

"I eventually got to be prime minister, four years too late to be no1, but not too late to stir the pot mightily. If you stick around, we might eventually be tempted to give you a go. But, a thought crosses my mind that my good friends across the table, Kingston and Forrest, might seriously trample you to a horrible political death in the rush to get there first. Mind you, if I were them, I would put my hand up to very quickly, so everyone would have been aware of my intent."

Lyne was looking flushed with righteous anger.

"These comments of yours are an absolute lie, George. Hopetoun told me that you clearly advised him to invite me."

"Ah, William, why have you have not yet learnt the nuances of politics? As I indicated a moment ago, I told Hopetoun, when he sought my advice, that the prime minister had to be a New South Welshman and that the correct protocol would be to consult with you first and take your advice on the matter as you were premier of our great state. But, I did not specify that he should appoint you. With my usual humility, I hoped that he would invite me. If truth be known, it would be revealed that I tactfully planted that thought in his mind.

"Very specifically, I did advise him that there would be blood on the streets if he invited a bloody Victorian in preference to a noble son of New South Wales.

"May I confess that I was somewhat devious in making every one of my comments to Hopetoun as I was absolutely certain that no one would work with you and so I knew he would eventually have to call either me or Toby. Poor little me missed out, as usual, but such is the story of my tumultuous life of sacrifice to the nation.

"To make matters worse, Toby failed to invite me to be a member in his first ministry, yet he appointed two quite politically devious Victorians. And, when Dickson died, he appointed you instead of me. If I had complained loudly enough, I could have gained sufficiently massive public support to start a revolution. Happily, most Australians are aware that I am fundamentally a man of peace."

Who Was Guilty?

This brought a slight smile to Lyne's face, encouraging him to make further comment.

"I extend my sympathy to you, George. All that you say has some element of truth about it, but I was the democratically elected Premier of New South Wales which is clearly the largest state in terms of both population and economy. The first prime minister should have been me as the result of this indisputable fact. It was an insult to New South Wales that I was not given this vital role. It was more than disgraceful that every one of you here tonight deliberately blackballed me and many of you did so publicly. It was grossly embarrassing, absolutely unfair and patently discourteous. Your sense of decency should have directed you to give up your animosity towards me and get behind me so the nation would not be born in controversy."

As the representative at the dinner of the smallest state, Bird felt moved to intervene.

"It seems to me that New South Wales was not offended in any way, William. In truth, it was not possible for it to be so. A New South Welshman, Barton, got the job and he did it well in the very difficult days of the infancy of a nation. You could only have become aggravated if the job had been given to a Victorian and that was never going to happen."

"True," responded Lyne, "but it was still an insult to me."

John Forrest walked the length of the table with a carafe of wine in his hand to refill Lyne's glass and gave him a friendly pat on the shoulder.

"No one insulted you, William. Your punishment was self-inflicted. It came about because of your personal vanity. You are not a bad bloke, but politics is all about taking a lot of hard knocks. You took a huge hit with this matter, but we have to face the fact that you would have been a bloody awful prime minister.

"Besides which, I should have been given the job in acknowledgement of the fact that, had Western Australia voted No about Federation, then the whole continent would not have united. I should have been honoured for this reason alone as well as for the fact that my state occupies almost half of the continent. In addition, I was the longest serving of all state premiers at the time, a decade in fact. None of the rest of you came within a bull's roar of this. However, I will drown my sorrows with another glass of Red. I am giving you the chance to do the same.

"Can I add, Toby, that, at future dinners you host, you ensure that the wine will be chosen from the superb vineyards of the Swan River Valley, just upstream from Perth? Our wine is infinitely superior to anything that Charles has in South Australia as we have a genuine Mediterranean climate over in the West, the exact same one as enables Italians and Spaniards to produce such great vintages."

This gave Charles Kingston an opportunity to weigh in.

"I will humbly ignore this patronising comment from my sand groper friend from Western Australia and I won't mention the indisputable truth that Western Australian wine invariably tastes as though it has sand in it, blown in from the Nullarbor in horrendous quantities.

"Be this as it may, let me say this to you, William. You were never within a cooee of getting the job as our first prime minister. Hopetoun had absolutely no idea of how Australians thought and acted. He was an elitist British aristocrat with a narrow mind and a shallow brain whom I found to be hopelessly out of his depth and quite obnoxious. Everyone in Australia except you and Hopetoun knew that the job would go to Deakin, Reid or Barton. If he had sworn you in as prime minister on 1 January, the whole nation would have groaned and you would have been mercilessly thrashed by the voters at the General Election on 1 March. That disaster would have created a strong movement to have Hopetoun recalled to London as a total failure. We would have packed him home just to let the Poms know that we were exercising our independence from their ancient and illogical protocols that have constantly filled the House of Lords with dribbling idiots."

The Villain Was Affable Alfred

Lyne ignored Kingston and now trained his sad eyes on Deakin.

"You were my chief destroyer, Alfred. You, encouraged by your Premier, Turner, sent several angry messages to Hopetoun saying that you would not serve with me under any circumstances. I know this because he showed them to me. Even worse, you and Turner made a veiled threat to recall the Victorian Parliament to vote on having Victoria withdraw from Federation unless he recanted from his choice of me."

"I did," responded Alfred in his softest, quietest and most threatening voice. Looking Lyne squarely in the eyes, he made a cold response, "And I would do it again if I had to, even more loudly and strongly and harshly. Hopetoun was a pathetically ineffective Head of State who insulted an entire nation which is based on a firm belief in decency and fair play that he could not even remotely understand. His foolish decision to call you was a travesty of the whole notion of democracy. Every citizen except you and a few of your closest friends knew that Toby had not only earned the right to have this honour, he was the right man for this crucial moment in our history."

He continued to hold Lyne firmly in his gaze. It was Lyne who blinked first.

Then Deakin added a compliment, "Let me now add and important acknowledgement.

"You acted with honour when you resigned promptly after discovering that none of us would serve under you. Had you been arrogant enough to go to extreme lengths to ensure you would be prime minister, you could have chosen half a dozen second rate politicians and submitted their names to Hopetoun who would have been spineless enough to accept them and ignore the rest of us. You did not do that. For this, we all thank you and so does Australia."

A profound silence engulfed the Dining Room. Griffith now felt that it was appropriate for him intervene. It was a mistake.

Slippery Sam Is Slammed

"William, I can't understand why you have chosen to single out Alfred for a verbal assault alone. As I recall it, George and Charles and John all refused to serve with you and did so quite volubly. I feel certain that Queensland Premier, John Dickson, did likewise. Alfred may have been the most vocal, but in doing so he represented a huge mass of shock and dissent about Hopetoun's unfortunate invitation to you to lead the nation.

"I must say that I have not come across one influential person who supported you among all the leaders I know. After your consistent opposition to Federation, your own personal integrity should have told you that it would be seen as a huge breach of ethics for you to be seen as even remotely considering a role as our first prime minister."

Lyne was not of a mind to accept Griffiths comments in any shape or form.

"My attitude was one of respect for democracy. I had huge reservations about Federation, but when a majority voted for it, I accepted their decision and wanted to do my best to make it successful. This was shown by my subsequent action in resigning as Premier of New South Wales so I could seek election to the Federal Parliament. This clear intent qualified me for consideration to have the role of prime minister if I was to be called upon by the Governor General. Had you given me the chance, I would have given it my best shot. None of you gave me any credit for having fully participated in the democratic process in an open and honest manner."

His fellow dinner guests had an uneasy feeling that Lyne was not yet finished. They guessed correctly.

He was about to deliver what he intended to be a killer blow with as much invective as he could muster.

"Now that you have chosen unwisely to speak on this matter, Sam, let me spell out to you a few words of truth that the whole world should know relating to your own appalling behaviour. No matter whatever sins I may have or what vanity I possess, I did not follow your appalling example of blatant self-aggrandisement. You outrageously campaigned for years to be appointed Chief Justice of the High Court. Even worse, you spent most of that time deliberately denigrating Toby so that you could make certain he would not get the nod as Chief Justice ahead of you when the High Court was established in 1903. He had voluntarily retired as Prime Minister in 1903 and had earned the honour of heading the High Court. He should have been given the role as a mark of respect for his splendid legal work on the Constitution and the successful establishment of a sound, working government. If anyone strove to do Toby in, it was you in 1903, not me, in 1901. You are an incurable hypocrite."

Like a bolt of lightning, Griffith rose from his seat, his nostrils flaring, his whole body shaking. For the first time in his life, he stumbled to find appropriate words with which to respond to what he regarded as a hideously outrageous comment and a profound insult, even though even though everyone in the room knew that it was very close to the truth. His demeanour failed to hide his clear guilt.

There could be no doubt that it was time to stop the blood-letting and restore order.

Barton was so taken aback by this outburst he simply stared at both Lyne and Griffith.

Bolton Stafford Bird rose to the occasion. As a wise old clergyman, used to the settling of family disputes, he firmly interrupted Griffith and requested the floor once more. Without waiting for a response from Barton, he took control of the debacle.

"Sam, may I politely invite you to sit down and calm down and say absolutely nothing more. May I tactfully suggest that you do likewise William.

"It will be both wise and appropriate if we all rise above personal denigration for the remainder of the evening. This last conversation lowered itself to a level of behaviour bearing a close proximity to that of undisciplined school boys. Can I, as a minister of my church, call for us to follow the Lord's advice and turn the other cheek, no matter what provocation comes our way.

"May grace and peace be with everyone here at this table."

George Reid applauded loudly. A sigh of relief spread through the gathering.

Tasmania Misses Out

Bolton continued, "Having tendered this advice, Toby, can I, in a similar spirit of goodwill, change the subject? May I ask how you went about choosing the First Ministry?

"You had to gather it together very quickly, thereby enabling Hopetoun to swear you in to govern the country in an executive capacity until the people could vote in a democratic election to choose the First Parliament? I am chiming in here because it was a massive disappointment to me, and all Tasmanians, that you did not appoint one of our parliamentarians to your ministry."

Relieved that Bird had deftly changed the course of the conversation, Toby responded warmly, "Bolton, I am very aware that my decision was an affront to you and many Tasmanians. I now admit that it was a mistake to do that. The man I wanted to appoint was Andrew Clark, but his health would not allow it. Your Premier at the time, Braddon, said that he did not want to leave Tasmanian politics and you were of the same mind. Frankly, I could not find a man of stature among the others, so I looked elsewhere. I should have looked at Tasmania again shortly afterwards when, as Andrew has already reminded us, our minister from Queensland, John Dickson, died one week after he was sworn in. This tragedy meant that I had a second chance to appoint a Tasmanian, but erred again."

"There are two important points for all of us to remember," intervened Deakin. "The first is that the Ministry was only a small one, just six men, so it was not possible to include everyone who deserved a place or try to appoint someone from every state.

"Secondly, it is an undeniable fact that the ministry Toby formed was able to work together well and establish a small public service that was seen to start governing responsibly prior to the First Election. Indeed, Toby, you prepared the nation well for that election. It was organised smoothly and without any sign of abuse of democracy, despite the vastness of the nation and the isolation of so many voters who knew very little about Federation and cared even less.

"May I also remind us that on the day we were sworn in as Ministers of the Interim Government, we had only one public servant, Sir Robert Garran? He had the honour of heading up the smallest bureaucracy in the world. More importantly, he was an excellent choice as he had been a key figure in organising the Federation Conventions in the previous decade. A superbly loyal public servant whose service to Australia has never been adequately recognised."

Lyne, who by this time had somewhat restored his composure as a result of several huge breaths of discipline, had an extra word and it was kind, a sharp contrast to earlier moments.

"Bolton, I was the representative of Tasmania in the ministry. I was born there and spent the first twenty years of my life on your pleasant island in the lovely village of Ross. Be assured that Tasmania was not forgotten.

"As you know, I am very parochial and I have never forgotten the happy days of my youth spent in what is the loveliest part of Australia. So, I looked after your interests as diligently as I could."

"My apologies for forgetting this important fact, William. And thank you."

"One more point, Bolton. You have overlooked the fact that Toby did invite a revered Tasmanian, Sir Phillip Fish, to attend Cabinet meetings as an observer."

"Point taken, William."

"Can we move into a more celebratory mood?" enquired Chris Watson.

"What do you have in mind?" queried Toby.

"It is time to talk about 1 January, 1901."

"Go ahead."

The Great Day

As Watson had been a high-profile opponent of Federation, he was the right person to give an objective comment on Federation Day.

"What a memorable occasion it was when we celebrated the birth of Federation on this day ten years ago. According to the New South Wales Police, there were more than five hundred thousand people watching the Federation Parade in Sydney. They had travelled from all states to be there and they occupied every possible vantage point in the city. We all recall that the participants had gathered in the domain in downtown Sydney and their parade wound around the city streets for several miles before reaching Centennial Park where Hopetoun swore in Toby as Prime Minister and then the five members of his ministry – Deakin, Turner, Kingston, Forrest and Dickson. Sadly, none of them represented the Labor Party. We had earned our rejection due to our stubborn opposition to Federation."

"What was impressive was that every major institution in the nation arranged to have a float or band or choir marching in the parade, even the Labor Party. There were even brigades of British and Indian troops, paid for by Queen

Victoria, who had made long boat trips to Sydney so they could march in honour of the new nation," added Deakin.

"I had arrived from Melbourne on the previous day and Toby kindly invited me to stay at his home for a few days, a sojourn I greatly enjoyed. We could not get any sleep on New Year's Eve. Revellers were out celebrating the arrival of 1901 and were still celebrating when the Federation Parade began at 10.30am. Our carriages were cheered every inch of the way and, to the surprise of none of us, Toby enjoyed much louder cheers than Hopetoun. In fact, as I remember it, Hopetoun received only a few polite claps and was fortunate to get them."

Watson took up his comments once more.

"After the swearing in, Toby made his first speech as Prime Minister. I must acknowledge that it was well received even though I did not agree with its politics.

"Even more stunning were the huge crowds who then spread out around the Harbour. They watched in awe a spectacle that the organisers called a 'pyrotechnical illumination' of that magnificent stretch of water that we all know to be the finest harbour in the world.

"By midnight, I had come to the conclusion that Australians had warmly accepted Federation. I had been amiss in my opposition to it. Griffith gave an image of having calmed down considerably by this time and had decided to create the impression that he had been absolutely unruffled by Lyne's accusation. He would follow the good advice Bird had given, joining in the discussion with good grace and putting William's accusations firmly in the furthermost corners of his mind.

"My understanding is that every community in Australia, no matter how small, staged a celebratory event on that momentous day when we became a nation. All political controversies were forgotten. National pride reigned supreme and it remains evident today. May that spirit continue."

"Hear, Hear," was the enthusiastic response.

Voters Have Their Say

Sam moved on, "Rejoicing in this, I think that it will be a good plan if we continue to take our conversation forward on the happy course we are now following. Allow me to remind you of some key facts.

"We are aware that the second notable event was the Federal Elections held on the first day of March to elect our first Federal Parliament. For each one of you, your campaigns were highly personal because your careers as national statesmen depended on the results.

"Having personally decided not to be a candidate in the elections for the First Parliament, I was able to take a detached view of it and found that the results were reasonably close to what I expected them to be.

"Toby had 32 of his Protectionist supporters elected while George's Free Trade Party scored 26. This left Labor with 17 MPs and holding the balance of power. Fortunately, their caucus promptly announced that they would support Toby as Prime Minister.

"This meant that his appointment by Hopetoun he was now confirmed by the voters. Importantly, all of the nation's newspapers reported that it had been a free and fair election that enabled people to vote even if they lived in the most remote places. The postmen delivered their ballot papers, waited while they filled them out, then delivered them to the election officer.

"Sadly, the Senate Elections produced a myriad of political factions. That none of whom were state based parties was a relief to us all. The fear of New South Wales, that voters were supposed to have, proved to be a myth. By a stroke of good fortune, the new senators had generally cooperated with Toby on key legislation.

"This was interesting when we consider the long and often bitter constitutional battles we had over State Rights. It has placed into question the issue of whether we ever did need to have a senate."

Lyne interrupted, "Let us be honest with ourselves. The creation of a senate was a total nonsense. It was established just to pander to parochial attitudes. It will be a monster that will plague our progress for centuries to come."

Suppressing once more his earlier altercation with Lyne, Griffith made a comment of intended goodwill to Lyne.

"You have a valid point, William, but I am sure you and I can agree also that it will be very difficult ever to remove it."

Toby intervened, "The spirit of democracy having prevailed, it's time for us to recall that our nation moved on to another tremendous day. 1901 was proving to be a very historic year."

Royals Add Their Blessing

"Most political commentators have reminded us over the past decade that Australia did not actually become a democracy on 1 January, 1901. They declared that this did not happen until the first elected Parliament held its first meeting. Over to you once more, Sam."

Griffith acknowledged the importance of the birthday of the Parliament.

"What a magnificent occasion it was when the First Parliament assembled in Melbourne for its inauguration on 1 May, 1901 when all MPs and senators were sworn in by Hopetoun and received the royal blessings of Queen Victoria as conveyed by the presence of the Duke of York. 15000 people attended that ceremony.

"We finally had a new nation with a democratically elected Parliament and a ministry that was already working effectively because all of its members had long experience as ministers in state governments over many years.

"Even more extraordinary is that the vast majority of Australians at that moment expressed great confidence in the future of the new nation. The goodwill that abounded across the continent was a joy to experience. As Toby has already indicated, many felt that the Australian nation began its life at the moment the Parliament had been sworn in. But then, there are some people who believe that we became a nation when the First Fleet arrived in 1788.

"Such were the scope of the festivities that there were many days and evenings of quite spectacular events to celebrate this historic event. Almost two weeks passed before the celebrations culminated when the Duke sailed home. It was only then that the Parliament was able to meet formally to transact legislation."

At this juncture, Griffith decided it was appropriate to take a jocular shot at Reid who seemed to be the butt of everyone's humour that evening, but George did not appear to be put out about it at all. Actually, he appeared to be enjoying it immensely and would have been highly offended if his presence had been ignored.

"You made an enormous blunder, George, when you allowed Federal Parliament to establish its initial headquarters in Melbourne.

"You should have been as upset about that insult as William was, and obviously still is, about the prime ministership. If William's assumption is indeed correct regarding his claim that deference must be given to the largest state on all important matters, you let the show down badly by not indignantly insisting that Parliament sit in Sydney. Your blunder in tolerating this will, in all likelihood go down in history as possibly a worse political gaffe than the one that Hopetoun made."

Reid once more patted his spacious girth contentedly and put on a broad smile.

"Sometimes, but hopefully not too often, one has to be gracious, and the Lord has bestowed upon me a particular talent for graciousness.

"At the time that this ghastly decision was made, I had to admit, with great reluctance mind you, that it is easier for boats to get to Melbourne from Perth, Adelaide and Hobart than it was for them to sail all the way round to Sydney. But, we will soon get our well-deserved and long overdue revenge.

"It must never be forgotten that the Federation Agreement says the National Capital must be located in New South Wales, specifically somewhere other than Sydney. You will all recall that this was the pay back that we demanded for allowing the first Parliament to sit in Melbourne. We will get around to choosing the site one day soon and I will use whatever influence I have to ensure that it is placed as far away from Melbourne as I can achieve so that Victorian MPs will have maximum inconvenience in getting there, preferably having to cross many flooded rivers. It will do their souls an infinite degree of good. They need to experience a healthy dose of humility after decades of unwarranted displays of blatant superiority in every comment they make about the fine State of New South Wales which is a close to Camelot as you will ever find.

"Besides which, we rejoiced about the way in which we made the Victorians grovel in order to become the centre of national power. They were forced to give up their Parliament building so the Feds could use it while their own State Parliament was despatched to the back blocks. There was no way that we would ever give up our lovely Parliament building in Macquarie Street to allow it to be used by 'foreigners' who lack our cultural values."

Flaws in the Constitution

Griffith changed the subject before George could get overly humble.

"When we framed the Constitution, we did not mention political parties anywhere in its wording and, therefore, did not authorise their existence. This has already proved to be a sad omission which will become even more obvious as the years pass and power brokers manipulate them to enhance their own personal power.

"Nevertheless, they emerged from the opening day of Parliament as part of the political establishment, as they had naturally done previously in all State Parliaments in a rather casual fashion. You will remember, Alfred, that, at the Constitutional Convention just prior to Federation, you predicted that political parties would become more tightly organised and highly factional once political power became focussed on the Federal Parliament.

"You were quickly proven to be correct as party politics emphatically dominated the Senate whose members were supposed to be there for the sole purpose of defending their states. Clearly, they had no intention of ever doing that thus making it clear that we now need a clause in the Constitution that strictly controls their formation, activities and operations. Importantly, we should have stated in it that no party could legally or politically bind its members to vote the way its leaders determine. In the long term, Australia will suffer from our failure to enshrine in our Constitution some appropriate words that would ensure the absolute autonomy of individual members and senators from their political bosses so that they could discharge their duties with responsibility solely to the voters who put them there."

Fisher disagreed. He believed that disciplined political parties were essential to democracy, provided that the factional leaders and political ideologues within each party were kept under control by binding them to operate their factions by conducting democratic votes on all policies.

"We need to take steps to deter the growing practice of factions seeking iron clad commitments from their members to vote is a confirmed manner on every piece of legislation. Factions must have their dictatorial powers blunted."

Barton pointed out another constitutional error.

"We also omitted to make any mention in the Constitution of the office of Prime Minister. Nor did we mention the existence of a Cabinet, probably because British law does not mention them either. We made reference only to ministers, but did not state that one would be chosen as Prime Minister. Therefore, the Prime Minister is in actual fact a non-person who operates with no constitutional authority. It is the Governor General who has been given the power to appoint all ministers, but the reality is that he doesn't do so in practice. It is an unconstitutional prime minister who appoints them and asks the Governor General to swear them in, a task that he usually performs without question. This is fundamentally no different to the way that the prime minister functions at Westminster, but it is open to manipulation if dishonest people ever attain positions of power.

"We will discover to our regret one day, that some supreme egotist with a powerful personality will become Governor General and brazenly decide to exercise his rightful legal powers under the Constitution. He will do this either in league with a weak or consenting or manipulative prime minister or by telling the prime minister of the day to go to hell, while he appoints his own team of people whom he believes are best qualified to hold office. This is destined to be a landmark day in our history. We can be sure that one day it will happen.

"The President of the United States has the power that our Constitution gives to our Governor General and the President does exercise it. Whenever this inevitable event occurs in Australia, it will make the Governor General more powerful than the Prime Minister. Indeed, it will create a major constitutional crisis, but no one will be able to move against the Governor General as he will be acting totally within the powers granted to him by the Constitution. In the long term, such a crisis may not be such a bad thing. It could create conditions whereby we can achieve an improved Constitution as a result."

Toby paused as he summoned Giles to graciously invite him to serve coffee and port, while noting that a few loyal British subjects had sternly requested tea. More than a few signalled their need for a cigar. In the interests of maintaining and enhancing his figure, Reid requested that chocolates be served also.

He carefully and authoritatively explained that good dark chocolate gave him the vital energy he needed to fulfil his onerous civic duties and strongly recommended that everyone should re-energise themselves, as there were still many matters of importance to discuss and he wanted all of them to be in top form.

Coffee, Tea, Chocolates, Port, Cigars

How Successful Was Federation?

"Now my friends, let us set forth on the culminating debate of our evening," intoned Barton.

"It's time to review what we have achieved together in the decade since Federation and what we failed to do. I am certain that some frank comment is needed or we may well regard this evening as somewhat less satisfying and constructive than we had hoped."

He invited Affable Alfred to open the discussion. Most likely the deepest thinker in the room, Alfred paused briefly as his hyperactive brain marshalled his thoughts so that his very persuasive tongue could achieve its greatest impact, a goal that he tried to achieve with every remark he made. Slippery Sam had a similar approach with his oratory but he lacked the charisma of Deakin.

"The fact that we are all still here is a notable achievement. Federation continues to have an aura about it that gives the appearance of having worked in the manner we hoped it would. Largely, it has.

"If our Parliament had descended into a parochial, dysfunctional rabble in the first few years, most of the states would have called referendums and pulled out of it. Such a debacle would have been quite legal as the Constitution clearly provides a mechanism for states to leave the Federation until there are none left. At that point in our history, the Constitution will be used to wrap up our fish and chips. But no state has taken advantage of this. Yet.

"There are a number of special achievements we can positively recall and humbly applaud. Firstly, we established a High Court that functions well and enjoys widespread public confidence and goodwill. We had a long battle with the State Supreme Courts to achieve this. You will recall how they stoutly defended their territory but it was a battle they were destined to lose.

"Then, we legislated to have an Age Pension introduced. It will grow to be the key element in the social fabric of our nation, allowing our people to grow old without fear of poverty. This was accompanied by the creation of an Arbitration System that provides workers with basic rights and fairer wages.

"We have created an army, plus the basis of a future navy as part of our contribution to the defence of the Empire and particularly our own security. We have done so in the hope that we won't always have to rely on Britain to defend us. We are on a clear path to independence.

"We determined a sound basis for the national control of immigration so that we have been able to entrench the aim of our nation being predominantly a White Australia. Significantly for our economic prosperity, we removed the charging of tariffs at State Borders. This has made a huge difference to interstate trade.

"Above all, we managed to balance our books financially. Australia is not in any danger of becoming bankrupt. The opposite is the case. We prosper.

"All of this indicates that our nation is, thankfully, a stable democracy, financially viable at all levels of government. Our commerce and industry is enjoying steady growth and society is becoming more cohesive. We could have done better, but we have not in any way done badly.

"It is fair to say that we now have every right to declare that Federation has been a success and our nation is at peace. The real debate before us is how we maintain this and strive to further improve it and progress it."

"You have missed one key achievement, Alfred, that has enhanced our status worldwide," said Charles Kingston. "In 1903, we granted to all women their long denied right to vote nationwide, with the full cooperation of every state, whereas a decade ago only women living in South Australia had this privilege. We were one of few nations in the world to do so at that time and I acknowledge William's role in managing this legislation through Parliament in his capacity as Minister for Home Affairs.

"England, our mother country, has not yet done this and has no plans to do so as they still operate their decadent class system on the principle that some must always dominate others. Lamentably, it continues to tear itself apart over the rights of women and will do so for some time to come as the suffragette movement inevitably grows stronger and more militant. However, it peeves me greatly that the New Zealanders beat us to it by a few years. Nevertheless, I rejoice that my beloved South Australia beat both New South Wales and Victoria to the starting gate on this significant social advance."

With a smile on his face, Kingston turned to George Reid and commented, "South Australia really is a state of perpetual enlightenment. We are the envy of all who live in New South Wales with the exception of my dear friend, George Reid."

George snorted. For once he was speechless.

Andrew Fisher stepped into the breach. "I hold the view that another milestone has been just as important as the achievements that Alfred and Charles have effectively outlined," added Andrew Fisher.

"It is this the Commonwealth has gradually increased its rightful authority over the states in many quiet, but significant, ways that the framers of the Constitution could not have envisaged would happen so quickly. Many people voted for Federation in the naive belief that the states would always remain dominant, with the Commonwealth rubber stamping whatever states wanted. Thankfully, we have conclusively proven that those parochial people were wrong. Federation could not have worked their way. We have a duty to encourage future Australian Parliaments to further strengthen the exercise of Commonwealth power in matters that obviously require a national strategy to achieve greater social and economic progress."

Griffith made an important point.

"Splendid observation, Andrew. While my record shows that I will always be a staunch defender of the rights of the states, it did take our states a long time to agree that the High Court should be established. As Alfred has already reminded us, they tenaciously persisted with the view that State Courts could legally and adequately control everything that occurred within their borders and so a High Court of Australia would not be needed. We can thank God that we won this battle, otherwise many people and institutions would have had to go to six independent courts to gain justice in a way that would be recognised nationally. This would have caused absolute chaos."

Barton added the comment that the Commonwealth was also transcending the power of London to interfere in its life.

"Our goal of national independence from the yoke of colonialism is being achieved by a strategy of gradualism. Piece by piece, and without the British being aware of it, we will continue to do so. We are gradually ceasing to operate in the manner of a colony. One day, we will remove every vestige of British domination to the extent that we will be enabled to break our legal ties with the Privy Council in London so that it will no longer have the power to override our courts. We spent many hours on the *Lucinda* discussing this very issue and agreed that, while it would take time, it must be achieved as it is a necessity of our independence."

Suffragettes

Kingston waved his arm and got the nod from the host once more.

"Other than for my earlier comments about their voting rights, there has been no mention at any time this evening of the active role of women in causing Federation to be achieved. In some ways, this is understandable because we did not appoint even one woman as a delegate at the two Federation Conventions or any of the Conferences. Even more lamentable is the well-known fact that my own State of South Australia was the only one to allow women a vote in the Federation Referendums. Quite unfairly, none of our Federal and State Parliaments has elected any women as Members or Senators.

But, in State of South Australia, I am proud to say that we did have some genuine patriots whose sterling efforts have never been adequately acknowledged.

The most notable is Catherine Spence who has been a fearless and powerful leader of Australia's suffragettes and a splendid symbol of what women can achieve in public life if they are given a fair chance to do so.

She was a committed supporter of Federation and did not let us take our eye off the ball at any time. She embarrassed us mightily when she became a candidate to represent South Australia as an official at the 1897 Federation. I voted for her, but most other male voters rose up in horror at the outrageous thought of a woman representing our great state on the national scene. They actually believed that all the other states would laugh at us. She was wiped out but she took her humiliation with good grace. At the very least, the history of Australia will record that she was the first female to become a political candidate for public office

She then commenced a strong advocacy of proportional representation in State and Federal Parliaments as this would enable a wider spread of society to participate in the halls of power. She wanted all parties that received more than 5% of the vote state-wide to be granted one seat in Parliament in addition to whatever specific electorates they may have won or even if they had won no seats. She was thrown to the wolves on that one too. Our males worked out that she was a person who had the ability to create a Women's Party that would easily get 5% of the vote and thereby enable a woman to walk around the hallowed halls of Parliament as a duly elected MP.

Those humiliations strengthened her belief that a National Parliament would be an essential platform from which women could gain equality with men in all matters of human rights.

I want to propose a toast to her as she is a special person and it is important that we honour her now as her health is failing rapidly. She is a great Australian and I intend to convey to her personally the manner in which we have honoured her tonight. She will be genuinely moved by this tribute, not just for herself. She will regard it as another step forward in acknowledging the injustices that women have had to tolerate in seeking the meaningful role in public life to which they are entitled."

"Let me now do something more positive and constructive than to lament the fact that you all blackballed me as Prime Minister. Charles, can I suggest that we make it two toasts?" asked William Lyne quite warmly.

"While wholeheartedly endorsing what Charles has said about Catherine Spence as an extraordinary person, I want us to include in our toast another splendid woman, Louisa Lawson. She hails from Mudgee in my home State of

New South Wales. She is of the same mould and has the same priorities as Catherine Spence, only more aggressive in the way she goes about it. Lamentably, she is an absolute pain in the backside when she is in full flight. But we eventually had no option but to listen to her. She was making a valid case on behalf of women regarding the role that they should have in the new nation that was about to be established.

She also had a personal battle to fight as everyone has constantly referred to her as Henry Lawson's mother and she has struggled determinedly to establish her own identity as a person. Which she successfully achieved. This was important to her because, while her literary son Henry is one of our most famous writers and poets, he is quite a drunkard who also has a sad record of domestic violence, especially directed at her. May I also comment Alfred that she, like you, is a spiritualist of some stature. You should go out of your way to meet her one day."

"This being so, it will be a privilege for me to drink her health," retorted Alfred. "This nation will be a far better place as the ranks of spiritualists grow. It will progressively give this nation more firepower.

Additionally, may I suggest that we include in our toast all women who worked actively with us to achieve Federation even though they were forced to work behind the scenes, usually doing the catering. There were many of them who voluntarily took up the cause of nationhood and they were magnificent, even though they were unheralded and unsung.

In drinking our toast, can we also include the suffragettes of our mother country over in dear old England which still has not allowed women to vote and are nowhere near doing so. In truth, they are probably decades away from doing so as their opposition to it often resorts to brutality. I find it extraordinarily difficult to understand in a nation that claims to lead the civilised world. English women need our total backing."

They all raised their glasses, perhaps a little sheepishly, but certainly with a pang of guilt.

Their male world had taken a king hit when women won the right to vote and they were now very unsure as to what further bastions of male power these female hordes would eventually assault. Unspoken, their deepest fear was that, one day, as Kingston had suggested, women might actually be elected to Parliament.

George added a pertinent comment to the toast.

"Any further thoughts about electing female parliamentarians must cease immediately for a very pragmatic reason. It is logistically impossible to allow women into our Federal Parliament. There are no female toilets in the main building."

Noting that this profound comment drew nothing but stares of bemusement, Reid decided that he had better redeem himself quickly.

'The Man in the Street' Takes Over

"One more toast," he added.

We have quite rightly acknowledged the constitutional work of Andrew Clark. We should also honour John Quick.

He was the man who, at the Corowa Convention of 1893, undertook significant negotiations which resulted in a resolution being successfully passed saying that, if Federation was to succeed, it had to be a movement of the people, not politicians.

He held the strong view that Federation could not be inflicted on the man in the street by the political power brokers who reigned over them. If this occurred, they would vote No in the referendums. This made a huge difference in grass roots representation at the 1897 Convention in Adelaide which finally agreed on a constitution for the new nation. That dramatic debate at Corowa was a very significant moment in the battle to achieve Federation. History may yet prove that it could have been the determining factor in swinging the Federation Movement towards its ultimate victory.

However, I am aware Alfred that you were not a fan of John Quick."

Deakin leapt into the fray. He was not a vindictive person, but he had issues with Quick.

"I acknowledge the significance of the resolution that Quick masterminded at Corowa. It was a significant step forward. However, whenever Quick mentioned 'the people' he meant the educated upper classes who supposedly had the wisdom and financial influence to decide what was best for all Australians. Fisher, Watson and I strived to make sure that those in basic employment had their voice heard by being invited to participate in the decision making as well.

Also, I am disappointed that Quick did not acknowledge the considerable help he was given, at all the Federation Meetings, by Robert Garran whose enormous service to Australia has never been adequately honoured. We would never have established the machinery for the effective operation of a Federal Government without him in charge of the Public Service on 1 January, 1901. And I exaggerate not."

Barton calmed the nerves.

"The simplest way to handle this is to toast both Quick and Garran. They are worthy of such a toast as they were both essential cornerstones of the new nation, especially noting that Garran was our first and foremost bureaucrat. I particularly endorse what Alfred has said about him. We note with pleasure that both were knighted by His Majesty."

They drank heartily.

The Convict and the Australian Dream

Chris Watson asked leave to speak.

"While we are in the mood to honour people, we should make mention of the remarkable speech made by the Member for Darling Downs, William Groom, when our Parliament first met.

After the Duke of York had opened our Parliament and had led and enjoyed the extended celebrations that followed, we spent many days setting up the mechanics of the way we would go about our work of ensuring that a stable democracy would be established so that we had a working Parliament and a functioning Government. Then we got around to making formal speeches recording how, for the purposes of history, our Parliament came into being.

We decided that a back bencher should make the very first one and we selected Groom because he was the oldest man in the Parliament and was also the only one of us who had arrived here as a convict.

His story is remarkable.

After gaining parole from his bondage as a convict, he had gotten himself in trouble once more and spent time in gaol as the result of being convicted for libel. His comeback after all of that was quite incredible. He decided that it was time to turn his life around and so he set about becoming a successful and respected business man in Toowoomba from where he easily won election to the State Parliament and then the first Federal Parliament. He represented the Australian dream by vividly displaying to us all that this was a land where anyone and everyone could rise from the depths of misfortune and win a place at the top. It was one of the few speeches by a capitalist that has ever made sense to me. I wish I could remember his exact words."

"I can help you," said Deakin, "I have a reasonable memory for inspiring words and feel that I know a few of his lines of it by heart, even though, like Chris, he did not belong to my political school. In my view, these two paragraphs from his speech capture the spirit of his message."

We are commenced on another page in our history.

I feel the responsibility of this occasion because we are now supposed to be rising above the provincialism of State Governments. We are supposed to be now in that higher sphere to which reference has so often been made, and I cannot but express the hope that, in the discussions and deliberations of this House, we shall set an example to other Parliaments in matters of legislation that will reflect honour upon the first Commonwealth Parliament.

I hope that we shall rise to the occasion and prove ourselves worthy. However, I feel assured that, knowing my fellow members, every matter coming before us will receive the greatest consideration and the most mature deliberation. I fervently hope that, on all occasions, our deliberations and discussions will be of such a character that people may point to us with pride and say that we are worthy of the great charter that has been conferred upon us.

"I may not have got that exactly correct, but I think it is a reasonable approximation. The issue now in my mind is to ask ourselves the question. Have we lived up to those lofty words spoken by Groom? Can we say honestly that 'we are worthy of the great charter that has been conferred upon us?"

Bird responded.

"As someone who has not been a member of the Federal Parliament, but a long serving Member of the Tasmanian Parliament, may I say that I am of the conviction that our Members and Senators have made a respectable attempt to live up to Groom's vision. There is room for improvement as some unfortunate blunders have occurred, but a fair start has been achieved. I know that this reminder of the words so splendidly uttered by Groom will motivate me to shake up our performance back in Tasmania."

Lyne added a comment.

"Thank you, Bolton. I am a conservative like Groom and he was a solid advocate of economic and social conservatism. It was a tragedy when he died, quite suddenly and unexpectedly just a few months after that speech. However, his son was elected in his place and, as we know from working with him, he has served with honour and distinction. The Groom legend lives on and it inspires our generation."

Griffith had the final word.

"Groom was the Member for Toowoomba in the Queensland Parliament during my time as Premier. He had been there for a long time before I arrived, holding his seat for almost four decades. He then moved on to the Federal Parliament as he fervently wanted to end his political career as an Australian rather than as a Queenslander. He told me at the Parliamentary dinner that we held to welcome the King to our shores that he had also wanted to show the Establishment back in London that one of their convicts had survived their brutality to take over the reins of government from them and handle its responsibilities far better.

It is important for us to applaud his total commitment to community service by noting that he was also Mayor of Toowoomba for seven terms, serving concurrently with his parliamentary service in Brisbane.

His honoured place in history as a member of our first Parliament was the just reward of a tumultuous journey through a memorable life that spanned both the northern and southern hemispheres and that few others could aspire to emulate. May his memory live on and may many others follow his example. It takes a great man to make a respectable and successful comeback from a life that involved two long prison sentences!"

Goodnight

The evening was moving towards its conclusion.

They indulged in some lively debate about the vibrant state of politics in Australia, being honest enough to acknowledge that politics will always be politics and will never fail to be turbulent.

No one could really give a rational explanation as to why it happened that there had been five prime ministers in ten years, with one of them serving three times. They came to a consensus that it had just happened and was not caused by any particular political strategy of disruption masterminded by any devious person or faction. By a stroke of good fortune combined with sensible compromises where needed, the Parliament had worked well. Good government had usually resulted.

Toby invited final comments.

Elusive Preamble

Bolton Stafford Bird took the opportunity to raise his vision of a Preamble to the Constitution and he was given strong support by Deakin who reaffirmed his long-held view that it was an unfulfilled issue of importance on the national agenda.

Bird stated his conviction that it was vital that Australians should have a clear vision of the values that had gradually become embedded in the life of the nation. They should also be aware of what it is they aspire to achieve. They needed an understanding of what it means to live in a good and just society and what responsibilities they had as proud citizens. This would ensure that the quality of lifestyle which they had been given the opportunity to enjoy in Australia was perpetually maintained and enhanced.

Alfred endorsed Bird's remarks with his usual passion.

Both were completely surprised that there was almost unanimous sympathy from their fellow diners for the concept of such a Preamble.

To their dismay, there was also a universal view that it would be almost impossible for Australians to reach consensus on words which would generate a majority of votes in a referendum on the matter as there was such a wide diversity of people who now had the right to vote. Some expressed the view that the exercise, noble though it was, would be a frustrating waste of valuable time as it was doomed to failure.

George Reid colourfully spelled out the rationale behind their thinking.

"The Micks and the Prods will never agree on what words should be used to describe a Christian way of life to which most Australians can aspire. If we give them such a task, we will wind up with blood all over the floor. On top of this, there are a million or more religious back sliders will want to continue with their ingrained habit of not wanting to believe anything."

Prime Minister Andrew Fisher was a little more positive.

He offered to look wholeheartedly at a draft Preamble when Bolton was in a position to place one before him, even though he thought that it would die of disinterest when it was debated in Committees of the Parliament. It would take much hard work to gain an acceptance of a belief that this was a priority for Australia for Australia at this moment. Nevertheless, he was willing to give it his best shot.

Bolton took a deep breath and indicated that he felt a calling to give it a go. Many wished him well without displaying any enthusiasm. Even so, they quietly gave thanks that Australia still had leaders of moral and ethical fibre of the quality of Bolton Stafford Bird.

Creating Small States

Bird was so disappointed that he had again failed in his mission to gain genuine traction for his dream of a Preamble, he forgot to raise the issue of creating small states that he had been discussing with Sam during the break.

Griffith himself came to the rescue, but used a different approach to the subject.

"In looking at the future of our nation, it seems to me that the Senate needs reform in many ways as it is not operating as a genuine House of Review.

"Our states are far too large for voters to feel any close relationship with any of the senators they elect. The best way will be to create new states so people can feel that those who are governing them are operating at 'the grass roots' of society.

"New South Wales and Victoria should be broken up for population reasons and Queensland and Western Australia for geographical reasons. Then, there will be less fear of small states being dominated by large ones as many will be of the same size. This will give us the opportunity to alter the Charter of the Senate so it can spend more time reviewing legislation, rather than stopping it."

Andrew Fisher responded, "You should have raised this earlier in the evening, Sam, as it is an important matter. Right now, we don't have the time to do it justice as the hour is late.

"Could I suggest that you might send to those of us who are currently members of Parliament a memorandum about it. This will enable us to start a discussion in Cabinet as to what it may be possible to achieve with Senate reform as the result of smaller states being created. If this can be done, it will certainly remove the fear that some states will be overrun by larger ones. I don't think that it will be an impossibility to create a nation of states that are fairly equal in size and influence."

"I will do that with pleasure."

Having generated much nostalgia, the evening was now reaching a pinnacle of goodwill that indicated that it had reached a point where its close would be appropriate. Barton decided that it should conclude by remembering giants of Federation who were not present tonight.

Team Players

"Could I suggest that we bring our grand evening to an appropriate close with a final toast to absent political colleagues who were an important part of our journey to Federation but whose names have not so far been mentioned?

"Those who readily come to mind are George Pearce of Western Australia, Frederick Holder and John Downer of South Australia, Henry Turner, Charles Pearson and George Higginbotham of Victoria, Bernard Wise and Arthur Bruce Smith of New South Wales, Edward Braddon of Tasmania and Anderson Dawson of Queensland. They were genuine patriots."

Lyne had an extra thought.

"Let us also toast the most influential of the fellows who opposed Federation. Their efforts show that democracy was allowed to work throughout the Federation process.

"Other than Chris Watson and me as prime evidence of guilt, there were John Want and Julian Salamons, eminent barristers, both from New South Wales. Those two had a powerful influence in generating a large NO vote in my state."

"Good thought, William," said Chris Watson. "But, we must toast also the positive campaigners for Federation who were not politicians. I reckon that they were very well represented by a newspaper editor who was a thorn in the side of the Labor Party as we strove to generate a stout opposition. He was Andrew Garran, Editor of the *Sydney Morning Herald*, who pounded us daily because we opposed Federation. He was a major factor in stopping us from defeating Federation in the New South Wales vote."

Deakin had a word.

"If you honourable gentlemen from New South Wales want to revere someone of stature, lets include James Macarthur, son of the rebel sheep magnate John Macarthur. He campaigned mightily about fifty years before Federation to sever our connections to England. He was a visionary who was way ahead of his time."

"I have no problems with that suggestion," said George Reid who, wanting to mock them just a little more, rambled on.

"So, let us really go out on a limb and include the bloke who tried to shoot the Prince of Wales in 1865. The infamous Henry O'Farrell has already been mentioned. Had he been a straight shooter, the Prince would have been history and we would have been banished from the Empire by Queen Victoria. We would have accepted her wrath with some alacrity and set ourselves free 35 years sooner than we eventually did."

"That has just got to be the cue to leave," opined Charles Kingston, who eyed Reid with disdain.

The Prime Minister arose from his chair.

"I warmly propose the toast to all those who have been mentioned except for O'Farrell. He was depraved. In his place, let me include every Australian who voted Yes in the Referendums. Cheers."

A hearty response resounded around the room.

Even Lyne rose to the occasion.

Cheers for Toby

They rose to take their leave and, as they were so doing, Griffith decided that it would be appropriate for him to make a kind gesture to his old rival, their host for the evening, Edmund Barton. There was a slight niggling of his conscience about the way in which he had demeaned Toby down the years in order to enhance his own career.

"We should all remember that Toby has made many sacrifices in his service of the nation. One outstanding one was that occurred when George Reid was Premier of New South Wales. He offered Toby the eminent honour of becoming

Chief Justice of the Supreme Court of his state. Toby graciously declined, telling George that he wanted to devote all his efforts to achieving Federation. We thank God, that Toby made that choice."

Slaps on the back all around for Toby.

He was greatly moved by the tribute.

So, it was. aAnn historic dinner ended late in the evening and most took time to offer sincere thanks to their host.

They complimented Barton on his superb organisation of it and there was a unanimous commitment to strive ever more diligently to advance the cause of a strong Australian nation. While the imbibing of good wine had made them all somewhat profuse, their sentiments were genuine. They had worked together to create a nation and none of them were now about to allow it to go into decline.

Finally, warm words of farewell were expressed to one another as they headed towards their homes or lodgings, all of them in good heart.

The Founding Fathers strode out into history and, beyond it, to the realm of dreams.

Loner

William Lyne took his time strolling along quiet streets to the residence of his friends in North Melbourne.

To his surprise, he had enjoyed the evening.

He was in a better frame of mind than he had been when he had walked to the club a few hours earlier. The dinner had produced more satisfactory results than he had anticipated. He had been able to say things that had been bottled up in his heart and soul for a decade.

It would always remain in his conscious thought that he had been treated shamefully in 1901, not just by his fellow travellers in the world of politics. He had been let down by Hopetoun, the tragic Governor General. Hopetoun should have stared down Lyne's opponents and told them to get behind him or expect the wrath of the Crown to descend upon them. Had Hopetoun been strong enough to insist that he, Lyne, was to be Prime Minister, then Barton and Deakin and Reid and others would have been forced to accept that. But, Hopetoun was a gutless ditherer, typical of too many of the British aristocracy who lived pampered lives somewhere outside of the real realm of humanity.

He was certain that Barton did not realise, then and now, that had he, Lyne, had been made Prime Minister, he would never have appointed that utter infidel Griffith as Chief Justice. He would have anointed Barton and given him a lifetime job as the first Chief Justice of Australia. Barton had made the wrong choice, but that was Toby's problem to live with forever.

He reached the door of his friend's home. They had anticipated that he would be arriving home late and had given him a key.

Quietly, he let himself indoors, closing the doors on his encounter with those who had caused him pain.

He was at peace.

He slept well.

Confession of Slippery Sam

Sam and Chris shared the ride once more in the comfortable carriage that was part of the trappings of the Chief Justice of Australia.

Chris gently posed a question about which he had been thirsting for an answer since Lyne's outburst midway through the evening. He steeled himself to face whatever invective may come from Griffith if he chose to respond.

"Sam, our angry friend William made a very pointed accusation tonight alleging that you used less than savoury tactics to gain your appointment as Chief Justice. You admirably refrained from responding, but were nevertheless clearly upset. Would you care to share with me your side of this story?"

To Watson's surprise, Griffith showed no embarrassment nor hesitation nor anger.

"You will have noted that my initial response was to rise from my seat in a state of total anger. Bolton saved the day with an astute intervention and appropriate comments so I refrained from defending myself. There seemed to be no point in creating an unseemly scene after Bolton had taken the heat out of the situation.

"On top of that, to have carried on with a turbulent debate would have unnecessarily embarrassed Toby for a number of reasons, not the least of which being a detraction from his role as our host tonight.

"When I did my work on the Constitution with Toby and Charles on *Lucinda*, I was Premier of Queensland. Not long afterwards, I resigned to accept appointment as Chief Justice of Queensland. Because I held that position, the government of the day deemed it inappropriate for me to take part in the 1897 Constitutional Convention as a delegate from Queensland. They considered that it would quite likely turn out to be a highly political scene from which a Chief Justice should absent himself. So, I worked behind the scenes, sending letters and cables to delegates and conveying lots of advice on crucial drafting issues that I anticipated would arise. I wanted them to be very aware that I was still around and actively influencing events even though I had to appear to be above the fray.

"Then, a couple of years later, to the horror of the Queensland Government, I campaigned openly to make sure that my State voted Yes in the Federation Referendum. I told the Premier that I was campaigning as a private citizen, not as Chief Justice, which I believed I was entitled to do. He was not happy with my decision, but I took great care to ensure that I was never introduced as Chief Justice at campaign meetings. I was Samuel Griffith, chief author of the Constitution, who was there to explain the content and intent of that historic document and answer their questions about it.

"As you will have already surmised, I had two reasons for breaking tradition. Firstly, I had devoted 12 years of my life to working for Federation and I wanted to ensure that it finally happened as I was a true believer in the cause. I held the view that in the history of the continent, this was the pinnacle.

"Secondly, I again wanted powerful people to be aware that I was still a force to be reckoned with on the national scene. Had I not participated, I ran the risk of being forgotten as I could not be a candidate for election to the First Parliament without resigning my position as Chief Justice of Queensland.

"Once Federation was a reality, there were many of the states that wanted to oppose or delay the establishment of the High Court of Australia. As you are aware, they felt that their State Supreme Courts were sufficient and that the existence of a High Court would mean that too much power would be passed over to the Commonwealth. So, I corresponded long and hard by writing to as many judges as I knew around Australia to gain their support for the High Court to become a reality. In their minds, this established me as its prime advocate and the right choice to lead it.

"I also aggressively courted votes in Parliament for my appointment as the founding Chief Justice. You will recall receiving letters from me which declared my interest in serving in the top role on the Court.

"Belatedly, Toby let it be known that he wanted to resign as Prime Minister and seek appointment to become Chief Justice. This upset all of my planning, but I was able to gather more support than he did.

"As Prime Minister, he had quite naturally accumulated political enemies who wanted revenge. This happens to all Prime Ministers. Additional to this was the fact that his duties as the nation's leader did not allow him time to campaign in the manner that I did. As you will readily appreciate, this gave me a huge advantage.

"Therefore, my answer to your question is that I absolutely confess that I did aggressively and persistently campaign to get the job ahead of Toby. And I won."

Watson pondered this for a moment, then responded, "As a politician, I can understand how and why you went about convincing the Parliament to vote for your appointment as Chief Justice in preference to Toby, but is it not true that a Chief Justice really should stay aloof from politics. You ran the risk of being beholden in some way to those who voted for you?"

Griffith was quick to respond and again did not seem to take offence.

"I made very certain that I did not allow myself to be placed in a position whereby I owed any political debts to anyone who supported me."

"How did you achieve that?"

"I simply promoted my legal qualifications and my experience in dispensing justice as being superior to Toby. I had been Chief Justice of Queensland for ten years. In the legal world, Toby had only the status of a respected barrister who had once served with distinction as a Magistrate. In addition, Toby and I had worked long and hard to bring about Federation. We both deserved honours as a result. Toby became our first Prime Minister. It would have been both inappropriate and unfair for him also to become our first Chief Justice. That honour was mine, so my appointment meant that we shared the spoils of office equally."

"I don't think Toby would agree with that assertion."

"He doesn't, but it is the way the cards fell and they fell justly."

"They didn't fall naturally. As you have so honestly and openly conveyed to me, you pushed those cards to the limit in a highly-planned manner and with considerable determination."

"I plead guilty. To pretend otherwise would be to lie."

Griffith felt more than a little uncomfortable that Watson had approached this conversation with such frankness and persistence. After all, he personally believed that he was entitled always to be treated as a revered and eminent citizen of the land who deserved respect at all times, no matter what the circumstances.

But, he decided not to make an issue of it. Watson was not acting rudely. He was certainly posing his questions in a far better way than Lyne had so viciously done with his full-on blast an hour or so ago.

Watson had similar thoughts in his mind. He had extracted what appeared to him to be an honest confession from the Chief Justice. Let sleeping dogs lie.

He chose a new tack.

How Do We Solve the Problem of the Senate?

"Sam, if you could relive your weekend on the *Lucinda* with Toby and Charles drafting the Constitution, what would you change in light of almost two decades of subsequent experience that led to the actuality of Federation and the Parliament's subsequent implementation of the Constitution?"

Griffith's reply was instant.

"I would comprehensively revise those parts of the Constitution that refer to the Senate.

They are too vague and capable of wide interpretation. Someday, someone with the power to do so will bestow in the minds of senators the thought that they have powers we did not intend them to have. It could well be that the Senate will become a House of Obstruction, not a House of Review and a Protector of States as we clearly intended it would be."

"What specific changes would you make?"

"The sole reason for the birth of the Senate was the determined insistence of the small states that it be a House that enabled them to enhance and defend their rights. We had no option but to agree that every state would elect the same number of senators, irrespective of population. The small states demanded that they be given the power to stop New South Wales and Victoria from dominating the Parliament. It was a matter of hot controversy at both of the 1891 and 1897 Conventions. We were faced with the very obvious hurdle that if we could not reach agreement with this demand, then Federation would not have occurred. It was an immovable obstruction blocking the pathway to the creation of the Australian nation.

"As a Queenslander, I certainly did not want the larger states to have the ability to dominate us just because they had far larger populations, but I did not see them as awful people who would deliberately smother us. As you know, Deakin and Barton were not the sort of people who would have allowed their states to do this. Nevertheless, the small states were solidly united in their determination to stop them in their tracks. They were worried that the successors to Alfred and Toby may prove not to be gentlemen of their stature. I accepted equal representation with great reluctance.

"Then came the sticking point. What powers would the Senate have, beyond being a protector of the states?

"Watson commented that in the first decade, the Senate had not caused a government to fall?"

Griffith agreed, but added, "Technically it could have done so, but, in the minds of our current senators, it is a power that is meant only to be used in the most extreme circumstances and they did not encounter such circumstances. It was recognised that this was never the explicit intention of the Constitution."

"The Senate has, however, consistently delayed legislation by referring it back to the House of Representatives for amendment?" was Watson's response.

"Correct. We intended it to have this right."

"Yet, it has gone further on a few occasions and has defeated legislation?"

"It has done that, but not in a destructive way thus far. It has had to recognise that the House of Representatives is the powerhouse of government from where the Prime Minister derived his ability to implement policy. They have not stopped a PM from doing what he promised voters he would do if elected and, up until this moment, there have been only one or two instances where the Senate has misused its power. Nevertheless, this unfortunate practice is likely to grow to the detriment of Australia. As political parties grow more powerful, they will be tempted to use the Senate as a vehicle to manipulate the legislative processes."

Chris was silent for a moment as he considered Sam's responses, then asked, "Can the Senate legitimately deny a Prime Minister the money he needs to govern?"

"If this matter ever comes before me at the High Court, I will rule that it cannot do this. But, the problem is that the Constitution is not crystal clear on the matter. It is open to abuse by political blackmailers."

"It seems inevitable that future generations of Australians will inherit a problem."

"One day, the Senate will overstep the mark to such an extent that a referendum may have to be held in which it is proposed to abolish it."

"Can good government be achieved with only one House of Parliament?"

"Yes. New Zealand has only one House and its people do not seem to be unhappy about that."

"There would surely need to be some checks and balances in place so as to restrain corrupt governments."

"Outraged voters have the right to go to Courts if corruption occurs. They can also vote out a bad government at the next election."

"Perhaps the answer is to always ensure that we only ever have minority governments. This means that for a government to be corrupt, it must convince the rest of the Parliament to join them in that corruption I believe that Australia has done well in the first decade of Federation because we have always had minority governments."

"There can be no doubt about that. Bolton and I talked about this during the break earlier this evening."

They had arrived at the house where Watson was staying so the Chief Justice had the last words on the Senate.

"There is no perfect form of democracy. Someone will always try to corrupt it. For example, I believe that democracy is not practiced in the United States of America. Their entire system enables power brokers to come to deals that often enrich them personally to the detriment of others. We are better served than that, but we have ample room for improvement as we strive for a more perfect exercise of democracy."

Chris Watson alighted, then reached back into the carriage to shake Griffith by the hand.

"I admire and envy you, Sam. I wish I could have experienced your enormous achievements in politics, government and the law. Your record in public life is absolutely extraordinary. Thank you for befriending me tonight, answering my questions frankly and giving me such wise advice. May Australia continue to have the benefit of your wisdom for many years to come."

"I appreciate your kind and generous words, Chris. May I reciprocate by saying that I have not the slightest doubt that your greatest years lie ahead in your career outside of Parliament. Enjoy them. May you prosper. Goodnight."

Griffith pondered his encounter with Watson. He had enjoyed his company.

He came, sadly, to the belief that Watson's frankness and honesty and decency would one day get him into huge trouble.

(Griffith would prove to be correct in arriving at this conclusion. In fact, he would still be Chief Justice when it happened to this idealistic young leader only a few years later.

He would watch with agony as those two virtues would cause Chris Watson to be brutally expelled from membership of the Australian Labor Party that he helped to found and which he led to forming a government. It would occur when he stuck by his beliefs over the highly controversial issue of conscription during World War I.

Politics is a perilous profession, particularly for those whose prime tendency is to speak the truth.

A 'Slippery Sam' is more likely to go much farther in politics and government and life than would an 'Honest Chris'.)

The Believers Continue the Good Fight

Similarly to Griffith and Watson, Deakin again invited Bird to share his carriage to South Yarra.

Bird was clearly troubled.

"Except for the much-appreciated expressions of goodwill, I clearly failed in my advocacy of a Constitutional Preamble of Australian values. Even so, I will not drop the matter. But, after listening to Andrew's comment about his anticipated reaction of Parliament, I am not sure which is the best way to proceed at this point. I really do need to keep the issue in the limelight and make a considerable effort if I am to finally get a positive result before my days are over. Sadly, I may be wasting my time. It could be that it is, quite simply, an impossible task."

Deakin felt some guilt in the matter.

"Well, you tried, and you tried sincerely. You may have done better without my backing, as playboys like George Reid will never cease to ridicule anything that has religious overtones, especially if he feels that I had a role in its origin.

"I venture to say that, a century from now, a debate about a Preamble may still be on the agenda, but getting nowhere. There does not seem to be a common mind about what a nation like Australia clearly stands for at this time or aspires to have as its foundation for in the future. Nor is there any evident will to actually settle the whole matter conclusively. There is absolutely no sense that a statement of values is a priority for Australia.

"It could be that, if we were physically able to interview every voter in Australia, we would discover that the vast majority would tell us that they couldn't care less about what the values and ethics of an Australian should be. They just want to be good blokes and get on with their own lives. It is not a good look."

"You are most probably correct in that observation, Alfred. However, If I may say so, we must firstly gain a political mandate to hold a referendum in which all Australians can vote on a Preamble. The weakness of our position is that you and I represent only one side of a vast scope of beliefs that are represented in one way or another across the nation.

"Our power base is too small and narrow to bring the public along with us as I am a Christian and you are a spiritualist. We must assemble a much broader team that has in it deep thinking people of influence. I have in mind persons such as an articulate atheist, an agnostic of similar talent, a revolutionary socialist, a risk-taking capitalist and a bushman who doesn't go to church, but blames God for everything. In addition, and from a Christian perspective, it will be vital that we enlist a Roman Catholic in to our ranks or we will certainly lose the votes of about a quarter of the population. Once we can assemble a formidable group, we can then try to find common ground on appropriate words that hopefully won't be so bland that they mean nothing."

"Bolton, your comments have genuine merit, but we must include a member of the Melbourne Club. Nothing happens in Australia without the approval of the club.

"You are becoming more than a little cynical, Alfred."

"I am, but my comments on the Melbourne Club are nevertheless quite close to the truth. They have huge political influence. Acknowledging this, let me become even a little more cynical. In getting started, we could fairly easily enlist David Syme into our team as its socialist member. He loves being involved in controversy and is a hugely influential member of the club. He will serve positively so long as we tell him that, if it all eventually happens, he can claim that 'The Age' masterminded the entire campaign."

Bolton was encouraged by this suggestion.

"Despite all of the sins of David Syme, it would be a splendid start to get him onboard, Alfred. I think that I could enlist Hugh Victor McKay who owns the Sunshine Harvester Company. He can be the capitalist in the team. I understand that his company is now the largest manufacturer in the Southern Hemisphere and he is most probably Australia's finest philanthropist. He is also a powerful Presbyterian Elder."

"Go ahead and get him involved, Bolton. We will have to think hard to find a broadminded atheist, but there has to be one somewhere in Australia. George Reid could be a candidate for the job if only for the fact that he loves playing games with anything religious and would be fascinated by all the political challenges involved."

"Alfred, after we give it much more thought, we must exchange letters regularly with firm ideas as to who the other candidates may be and how we will enlist them. Could I suggest also that we each draw up some possible wording for the Preamble that we would like to have accepted and work at it until we find common ground. Then, we can get the others working on it with us. My feeling is that it will take a year or so to achieve unanimity, but we will then have something to take to the Prime Minister and invite him to take whatever political steps will be needed to get MPs to vote for call a Referendum in which the Preamble can be placed before the people."

"Done."

"Great. This discussion has given me some hope that all may not yet be lost. We may be able to get somewhere if we persist with it."

Deakin was not finished with the matter.

"Does it not strike you as odd, that our mother country over there in the British Isles has neither a constitution or anything that faintly resembles a preamble?"

Bird admitted guilt.

"I have never given that any thought. I just assumed that Magna Carta was the basis of their Constitution."

"Magna Carta is now so out of date that it does nothing except to provide a basis for learnt debates from time to time. The British have never ever adopted a constitution. They operate the entire Westminster system of government on a basis of laws created by thousands of Acts of Parliament that have evolved over the centuries. And I am willing to wager that our late Queen Victoria could not have told you what the fundamental beliefs of the Church of England are, let alone those of the nation she led. Yet, she was the revered leader of that Church, and therefore beyond criticism."

"So," said Bolton, "we are all alone with this."

"We are," said Alfred. "But this is a good thing. We are not tied down by a lot of old hogwash and ancient baggage. We can start our journey with a clean sheet."

Bolton nailed the issue.

"It will require all the literary skills that we have to find wording for a preamble that will make sense to the Afghan camel drivers of the Northern

Territory, the football fans of Melbourne, the thousands of Australians who own a small business somewhere and the school teachers of the nation who mould the character of the young."

They had reached the Congregational Manse in South Yarra.

After reaffirming their intent to work together to keep the Preamble assignment moving forward, and bidding warm words of thanks and farewell, they went their ways.

Bolton committed the task to The Lord in prayer.

Alfred meditated with the Great Spirit.

Their sincerity could not be doubted.

(Nevertheless, it may not have surprised them had they known that a century later the Australian Constitution would still not have a Preamble.

They would have agreed that it will never get up unless a powerful personality with huge community clout takes it on as a priority commitment and refuses to relent until it has been enshrined in the Constitution.)

Cheers for the Founders

The guests of the Hotel Windsor walked slowly back to their prestigious lodging house. Their happy frame of mind was not conducive to speed.

George Reid was, as fully anticipated by the others, dominating the conversation.

He had over imbibed, and to a much greater degree than the others, but was not anywhere near being drunk. It took an enormous amount of alcohol for him to achieve that status. He just had a pleasantly happy glow and a growing sense of merriment. Forrest and Kingston were happy to listen to his jovial banter.

"That was a good dinner. I finished the evening with a much better opinion of people who have the unfortunate status of not being New South Welshmen. It is now within the realms of possibility that one day we will welcome all of you to Sydney."

"We actually have reasonable goodwill towards you too, George. I think that I may be able to get a few good citizens of Adelaide to give you a warm welcome if you should grace our city with your presence one day. It is our social policy to look after lost souls," was Kingston's tender response.

John Forrest was determined not to be left out of this.

"George, if you can ever muster the courage and good sense to travel across the Nullarbor during one hot summer without dying of thirst, I am sure that some of our folk would happily buy you a drink."

George was so moved by all of this, he decided that he should make a practical suggestion about the future well-being of the nation.

"Well, while such goodwill abounds towards me and you treasure my invaluable and unfathomable wisdom, we should talk about the suggestion made by Sam that we should do more about the business of creating new states and do so soon, while we still have some political clout amongst us all. We can never overlook the fact that we deliberately made provision in the Constitution for new states to be created by breaking up existing ones. We are all anticipating that this will occur one day but we continue to do nothing about it. We will have to make it happen.

"John, you were right with that wisecrack of yours about Riverina and New England becoming states. Sydney does not need those regions for its economic survival and those same regions will grow much more quickly if they are able to govern themselves and put more emphasis on their local economic development. No one in Sydney really knows anything about their potential or is willing to do something specific about it."

Forrest agreed, "Since you made an issue of it earlier tonight, I think that it could be time to seriously look at the idea of Kalgoorlie being set free from Perth, I have given that task some thought and I reluctantly admit that you have a point. We can include Esperance and Albany as the ports of a new state, plus a large slab of mining land to the north of Kalgoorlie, stopping just short of the Pilbara. Perth will actually be better off not having to worry about them from an administrative viewpoint and can concentrate on making itself more economically self-sufficient, which it is not at present."

Kingston piped in, "Western Australia, John, is altogether too big in terms of the vastness of its geography. You should give the Kimberley and the Pilbara to the Northern Territory. This would give it the means of becoming a viable state that we could call Northern Australia. South Australia would back that move. Having the Federal Government looking after the Territory as it now does is a political and administrative pain for us all. Its huge potential is there to be unleashed if we empower the locals."

George was developing a few more thoughts.

"We must talk to Andrew Fisher about splitting up Queensland too. There needs to be new states based on Rockhampton and Townsville and Toowoomba. Even the smallest of the four states created by that move would still be larger geographically than Victoria. But, it would be part of a solution to decentralise the nation and help to bring State Governments closer to the people?"

"That's important," said Forrest. "Too many rural Australians feel that they are much too far away from their governments to have any influence with them. So, it is imperative that we get more population into those rural areas. This will happen only if we can achieve smaller governments which will deliberately invest in rural industries and add value to them."

"Well," said Kingston, "this means we have work to do before we can have a genuine and binding Federation. But, life would be boring if we didn't have a steady flow of challenges ahead. I will prompt Griffith to get moving quickly on his memo to the Prime Minister. We don't want our Parliaments still thinking about this a century from now."

They were now entering the foyer of The Windsor.

At that precise moment, a large dinner party was breaking up and heading for the doors.

The guests quickly recognised the three Founding Fathers and came over to introduce themselves, with goodwill genuinely abounding.

One asked the obvious question, "What brings three great Australians to Melbourne from places far away on New Year's Day?"

Totally in character and with expansive bonhomie, George took it upon himself to be the spokesman.

"We have been at a splendid dinner at the Melbourne Club hosted by Sir Edmund Barton."

"Just the four of you?"

"No, we were a humble minority. Our fellow guests were Alfred Deakin, Samuel Griffith, Andrew Fisher, Chris Watson, William Lyne and Bolton Stafford Bird."

"Goodness me. What a wonderfully interesting evening that must have been."

"It was."

"Did you mutually decide to do something magnificent for Australia in the new decade that is ahead of us?"

"Yes, we did."

"Is it courteous for us to ask what it was?"

"We agreed on visionary plans that will eventually make Australia the greatest nation in the world."

"I don't want to appear to be rude, Mr Reid, but we all believe that it already is the greatest nation."

"Then," said George expansively, "we will plan to leave the world behind."

Enthusiastic applause broke out.

They asked the great men to sign the dinner menus the Windsor had given them as a New Year gift, after which the three musketeers took their leave, greatly pleased to hear more applause breaking out.

"Let me have the last word," said Forrest.

His two companions invited him to do just that.

"I intend to make sure that Western Australia never secedes from the Federation."

"Hear, Hear!"

(It would have greatly saddened John Forrest to learn that Western Australia would try to do just that 15 years after he died. He would have been delighted that they failed.

All three would have been profoundly disappointed had they peered into a looking glass and found that, a century later, no new states had been formed despite determined attempts by New England and North Queensland to do so. The status quo, being the most powerful source in Australian society, had once more resisted progressive change.)

White Australia

Barton invited Prime Minister Andrew Fisher to remain behind for a few moments of private conversation, whereupon they retired to the quiet seclusion of the Gun Room. Toby was served with a fine single malt Scotch whisky by the ever-faithful Giles who also cared for Andrew with a cup of fine Ceylon tea.

The whisky of Toby's choice was a Talisker from the Isle of Skye, the historic distillery in which Bonnie Prince Charlie took refuge. This particular bottling was twenty years old.

Toby toasted Fisher's homeland and the Prime Minister responded with delight. He would never forget old Scotland and its primitive coal mines.

In response, Fisher toasted the High Court and the contribution that Barton had made to its stability and the public trust it had earned from its consistent integrity. With a smile, he also expressed the hope that the Court would unfailingly rule in favour of the Commonwealth in all future disputes with the States over where the power actually lay.

Thanking the Prime Minister for staying on for a chat, Barton raised two issues that were troubling him.

"Andrew, despite the fact that you and I enjoy a respectful professional relationship, we embrace different political ideologies. However, there are two matters that I think will transcend our ideologies as they become major issues of concern for us both in the years ahead. I hope that we may be able to work together closely to ensure that they can move along a pathway that will be for the common good of the nation.

"One is the future of aborigines and the other is the unlikely maintenance of a White Australia. We deliberately ignored aborigines in our preparation of the Constitution because we did not want them to have any land rights. We knew that any such claim would become a hugely formidable hurdle for the states to overcome in accepting Federation, especially Western Australia where there was a large indigenous population who had not been well treated by white settlers. In fact, those relationships were so bad over in the West that London had found it necessary to delay their self-government until 1890 in an attempt to sort it out.

"At the same time, we adopted a policy of ensuring a White Australia because the states also insisted upon it as a condition of Federation. I don't think that this policy is working to our national advantage in the manner we had hoped it would a decade ago."

Andrew Fisher was quiet for a moment, then answered carefully.

"I am certain that it is absolutely correct to say that we would never have achieved Federation without handling both of these issues in the manner that we did at that time. Assuredly, the entire Federation movement would have foundered over either one of them, certainly over both of them.

"Our states determinedly wanted to maintain control of aborigines as they feared that a Federal Parliament may eventually get around to declaring them to be citizens. The truth is that the general ranks of politicians who serve in State Parliaments feel that Aborigines will soon die out as the result of the ravages of white civilisation, so why worry unduly about them or enshrine them in a constitution. One of them said to me recently, 'Why smooth out a dying pillow.'

"This attitude really is demeaning to all sides of this issue, if only for the reason that there is now no genuine evidence that they will die out. Even more importantly, they are human beings who have rights and needs even though they are considered primitive by our standards and don't have the benefit of a

European education. Be this as it may, it was such a hot issue that it could have caused every Federation Referendum Campaign to be fought over this matter alone. All other issues would have paled into insignificance. The results would have shown to the world that we had no respect for or guilt about aborigines.

"When you add to this the fear that many Australians, including aborigines, have about a possible Asian takeover of our continent, we had to face the fact that this too was a huge factor in the background when most people decided which way to vote in Federation Referendums. Many voters wanted no more Asians here. They held the firm belief that we made a huge error in allowing any Chinese to come here during the gold rush. So, their worry was that if Aborigines were formally recognised, it would become inevitable for Asians to be recognised too, with the consequent fear that we would be overrun ultimately by non-whites."

"Your words are true, Andrew, but we must face an historic fact that one of the reasons why New Zealand withdrew from Federation negotiations very early in the piece was that their colonial government had signed a Treaty with the Maoris in 1840 and this led to them being represented in Parliament with a specified minimum of four seats. We wouldn't do either of those things for our aborigines. So, New Zealand decided that they would lower their community standards if they joined an Australian Federation. How could a Federal Government allow Maoris to vote but refuse the same right to aborigines?

"I don't have an answer to this dilemma, but the controversy about the status of aborigines will continue to grow and become a festering sore. As a High Court Judge, I am expecting more and more cases relating to the rights of aborigines to come before me. They will become increasingly difficult to handle on any basis that may be favourable to white men. The decisions we hand down will become matters that will foster public unrest, no matter which way we make rulings and how wise and fair our adjudication may be."

Fisher expressed an opinion on the religious history of both nations.

"New Zealand was able to bring the Treaty of Waitangi into existence without too much delay because Maoris embraced Christianity very quickly. Australian Aborigines proved to be highly resistant to it, so much so that Australia's revered Christian leader, Samuel Marsden, made no converts during his time here, so he moved over to New Zealand where he was quite successful among Maoris. This situation is now slowly changing in Australia with the establishment of our Aboriginal Missions mainly in the Gulf country but we are a century behind New Zealand."

He moved on to the matter of non-European immigration.

"I have no doubt that, at this time in our history, a very clear majority of voters still want a White Australia free of all Japanese, Chinese, Indians, Malays and others. They will defend this conviction with vehemence as most feel that the legislation we have about White Australia has been a great achievement. However, we will not be able to sustain such a ban forever and it may not be smart for us to do it anyway.

"We are all aware that many Chinese are good businessmen and their labourers are extraordinarily hard workers, while the Japanese are great industrialists and many Indians are fine bureaucrats experienced in the ways of the British Civil Service. Some of them could help us grow as a nation rather than be problems for our society. I am very conscious of the fact that, if the newspapers ever report these comments of mine, I will lose the next election in a massive landslide, such is the passion that voters openly display about the necessity to preserve and expand the white race.

"As an example of just how difficult an issue this matter is, we should remember that one of Alfred Deakin's most memorable speeches, which he made to the Federal Parliament in September, 1901, was about the importance of maintaining White Australia, and yet he is most probably more to the political left than anyone else in the Parliament, including every one of the members of my Labor Party. What is abundantly evident is that neither he, nor the majority of Australians, have ever thought that he was a racist or an extremist.

"In that particular speech, he actually said this. I can quote it as it was reprinted in a magazine I read recently. I tore it out and put it in my pocket in case the issue arose tonight."

Members on both sides of the House, and all sections of all parties – those in office and those out of office – with the people behind them, all are united in the unalterable resolve that the Commonwealth of Australia shall mean a White Australia and that from now henceforward all alien elements within it shall be diminished. We are united in the resolve that this Commonwealth shall be established on the firm foundation of unity of race, so as to enable it to fulfil the promise of its founders, and enjoy to the fullest extent the charter of liberty which we now cherish.

Barton was frank and honest in his response.

"I was in Parliament on the day he made that speech, and so were you. We voted with him and the count was almost unanimous. We now have to live with the nest we built until the winds of change gradually blow it away, hopefully without us experiencing anything like the American Civil War."

Fisher went on to say, "Toby, I don't think that you and I will be around to see either of these issues finally resolved, but we should at least use our current positions of influence to ensure that Parliament and significant community institutions such as the Australian Natives Association begin to have open debates about both of them so as to keep them on the public agenda. Nevertheless, it may take fifty years before enlightenment on these matters actually impacts on Australian voters."

Barton closed it off.

"If the British intended that Australia should be a white Anglo Saxon Protestant nation, they wrecked any hope of it when they sent out so many Irish convicts. But, then again, their entire planning of Australia has been very ad hoc, often most haphazard. We live with all their legacies."

All Whites and All Blacks

Before Barton could comment, there was a gentle tap on the door.

Giles appeared.

"Gentlemen. I bear a message from Thomas Seddon, son of the former Prime Minister of New Zealand, Richard Seddon, who led his nation out from Federation with Australia. His father has long since passed away, but Thomas is here tonight, experiencing the fine menu of the Club Dining Room. I understand that he is enjoying a private holiday in our fair city. He noted earlier in the evening that you are both in the club. He realises that the hour is late, but would greatly value a few moments of conversation with you. How should I respond?"

Fisher replied first, "I am aware of Seddon's arrival in Melbourne as he has made an appointment to see me for an informal talk next week, but I am certainly happy to also spend a few minutes with him now. When his father died, Thomas won his seat in Parliament and is reported to be serving with distinction. The family 'fiefdom' is based at Westport in the South Island. It has coal mines, just like the ones I worked at in Scotland."

Barton willingly agreed.

"I met his father at the first Federation Convention when New Zealand was seriously considering joining with us. It will be good to find out what his son will say to us about the way in which Federation has worked out. Many New Zealanders regard his father as the finest Prime Minister their nation ever had. He certainly held office for a long time and achieved much for his people."

"I will arrange a drink for him and escort him upstairs to be with you here in the Gun Room," declared Giles. "I will refresh your drinks also."

He returned with Seddon a few minutes later, the New Zealander expressing his gratitude for their willingness to meet him so late in the evening.

At Seddon's request, Barton and Fisher opened the discussion by relating to him the list of guests who had attended the Founder's Dinner and outlining the highlights of its discussions. Seddon listened to them with considerable interest and asked relevant questions here and there. His desire to be briefed of the progress of Australian Federation was obvious.

Fisher then raised a question relating to New Zealand's decision not to join the Federation.

"A few minutes ago, Toby and I were, by sheer coincidence, and not knowing you were here at the club, talking about the impact of the potential relationship of your Maoris and our Aborigines on the failed negotiations for New Zealand to participate in Federation. We are of the opinion that this was the key factor in New Zealand making its decision to withdraw from any further deliberations in 1893."

"The status that Maoris would have in a Federation was a factor of genuine importance to us," replied Seddon. "We had signed the Treaty of Waitangi with the Maori people half a century earlier and, while in many ways our colonial government failed to fully honour its obligations under that Treaty, the fact was and still is that Maoris have attained a citizenship status in New Zealand that

Aborigines do not have in Australia and are not likely to attain in the foreseeable future.

"I do not want to cause any offence, but my father told me that many of your delegates in attendance at the initial Convention did not want even to have this matter on the agenda. Indeed, some of them were quite rude about it and fobbed off all of his efforts to open a preliminary dialogue about it. One or two of them told him that we were fools to have signed our historic Treaty of Waitangi and would live to regret it.

"It was a killer blow to our chances of joining you because we knew that Waitangi was a good and just treaty. We could not retreat from the historical fact that white men had come and stolen New Zealand from its rightful owners, the Maoris. They had been present throughout our islands in strong numbers for many centuries. The truth is that white men had unfairly taken land from aborigines in exactly the same way as in Australia, except that you have not acknowledged their original ownership and I doubt that you ever will.

"May I also add that we had a pragmatic reason for coming to a settlement with Maoris at Waitangi. They were renowned warriors with highly organised fighting units so it made sense to become their friends. Your aborigines were not disciplined fighters in that same mould."

"This is a truth that, one day, Australians will be called upon to face the issue of an Aboriginal Treaty," responded Fisher quietly, but profoundly. "Sadly, as you have rightly suggested, it will take a long time for us to reach this inevitable point in our history. It may well be that our courts may make a ruling on it long before the voters and their parliaments get around to it. We will then be forced to clear the ledger and start again."

Seddon added an important comment, "It may be irrelevant to this discussion but we should note that neither the United States nor Canada treated the American Indians in a democratic fashion or with any sense of equality. New Zealanders decided to learn from this mistake but Australia chose to ignore it."

"Was the aboriginal issue really the major turning point in New Zealand's decision not to become part of the Federation," enquired Barton. "I thought that economic concerns were a prime factor as well."

Seddon responded honestly, "The fate of Maoris was not alone as a major reason for New Zealand saying No, but it was the crucial one.

"The collapse of your property market, which destroyed many of your banks in 1892 was an enormous deterrent for us, as was the impact of your horrendous drought. New Zealand was not heavily impacted by those economic events, but we wanted to be sure that we could barricade ourselves safely away from them. So, in our view at the time, the best way to avoid an economic downturn was to turn our backs on Federation. Frankly, this was a rash, short term decision as it was inevitable that Australia would recover economically after a few years. It would have been wiser to request a delay with our decision rather than just saying no."

Barton persisted.

"Happily, there is a clause in our Constitution that allows for New Zealand to join someday. It will remain there as a symbol of hope. But, let us move on. I think that there was third factor that heavily focussed your minds and that was your concern was about the power of states. Many of your people disliked the idea that New Zealand, at that time a separate nation in its own right, would simply become just another State of Australia. It looked like a huge step backwards in status."

"Yes, on reflection, this was another important factor. It may have been the biggest issue in a populist sense."

Fisher had some thoughts on the matter.

"Did you ever give consideration to dividing New Zealand into four states, each of which would have had equality with any Australian State. You could easily have created states around Auckland, Wellington, Christchurch and Dunedin. It would have given them an autonomy that they had never had before in your history, even though they were becoming part of a larger nation."

"We did think about it, and actually worked out that it could be achieved with a minimum of fuss. In hindsight, we didn't push it seriously enough. I guess that our desire for Federation was waning, particularly as we believed it would falter on the status of Maoris, and so all other issues finally became irrelevant."

They chatted on purposefully about peripheral issues that would lead to greater cooperation between the two neighbouring nations and then Seddon rose to go.

"Thank you for making time to meet me. It has been a pleasure and a privilege to make your acquaintance. In parting, can I express the hope that at some time in the future our nations may look again at the possibility of a binding union? It is a tragedy that my father is not alive and present tonight. He had the political standing to make it happen. He had that magic talent that we call vision and he had the clout to carry it out. In truth, he was always willing to use that clout, hopefully always for the right reasons. I am a shadow of his stature, but I am willing to take a lead in starting the ball rolling once more if there is reasonable hope of achieving a positive result."

Barton and Fisher responded with a warmth that endorsed that hope and Seddon took his leave, with Fisher commenting that he looked forward to their meeting next week. There were trade matters he would like to discuss in some detail.

After Seddon's departure, Barton had a comment for Fisher.

"You know, Andrew, I think that we made a huge blunder in not working much harder to get New Zealand into our Federation. They could have become the food bowl of the nation and a great base for generating a prosperous tourist industry."

Fisher had no difficulty in concurring and added that it may have be possible, in the not too distant future, to use a debate re the stature of Maoris in Federation as a political lever to raise the status of Aborigines with Australian voters.

Forgotten Fijians

Barton added a further thought, "We have forgotten the fact that Fiji had attended the first Federation Convention in 1891 and we did not take them seriously, probably because of their small economy. More likely, it was because they were not white.

"Adding to that problem was the reality that a large number of their population were Indians, brought there by an incredibly insane decision of the British to have labourers in the cane fields, a task that native Fijians were reluctant to undertake. Without giving it much thought, we formed the view at the Convention that Fijians could well become a bigger problem for us than Maoris or Aborigines.

"So, they went back home to Fiji and we somewhat rudely failed to invite them back.

"Upon reflection, it would have been smarter for us to consider the possibility that their involvement would have given us a strategic naval base and a trading hub out in the Pacific. However, it would have been a difficult task to agree on the terms of a relationship between all the racial groupings involved in a Union of Australia, New Zealand and Fiji that would not have mightily ruffled too many feathers. Happily, there is still an encouraging degree of goodwill between Australia and Fiji, even though they remain a Crown Colony with minimal control over their daily affairs and their future."

"Toby, if we are honest with ourselves, we can look back at it all objectively and acknowledge that, while we made many mistakes, we did make enough good decisions to achieve a Federation that is working well. We may yet enhance our nation by adding New Zealand and all the Pacific Island colonies of Britain in a partnership of equality before too many years have passed."

"This could well be achievable, Andrew. To pull it off, we will need to breed statesmen of genuine stature and power at some time during this century."

Relentless Murdoch

With that, two great Australians made their way towards the foyer of the club.

There, they found Keith Murdoch waiting to waylay them.

Both knew him reasonably well, having locked horns with him previously over the accuracy his political reporting in times past.

"Prime Minister and Sir Edmund. Could I have a brief word with you?"

"Go ahead, Mr Murdoch," responded Fisher with polite formality.

"I had an earlier conversation with the Chief Justice and Reverend Bolton Stafford Bird while you were taking a break during your dinner. They suggested that as Prime Minister you were the only one of the diners who could make a statement about decisions made at the dinner as you were the one with the current political power to take action on any matters.

"Can I be presumptuous as to ask if you can tell me what plans were made?"

Fisher's response would not please Murdoch.

"I will be pleased if you would publish this statement. Ten leaders of Federation dined at the Melbourne Club tonight. The host was Sir Edmund Barton and his guests were Samuel Griffith, Alfred Deakin, George Reid, Charles Kingston, John Forrest, William Lyne, Chris Watson, Bolton Stafford Bird and me.

"We reviewed the steps that we took to create a binding Federation of Australian States and we discussed how we could have done it better. We then carried out a critical review of how we had governed for the past decade and talked of opportunities for progress that we missed. Then, we spoke of the challenges that lie ahead of the nation and we agreed to face them sooner rather than later.

"We departed after agreeing that great opportunities lie ahead of Australia in the next decade."

"Thank you, Prime Minister. Did you discuss how a procession of minority governments has retarded progress since Federation?"

"No, we did not. We all enjoy working in situations where opposing ideologies have to make compromises. This is a wise way to ensure that democracy works at its best level. That way, everyone in Parliament has a part in the action. I hold the firm view that Majority Governments become lazy dictatorships."

"I must forcefully disagree, Prime Minister."

"Please say so in your next column."

"May I ask one more question, Prime Minister."

"By all means, but only one."

"How much longer will Australia keep close ties with England? When will we become a free nation?"

"We will remain close to our mother country as it is to our economic and political advantage that we do so. At this moment in our history, trade with Britain is vital to our economy and we would be foolhardy to drop it. And if Britain becomes involved in a war, we will back her as the vast majority of our citizens are of British stock who would want to serve. I hold the view that the situation will remain this way for at least a century."

Murdoch tried his luck one more time.

"Sir Edmund, would you like to make a comment?"

"Yes, I would. The quality of single malt scotch whisky in this Club is astonishingly superb and I want to recommend to all Australians that they should enjoy it as soon as possible. Goodnight and a happy New Year."

The Essential Giles

With the sheer depth of that profound response still reflecting upon Murdoch's face, Fisher and Barton headed for home, using the Prime Minister's carriage that was waiting for them in Collins Street.

The ever-vigilant Giles opened the doors and assisted them in.

They confided to him their high praise of his professional performance throughout the evening and their grateful thanks for it.

He was delighted. For him, it was a supreme accolade.

To the members of the Melbourne Club, he represented whatever was splendid about the old British Empire.

Indeed, he would have been superb as the senior butler in 'Downton Abbey'.

Fisher Speaks for the Nation

The short journey enabled the two Prime Ministers to chat further.

"You know, Toby. I have not yet decided whether it is good politics to have Murdoch as a friend or an enemy. We much watch him carefully. In years to come, he will not be an inconsequential figure. He will take over the mantle of David Syme."

This brought a smile and a nod from Toby. It would have amused him even more if he had known that his rival, Slippery Sam, held a similar view.

Fisher then thought it appropriate to comment on William Lyne.

"Our controversial friend, William, became very upset midway through our dinner, but he appeared to steadily calm his nerves as the evening progressed. He will be delighted that he was able to humiliate Griffith in the midst of his own suffering. Do you think he will ever accept that he was never destined to be Prime Minister?"

"No, Andrew, never. He may put it to the back of his mind, but it will forever lurk there. My personal view of the matter is that the blame clearly lies with Hopetoun who humiliated William unnecessarily. He did not formally consult anyone as to who should be the first Prime Minister and just had a few casual conversations with people like George Reid. He simply made up his mind that there was only one possible choice. It had to be the Premier of New South Wales and so he shot from the hip, caused a sad mess, then blamed his humiliation on us. He was a self-opinionated, second-rate aristocrat of limited ability who should never have left England."

"What it means is that we must arrive at the day as quickly as possible when Australians are appointed as our Governor General, not Englishmen. At the very least, an Australian would understand how the Australian way of life actually works."

"Ah," sighed Barton, "it won't happen while the current generation are in power at Westminster or while Queen Victoria's immediate family are in power. The ones I met in London had closed minds about everything other than preserving the British Crown. It will have to wait for a few decades. Britain has to come out of the past and embrace the future. It is a tragedy that so many Englishmen are unaware that their Empire is about to go into a steady decline."

"We can keep sowing the seeds in their minds. At some point, they will come to the view that it will be wise to allow colonials like us to determine our own destiny."

Barton's home came into view, bringing an end to their speculation about the virtues of Australian-born governor generals.

Neither of them would have imagined that the first to achieve that honour would be Isaac Isaacs who had been one of the staunchest opponents of

Federation. The passing of time always brought with it huge elements of change, especially in the minds of intelligent human beings.

As Barton alighted on to the footpath in front of his home, Fisher stepped down also and, gripping Barton's hands, was moved to say something that he genuinely believed.

"What you have achieved, Toby, in giving such sterling leadership to the huge task of attaining the Federation of Australia will be recognised and remembered throughout the world for a long time. It is a fine example of how a smooth democratic transition of power can be achieved. It will be noted that you made it happen without bloodshed and with maximum goodwill, while creating a platform on which future prosperity and social cohesion could be built. It is an honour and a privilege to know you and work with you. Thank you and goodnight."

He stepped back into his carriage and moved on before Barton could adequately respond.

All that he could stammer out was, "Thank you, Andrew, thank you. Goodnight."

Jeannie

'Tosspot Toby' remained on the footpath as if stranded, quite overcome by the Prime Minister's words.

A thought ran through his mind.

"If I had been born ten years earlier or later, I would not have been in the position in which I found myself at the time of Federation. I was in the right place at the right time by a fluke of history and I was able to position myself in a place of influence. For the opportunity that was presented to me, I thank providence."

He was not a religious man, but, at that moment, he was certain that the Good Lord had dealt him a fine hand of cards. He hoped that the same Good Lord would deal as fine a hand of cards to the Australian nation for the rest of the century. Most crucially, he must preserve and protect the Constitution from all who would use it wrongly.

His devoted wife, Jeannie, was waiting for him at the door, as always.

He embraced her for a little longer than he normally would have done.

She had been utterly loyal, devoted and loving throughout their many years together. She needed to be.

He had purchased the five homes in which they had lived without ever telling her of his intentions in advance. Nor did he show her any of the homes or seek her opinion or ask for her approval. On each occasion, she had dutifully packed up and moved to their new abode without complaint so that Edmund's life could move smoothly forward to its ultimate destiny.

Such was the almost total male domination of the Federation era. A prime quality expected of all females was that they must accept their place in society, not ask difficult questions or ever complain.

Thankfully for the wellbeing of most males, and towering above all the benefits that marriage afforded them, was the love and affection that most women had for the men to whom they were loyal, no matter how dominating or wayward they may have been.

Jeannie's commitment to Toby was total.

Without her, it was highly likely that his life may never have achieved the stability to become the Founding Father of Australia.

Indeed, without Barton having been in the right place at the right time and with loyal family support, Federation may have been long delayed or may have resulted in a different type of constitution being written by a different leader.

More significantly, Malcolm Fraser, Gough Whitlam and John Kerr may never have been in the position in 1975 to go within an ace of destroying the nation because a different constitution may not have allowed it.

Unknown at the time was that subsequent generations of women would gradually and rightly expect that the one-sided relationship experienced by Jeannie Barton would change.

The best example of the advance of gender equality is shown by a fact of history.

One hundred and ten years after Sir Edmund Barton became Prime Minister of Australia. Hon Julia Gillard became the nation's first female Prime Minister. Jeannie Barton would have been quietly delighted.

One day, in the not too distant future, an Indigenous Australian will be elected to lead the nation, even though his or her ancestors were not mentioned in the Constitution.

Book Two
Ninety Years Later

THE AUSTRALIAN CLUB IN SYDNEY
1 JANUARY, 2001, NOON
LUNCHEON TO CELEBRATE THE CENTENARY OF FEDERATION

Guests

Three giants of Australian history celebrate the Centenary of Federation at a private luncheon to honour the Founding Fathers and review the relevance to a modern nation of the Constitution they had written and implemented.

They are three unforgettable leaders.

GOUGH WHITLAM

Barrister from New South Wales. Former Prime Minister of Australia leading an ALP Government. Dismissed from office in highly controversial circumstances in 1975 by Governor General John Kerr. Legendary advocate of political and economic change.

MALCOLM FRASER

Gentleman Farmer from Western Victoria. Whitlam's successor as Prime Minister of Australia leading a Coalition of Liberals and Nationals. After leaving Parliament, he gradually adopted the ideology of the political left whom he had originally despised.

ZELMAN COWEN

Constitutional Lawyer from Victoria. Former Vice Chancellor of the Universities of New England and Queensland. Appointed Governor General of Australia after the resignation of John Kerr. Subsequently Provost of Oriel College Oxford. Peacemaker.

Visitors

GARFIELD BARWICK

Former, and longest serving, Chief Justice of the High Court of Australia. Informal Adviser to John Kerr during the Constitutional Crisis of 1975, in a breach of protocol that caused considerable controversy.

MANNING CLARK

Eminent Historian. A poetic and highly controversial interpreter of historical events. Huge critic of the 1975 Coup and an outspoken admirer of Gough Whitlam.

PONSONBY

Whitlam's driver. A fictional character typical of the team who drive Commonwealth cars. Reliable and respectful.

Towering Presence

JOHN KERR

The only Governor General in Australian History ever to dismiss a Prime Minister. His action was never envisaged by the Founding Fathers when they wrote the Constitution. Malcolm Fraser was the beneficiary. Few lamented his passing.

The Host

Gough Whitlam strode through the door of Sydney's Australian Club on New Year's Day, exactly one hundred years on from the memorable day in 1901 when the Australian nation was born and Edmund Barton became its first Prime Minister.

He recalled that on this historic occasion, the City of Sydney had led the national celebrations of the Federation of Australian States in grand style with thousands upon thousands of proud Australians flocking through the streets as the bands played triumphantly while the crowds sang happily and cheered with pride and enthusiasm at the dawn of a new era in the history of the continent.

The Australian Club had staged celebratory events for the high and the mighty on this 'once in a lifetime' occasion. However, Queen Victoria would not have considered it to be in the same pecking order as its counterpart in Melbourne. When it was founded in 1838, the heritage of Sydney was still considerably influenced by its convict beginnings, whereas Melbourne had a broader base of free settlers. Nevertheless, the Australian Club is clearly upper crust and it had affirmed this on Federation Day.

Gough glanced around the lobby in his delightfully imperious manner to see if he could spot his luncheon guests, Malcolm Fraser and Zelman Cowen, who had flown in from Melbourne for the occasion. They had stayed at the club the previous evening to enjoy the peace and quiet of its colonial ambience.

Whitlam had, some months earlier, invited Malcolm and Zelman to join him for lunch today. He had asked them to lock it in their diaries as he felt that the exact day of the centenary of the creation of the Australian nation was an appropriate time for them to dine together to plan a reformation in the way that Australians governed themselves.

Primarily, he had suggested that the agenda for the luncheon should centre around a debate on what damage had been done to the Constitution of Australia by the Senate and the Governor General in November, 1975, when their actions caused him to be sacked as Prime Minister. It was the first time that a Governor General had taken such an action in the history of the nation and, hopefully, it would be the last.

He had proposed to Malcolm and Zelman that, in the course of their discussions, they should consider what the Founding Fathers may have thought about this highly controversial debacle which had torn the nation apart at that time and about which passionate debate still persisted.

The plan was that they would then chat about the changes that should ideally be made to the Constitution to make it more relevant to modern Australia.

He had emphasised that, while a revolutionary century had followed on from the great work done by Barton's men, it was an undeniable fact that Australian society in the 21st century bore little resemblance to that of 1901.

Moreover, 90% of Australians had little knowledge of the tumultuous events that had brought Federation into being and had little desire to think about them. It was time for this attitude to be changed.

The Importance of Taking Charge

The Club Manager was in the foyer to meet Gough. He mentioned that Fraser and Cowen were already settled upstairs in a private dining room that had been reserved so the trio could dine in private 'far from the madding crowds'. He led Whitlam to the venue

Gough dominated the room from the moment he passed through the door, in exactly the same manner as he had towered above every gathering during his highly controversial term as Prime Minister of Australia from 1972 to 1975. In Parliament, his look of disdain for his opponents had always been withering. This air of dominance became his political trademark, even on the days when he had been under heavy fire, which were often. Other mortals would have shrunk away. Never Gough.

Today, he was determined once more to let Malcolm Fraser, who himself was physically a towering giant, know that there was a more formidable presence in the room. Stretching himself to his full height, he managed to achieve this by less than a centimetre, but this was enough to make the point that he was in control of the situation, as always.

Despite Whitlam's theatrics, Fraser greeted him as if they had been lifelong friends and Gough gave him a prolonged double handshake. Since the dramatic days of 1975 when they were bitter political foes, both had mellowed remarkably, to the astonishment of all who knew them well. This was important as, had they perpetuated the enormous venom of that era, both would have suffered premature heart seizures.

To Gough's delight, Fraser had, to the surprise of most, but not his closest friends, moved decisively to the political left, almost out of the reach of his old conservative allies who now regarded him as an infidel and a traitor.

Astonishingly, the two old warhorses were now staunch mates, happily finding a political home together out in the exciting domain of radical ideological thought.

Zelman Cowen received a prolonged bear hug from Gough whose words of welcome were as colourful and outlandish as one could possibly expect.

"Thank God, Malcolm appointed you as Governor General when that cur, John Kerr, resigned in an alcoholic daze after thoroughly disgracing himself by irresponsibly tearing our nation asunder. His treacherous coup flaunted the very fabric of the Constitution that had been drawn up so wisely by our Founding Fathers. But, Zelman, you calmed down the country magnificently. Had I had the wisdom to have appointed you as Governor General in the first place, instead of that law breaking and back stabbing Kerr, we would not have suffered the painful debacle that we did. As the nation's eminent constitutional lawyer, you have more knowledge of the Constitution in your little finger than Kerr had in that huge uscless frame of his that was bloated by a pomposity of the most obnoxious and repulsive kind."

With a smile, but no words of agreement, Zelman responded to Gough's passionate oration.

"We look forward to elaborating on every one of your moderate views as we dine with you on this historic day, Gough. Thank you for inviting us to join you. Malcolm and I have been reflecting on the key issues of 1901 and 1975 for the last few minutes. This leads us to believe that, with your enthusiastic input, our conversation over lunch promises to be colourfully enlightening."

Malcolm finally got in a word.

"May I also add my thanks to you for hosting this lunch, Gough. A quarter of a century has passed since November, 1975. With the wisdom of age, we both may have acted differently if we could now relive that fateful day. We shall find out over a good lunch, especially if it is accompanied by some fine wine to keep us in a jovial state."

Drinks

"Who would like a pre-lunch drink?" enquired Gough as he pressed the buzzer to summon the butler.

"I certainly will enjoy one, so long as it is of a class that will rejuvenate the soul of an old political campaigner. There is a chance that it may put my annoyingly hyperactive disposition at ease so I can adequately counter any old Liberal Party ideology and other trivial political nonsense that Malcolm may trot out and throw at me today. Mind you, he will do it in the delightful manner that he has so carefully developed into an art form.

"By the way, the Club President phoned me yesterday to say that our feast today is on the house. The blissfully unsuspecting members of this historic club are footing the bill. They are completely unaware of the largesse that the management dispenses to needy old pensioners like us. If we eat and drink enough, their membership subscriptions are likely to rise, an imposition that most of them can afford anyway.

"My carefully considered plan is to enjoy a generously sized gin and tonic in honour of Her Majesty. I am reliably informed that she drinks nothing else. As a passionate Republican, I feel that the minimum courtesy I should render on this memorable occasion is to do her the honour of drinking in the same manner on such a famous day which I am sure she is happily celebrating also.

"She is a far more gracious and intelligent person than that old witch Victoria who, unfortunately, was on the throne on the momentous occasion when our nation achieved Federation in spite of her opposition to it. Elizabeth is far better looking also. She actually gets on very well with me. If there is a Good Lord out there, may he bless her."

Malcolm and Zelman wisely chose not to comment on Gough's infinite wisdom regarding royalty or match his taste in drinks. When the barman appeared, they both ordered a glass of Shiraz from the Great Western Region of their home State of Victoria, close to Malcolm's former country estate. Their choice was made precisely because red wine is reputed to contain the essential chemistry to break up one's cholesterol. Even if it didn't, they would have ordered it anyway.

Arthur Phillip

While awaiting the arrival of the drinks, Gough suggested that their first item of business when they had drinks in hand should be to toast the Commander of the First Fleet, Captain Arthur Phillip.

"I will never diminish the stature of the Founding Fathers of 1901, but the fact is that Phillip was the very first Founding Father who operated under what can be regarded as the nation's first Constitution.

"It was a letter signed by King George giving him power over all things and authority to do anything he chose to do in order to keep law and order in the new colony."

"Gough, may I comment?" enquired Zelman.

"By all means."

"Arthur Phillip was not the founder of a nation. He established a gaol which was intended to be the largest in the British Empire. This was all that the letter gave him authority to do. Any farms and industries that he established were solely for the purpose of sustaining a penal colony. He went home believing that he had achieved what he had been instructed to do. If he returned now, he would be flabbergasted to find that a nation had arisen from his work. He cannot be ranked in the same status as Edmund Barton as a nation builder. Nevertheless, I am pleased to honour him with a toast. He was a brave man and a skilled seaman, as well being a good builder and manager of a gaol which he created in extraordinarily difficult circumstances of total isolation."

Malcolm had words to add.

"In toasting him, we should remember also that Phillip did try to make peace with the aborigines. He knew that he had invaded their land, but skirmishes eventually broke out, causing a war to begin that lasted for a century. Eventually, thirty thousand aborigines would be shot and killed while three thousand white men were speared to death. We now call it 'The Forgotten War' and Barton chose to ignore it when our Constitution was written. Aborigines were given no stature in it."

The drinks arrived.

"Here's to Governor Phillip," intoned Gough.

Malcolm and Zelman warmly responded.

Gough continued, "Phillip and Barton had one thing in common. They lived in an age of very sparse communications.

"It took Phillip six months to get a reply from London to any letter he sent. He had no other means of communication. He must have felt very alone.

"Barton had to sell the adoption of the Constitution to leaders and citizens of six independent states in an era where the only means of contacting anyone were newspapers, morse code and letters. He had no radio, television, telephones, or internet. He and his team won the day by addressing street corner meetings all over the continent. In my view, it was the greatest marketing exercise of all time. And he achieved the creation of a nation without any of the violence and bloodshed that the Americans, French and Russians went through to achieve their freedom."

Malcolm added some spice to it.

"Without meaning to further belittle our first Prime Minister in any way, can I add a reminder. Barton achieved Federation without involving the women of Australia, except for those in South Australia where Kingston insisted that they must vote in the Referendum. They were not even allowed to participate in any of the Federation Conventions that planned the Constitution. What an enormous difference a century makes."

Zelman closed the conversation.

"Can I say that if our current Prime Minister tried to achieve any major reform without consulting Indigenous Australia and the women of Australia, he would be dead before sunset. Shall we move on."

Chairman Zelman Examines John Kerr

Fraser and Whitlam had agreed beforehand that Cowen should have the role of independent umpire for today's debate.

Zelman decided to open the floodgates by immediately commenting on John Kerr, the man who had determined the destiny of both of his fellow guests and who had now passed on with little lament other than from his closest friends. It could fairly be stated that he had descended tragically to the status of having been an embarrassment even to those who, not only had thoroughly approved of what he had done, but had actually recommended to him that he should do it, indeed pressed him to do it.

"Let me begin today's luncheon debate by posing this quite blunt, but quite crucial, question to you, Gough. Your answer will set a course for the rest of our conversation. Did Kerr have the constitutional power to sack you?

"Now, let me answer it. Yes, he did. Let there be not the slightest doubt about this. It is incontestable and its basis is this fundamental truth.

"When it passed an Act of Parliament in 1899 to establish legally the Commonwealth of Australia in 1901, Westminster insisted on giving the Governor-General the reserve power that Kerr used to dismiss you. They wanted Queen Victoria's representative to have the right to be able to intervene decisively in the event that the colonials ever became rebellious against the Crown. In doing this, they made an incorrect presumption that the Governor General would only ever be an Englishman who would only ever take advice from a Queen or King on a matter of such importance as the dismissal of a Government.

"It is fundamental to note that, in 1975, Kerr did not seek Royal assent for his drastic action. May I also add that I do not believe that Her Majesty would ever have given her approval to Kerr. The Imperial Parliament of 1901 did not even remotely consider that such a breach of protocol by a Governor General would ever occur.

"Nevertheless, Kerr exercised a power that they had, by law, quite clearly given to Governor General"

Cowen paused momentarily.

"It is therefore logical to ask a second question at this moment. Should Kerr have used this reserve power?

"Allow me to answer this one too. No, emphatically no. In writing the Constitution, the Founding Fathers did not intend, or even imagine, that the Senate should have the right to refuse Supply to a government that had the confidence of the House of Representatives. In fact, their expectation would have been that the Governor General would have counselled and warned the Leader of the Opposition against such an action and advised the Prime Minister to take steps to resolve the matter. In modern Britain. it has always been the role of the Monarch to counsel and warn."

"And I did have that vote of confidence," exclaimed Gough with huge indignation. "That vote had been taken on the very day I was sacked. This emphatic proof is backed by the fact that the House had also passed a vote of no confidence in Malcolm on that same day, only hours after Kerr had appointed him as Prime Minister. Kerr ignored both of these legitimate votes and was either totally misguided or utterly corrupt in doing what he did. I am of the mind that it was the latter. In fact, it is quite possible that his birth was a corruption of all the noble attributes that motherhood represents. And may I say that this is one of my milder observations on the matter."

"Allow me to interrupt, Gough," suggested Zelman. "We are aware of your low opinion of Kerr. Can we get back to the subject matter in hand? Do you agree with my answers to the two questions that I posed to you?"

"With extreme reluctance, I say yes to the first while also saying that the British did not have any right to presume in 1901 that they could have the final say on how Australia should be governed. But, I give a loud yell of yes to the second. While I require a pledge from you that you will not convey it to another soul, I will admit to you the lamentable reality that the Governor General does have reserve powers. But, I would never have admitted it to Kerr, nor Malcolm for that matter. Indeed, I implore him to ignore my comments right now."

Zelman produced a piece of paper from his coat pocket.

"Gough, while you are in the mood to utter one or two conciliatory comments about your antagonists on that fateful day, can I read to you the speech that you made from the front steps of Parliament during the afternoon when the Governor General's Official Secretary, David Smith, had read to a huge crowd the Proclamation dissolving Parliament and calling a Double Dissolution Election.

"In my view, it was not the greatest speech you have ever made, but it was your most indignantly outraged oration and it is the one that most Australians are vividly reminded of when they think of you, which they do often, and not always kindly.

"I am sure that you both remember it well, but here it is for the purposes of enlivening today's debate.

"Well, may we say 'God save the Queen', because nothing will save the Governor General.

The Proclamation that you have just heard was signed by the Governor-General and countersigned by Malcolm Fraser who will definitely go down in Australian History from Remembrance Day, 1975, as Kerr's cur.

They won't silence the outskirts of Parliament House, even if the inside has been silenced for the next few weeks.

The Governor General's proclamation was signed after he had already made an appointment to meet the Speaker of the House, but before he met him. The House of Representatives had requested the Speaker to give the Governor-General its decision that Mr Fraser did not have the confidence of the House and that the Governor-General should call me to form the Government.

Maintain your rage and enthusiasm through the campaign for the election now to be held and until polling day."

Zelman continued.

"May I now make this suggestion, Gough? It was not your finest moment when you called Malcolm 'Kerr's cur'. Could I suggest that it is not too late for you to apologise?"

Gough seemed a little startled by this unexpected request so early in what he had planned to be a convivial luncheon.

"I did apologise to Malcolm in a sort of way a few years back and he sort of accepted it. But, he really did deserve a solid spanking on the day itself. Had his mother been there, she surely would have done so. Now, if we could re-write history, I could be moved to amend my words to utter a slightly more moderate tone in describing the predatory Malcolm of that infamous day. It would be something like 'Kerr's Conniver'. Perhaps that would have been seen as a more gentlemanly remark in keeping with the highest traditions of our Parliament."

"Now, now," said Malcolm who had maintained an admirable silence up until this moment, "let's set the record straight on a few things. I can understand the hurt you felt in 1975, Gough, and I am saddened that it was me who caused you such pain, but the prime factor in creating the conditions for your sacking was that Kerr was absolutely certain that you were about to sack him unless he got in first. You did nothing to allay that fear, even though others had made you aware of his fragile state of mind.

"In addition, had you advised him that morning to call a full election of the House of Representatives, plus a half Senate Election, on a date as soon as practicable after Christmas, he would have granted it. This would have placed you in the advantageous position of going into that election in the New Year in the more powerful role of Prime Minister rather than as a sacked one. And, you would have been in much better status with the voters after everyone had calmed down during the festive season. You would have won many more seats than the lamentable few that you managed to scrape together in December. As I remember it, you lost around 30 seats."

"Ah," responded Gough, "wisdom after the event always provides exhilarating clarity. You have actually got me seriously pondering the possibility that, had I done what you have just suggested, I might have beaten you in that election. In truth, now that I have pondered it for a few seconds and had a couple more sips of my gin and tonic, I become quite certain that I could have done so with a fair degree of panache."

Malcolm smiled kindly. He did not often do so.

"Gough, I have been in politics long enough to know that anything is possible.

"Be this as it may, we should now recall an indisputable fact. Your worst mistake of that entire saga was that, after Kerr fired you, you failed to call Ken Wreidt, your Senate leader, and instruct him not to proceed with the Supply Bill that was scheduled to be, once more, before the Senate for a vote of approval that afternoon.

"Could I comment firstly that you really did humiliate Wreidt quite unnecessarily and, had you talked to him, Wreidt could have withdrawn the bill from the Senate agenda that afternoon and this would have left me in the same situation that you had been in, a Prime Minister without money. Kerr's plan would have totally misfired at that point. He would have had to immediately reinstate you and you would then have fired him on the spot with all guns blazing."

Malcolm's smile became even kinder.

"And, may I say this with considerable acknowledgement of your infinite capacity for revenge, you would have been quite merciless in having his head chopped off. I can imagine that you would have insisted on doing the job personally so as to ensure that you could take half a dozen hits of the axe just to draw out the procedure with maximum pain for him and unbelievable joy to yourself."

With some solemnity, Gough replied, "Your prediction of what I would have done to Kerr is incredibly accurate, Malcolm. You are underrated in the world's view of you as a perceptive soul.

"As to your comment on Wreidt, alas, I have often lain awake at night wondering why I didn't call him, but it is a bit late in the relentless tide of the history of the affairs of men for me to consider slashing my wrists over it in a fit of self-punishment. Besides which, if the media of 1975 had been as hot off the mark with instant news as they are now, Wreidt would have heard of the drama all by himself and had a chance to plan an appropriate strategy with his colleagues. So, I must now, and with not the slightest pang of regret, place full blame on the negligence of the media for the travesty that occurred. They simply did not do their job. Let me phrase this better. They acted normally.

"May I add that I did not purposely humiliate Wreidt. I simply became consumed with a strategy to have a vote of no confidence passed against Malcolm in the Reps."

Zelman got a word in before Whitlam could continue with his colourful reminiscence of the most fateful day of his life.

"Can I affirm that Gough's failure to contact Wreidt was an enormous blunder in terms of political strategy. An even worse blunder was that Gough did not call Senate President, Justin O'Byrne, who could have cancelled the entire sitting of the Senate that day, using the constitutional crisis as the reason for doing so. That would have totally blindsided Kerr.

"Equally important is that Kerr did not have the right to call an election on Malcolm's advice as Malcolm quite clearly did not yet have the confidence of the House of Representatives. This was a significant breach of parliamentary protocol and procedure, and can I say, Malcolm, that you did have a constitutional responsibility to call Kerr and advise him that you had lost a vote of confidence in the House. You did not do so, but let us move on."

Malcolm asked Zelman to pause a moment. He was in a mood for confession.

"I can now belatedly admit that I should have advised Kerr of my defeat in the House. But, he had already appointed me as Prime Minister and so I made what I considered at the time to be an astute political decision. I acted on the basis that I had the job until he withdrew my commission, an action that he did not take. In the meantime, I wanted the election to happen and intended to do nothing to stop it as I knew with certainty that I would win it."

Zelman was not yet finished.

"May I add one more point, Malcolm. Kerr illegally called a double dissolution election on the basis that several of Gough's Bills has been repeatedly rejected by the Senate. These were bills that you had opposed and defeated. Therefore, you had no right to use their rejection in order to have a double dissolution on the basis that they could be passed at a subsequent joint sitting of both Houses of Parliament that you had no intention whatsoever of ever calling."

Malcolm's body language was one of acute pain.

"Yes, Zelman, in hindsight, the calling of a double dissolution election was a breach of the Constitution."

Gough walked over to Malcolm and warmly embraced him.

"At last, Comrade, at last. On the basis of your confession, I am prepared not to remind you that you knew that the Governor General was going to dismiss me before I did. He was totally in breach of protocol in contacting you as Opposition Leader before he spoke to me as his Prime Minister. You both know how assiduously I stick to protocol."

Sins of the Senate

Zelman paused to absorb this extraordinary moment, then went on.

"All of the miss-steps that the two of you, plus Kerr, made that day have subsequently become an intriguing study for students of political tactics. They highlight the ever-present potential for frailty by human beings at the extreme pressure points of life.

"Therefore, can I conclude our review of the Dismissal by re-emphasising the point that there were three guilty people that day – Kerr, Fraser and Whitlam? The three of you equally share the blame for the tragedy. You all could have acted more responsibly."

"Correct," said Malcolm.

"I remain in discreet silence," responded Gough. "Humbly so."

Zelman moved on, "Be this as it may, I want to come back to the real crux of the constitutional issues that were under extreme pressure that day.

"The fundamental question for which we must now seek an answer is this. Quite separately from the political conditions that prevailed in 1975, did the Founding Fathers, in drafting the Australian Constitution, ever envisage that any circumstance could arise in which the Senate could cause a Prime Minister to have no money to finance the basic requirements of keeping a government operating on a daily basis?

"My clear view is that they did not intend this to happen, ever. You, Malcolm, were in breach of the Constitution by asking the Senate to bankrupt a Government.

"The Governor General was in breach of his duties in not informing you that you were acting improperly. The Senate itself clearly violated the Constitution.

"Our Founders had it clearly in mind that the Senate should be able to reject a money bill relating to a particular matter, but they did not give it power to completely shut down a government."

"You have raised a valid point, Zelman," was Fraser's immediate confession, "I belatedly accept that your interpretation of the limits that the Founding Fathers placed on the powers of the Senate is hard to dismiss."

Gough was wise enough to say nothing, but he had a look of happy satisfaction on his face.

So, Zelman continued, "This raises yet another fundamental question. Did Australia ever need a Senate? Should the Founding Fathers have scrapped the whole idea?

"New Zealand has never ever had an Upper House. Queensland voted theirs out of existence. Both claim that this gives a democratically elected government the power to carry out whatever mandates the voters had given them at an election. They firmly insist that restraints of that fundamental democratic authority should never be applied. The power of dismissal must always lie with the voters and they have this power at every election. This is a very vital point. It is the core of the matter."

Fraser had a clear viewpoint.

"It is reasonable to assume that the three main power brokers of Federation – Barton, Deakin and Griffith – envisaged a senate that would basically have the powers of the House of Lords, but would have no aristocrats in its ranks. They were copying the Government at Westminster as closely as they could as this was essential if they were to gain their approval in order for Federation to proceed. They correctly assumed that the creation of a Senate would guarantee British approval of the Constitution.

"But, there was a second reason why they established a senate and it was a must more compelling one back here in Australia. This embraced the volatile issue of interstate rivalry in Australia. The inevitable existence of the Senate was based on an unshakeable acceptance of the obvious.

"The smaller states would not agree to Federation unless there was an Upper House in which all states had equal power. New South Wales and Victoria could not be allowed to occupy a position where they could overpower the smaller ones and dictate the decision-making processes of any government. Queensland, Tasmania, South Australia and Western Australia had a strong conviction that, together, they must always be able to have sufficient numbers in Parliament to outvote the Victorians and New South Welshmen.

"They were certain that domination of national destiny was something that the big states clearly intended to achieve if the MPs serving in the House of Representatives were elected on a basis of an equal number of voters in every electorate.

"It did not occur to them that, even though equally sized electorates in the House of Representatives would have created an opportunity for New South Wales and Victoria to combine together to have the numbers that would let them rule Australia, it was highly improbable that those two large states would ever agree anyway.

"If fact, Victorians had a high degree of suspicion about New South Welshmen and actually regarded them as second-class citizens who were descended from convicts and gamblers, quite distinct from the gentlemen of Victoria. In return, the New South Welshmen would have used even more colourful language to describe their Victorian brothers. They once called them 'a cabbage patch'. Nevertheless, the small states took no chances. They insisted that a senate must be established that would clearly and effectively curb the big guys.

"There is no way that Australia could have avoided having a senate. Nevertheless, its powers should have been defined more clearly by the Founding Fathers. It was one of the few major errors thy made."

Unsurprisingly, Gough had an unambiguous opinion on this matter too.

"A far more profound problem was created by the final decision of the Founding Fathers to have all states equally represented in the Senate, irrespective of size of population. It has since been indelibly proven that, never in the history of the Australian Senate, have senators ever voted together to defend their own state on any matter whatsoever. Not once has it happened in the century that has just passed and it never will happen. All senators are politicians who, above all other motivations, want their party to stay in power. If they are forced to choose between the welfare of their state and their own hold on power, then power will win every time.

"Except on one or two minor occasions when they found it politically useful to show some evidence of having a conscience, they have consistently voted according to how their political parties told them to do on every bill that has ever been put before them for a decision. The rights of a particular state have never ever been a burning issue and so the entire concept of protecting small states is an absolute nonsense, a total hypocrisy.

"Now, a strong case can be made to abolish the Senate totally and quickly. Its existence is an extravagant waste of public money and an insult to democracy. We have a ridiculous situation where Tasmania has twice as many senators as it has members of the House of Representatives – twelve senators and five MPs. This is absolute stupidity.

"It is ridiculous that each state elects twelve senators, no matter what the size of the state. This is caused by a Nexus which is spelled out in the Constitution which says that the Senate must be half the size of the House of Representatives. That Nexus must be removed via a Referendum as the House will keep growing in size as Australia's population grows. We must go back to five senators per state as this was the figure in 1901. There is no justification for any more.

"If we could start from scratch and plan Australia all over again, we would abolish all states, and as a consequence, the Senate. We would have a national government of one House and have many regional governments rather than local governments."

"In broad terms, I am in agreement with both of you," observed Cowen. "You have hit the crux of the national dilemma that we now have in determining the actual value, if any, of having a Senate.

"Especially, we must remember that the House of Lords at Westminster has no power to deny Supply to the House of Commons. It has only an ability to delay and amend legislation of any kind, not finally block it. In fact, it's once fundamental powers have been gutted in many ways.

"This first began in 1910 and a steady dilution of the power of the Lords has occurred ever since. Its origins were laid when the Conservatives in the Lords persistently delayed crucial Budget legislation put forward by David Lloyd George on behalf of the Asquith Liberal Government in 1909. They had reached a point of total exasperation and complained strongly to the new King who was of a mind to flex his muscles early in his reign.

"This was George V who had just ascended to the throne after the recent death of Edward V11. They gained a somewhat reluctant permission from the King to stack the Lords with a new set of Liberal Peers in order to have his Budget passed. After two elections were fought on the issue, the Conservatives admitted defeat and subsequently were forced to allow legislation to pass that curbed the powers of the Lords. This was a crucial turning point in British history as it began a long slide of irrelevance for the Lords.

"Australia should now do likewise. This would mean that those who want the Senate to remain in existence must legislate an indelibly clear constitutional change. This must place beyond doubt that the Senate's presumption of power to stop Supply, or deny a voter mandate given at an election, is abolished. But, at the same time, we should increase the powers of the Senate to review and delay and publicly embarrass the House of Representatives about legislation that they send to them, but not finally deny it. This would mean that key legislation would get adequate, high profile, public scrutiny within defined time limits before it becomes law. It is a basic fundamental of democracy."

"Let me repeat my heart felt observation that we should rid ourselves of this obnoxious leach that we call the Senate," said Gough.

"It is more obnoxious than the House of Lords has ever been and I say this having had no respect for the Lords from the day I first heard of them.

"To quote one of my successors viewpoint of our beloved Senate, 'It is a barnacle on the arse of progress'.

"Many have quoted this poetic remark made by Paul Keating as one of the great one-liners of all time and may I add that it superbly describes the undeniable facts of the matter.

"As Zelman has rightly pointed out, New Zealand prospers quite impressively without an Upper House and with no states. I greatly admire them and suggest that we should copy them on this crucial issue.

"The key matter for us to note is this. New Zealanders enjoy good government because they also have proportional representation in their only House which has consistently enabled minor parties to win some seats there, thus enabling minorities to be represented in the halls of power. Currently in Australia, minor parties can do this only in the Senate where they often undemocratically hold the balance of power.

"We should vote that same way in electing the House of Representatives here in Australia. Right now, those minor parties in the Senate, elected by only a few thousand voters, believe that they can behave with utter irresponsibility in dictating the future of the nation. They would need to gain many more votes if a five percent hurdle is set for gaining a proportional representation seat in the Reps."

Cowen added an important point.

"Despite their error of not clearly defining the powers of the Senate, I believe that we can say with conviction that the Founding Fathers did a remarkable piece of work in writing the Australian Constitution. It has served the nation for a century and will continue to do so for many years to come."

Creating More States

Fraser leapt on to Whitlam's remark on the inability of states to have any influence on legislation before the Senate and proffered a solution.

"As much as I would like to agree with Gough about abolishing the Senate, it will be almost impossible to achieve. Can we look at an alternative?

"While the comment that I am about to make will not solve the entire problem caused by a senate which is trumped up by its own misguided version of power, the best thing for Australia to do right now would be to rid ourselves of one level of government – local government – and create 44 new states to take the number to 50.

"This can easily be achieved as the Constitution quite wisely provides for new states to be created, but makes no mention whatsoever of local government, which I might add is quite odd. The Founding Fathers really slipped up there. They regarded local governments as being totally within the realm of state governments.

"A positive plan to create new states could be this. Each of our six states would amalgamate existing local governments into large enough entities to become states. Obviously, each of the capital cities would become a state in its own right, with the remainder of each state being divided into states based around a major regional city.

"This means that, in effect, the states would become large local governments delivering essential services to the people in a much better way than it is now done. While the states are doing that work at the grass roots level, the Federal Government can concentrate on raising revenue for the states to provide those services, while it continues to give priority to national issues. This would remove many of the stupid taxes that states currently inflict on their citizens for no valid reason other than to raise cash for their daily operations."

"I could be open to the thought that I may be convinced to go along with that," proclaimed Whitlam, "so long as each of the fifty states elects only one senator by direct franchise so as to remove the possibility that a senator can be elected with a tiny percentage of the vote as happens now. This process will cut the number of senators by a third."

Cowen expressed the view that Malcolm's proposal was worth looking at, but then offered a possible alternative solution.

"Difficult as it may be to achieve, it could still be possible to have the Senate abolished entirely and the composition of the House of Representatives changed so that each state elects the same number of MPs irrespective of population. This will give the small states the protection they appear to cherish, if indeed they still want it, thereby rendering the need for a senate to be absolutely unnecessary. This could make Malcolm's proposal for fifty states to be very relevant and urgent.

"The break-up of the population of New South Wales and Victoria into new states means that there would be more likelihood that a majority of new states across the entire nation would have more equal populations in regional areas and, as the capital cities became states like Singapore, they would offset one another in political influence. In the end, this would mean that there could, in reality, be no predator states."

Both Malcolm and Gough agreed that this dramatic proposal could provide a revolutionary solution to the good governance of modern Australia and was worthy of thorough examination, especially as it also would reduce the cost of government overall. In particular, they noted that it would remove all 75 senators, many of whom would not be missed as they were there as a gift for their long service to their political parties.

However, Gough finally came down on the side of Malcolm's earlier suggestion that there should be fifty states as it would be achievable within the current Constitution without amendment, whereas Zelman's suggestion, excellent though it was, would need several difficult referendums to achieve the number of significant constitutional changes that will be needed.

He then added a note of ultimate triumph, "Upon reflection, a substantial side benefit of Zelman's suggestion would be that we would eventually be able to organise a glorious funeral service for the Senate. It could be the most spectacular funeral in the history of Australia.

"I would insist that I be granted the historic privilege of being the preacher on this momentous occasion and I shall wear specially prepared religious robes to vividly indicate to the masses that I am more than a little agnostic. Be assured that the words I will utter will absolutely guarantee the descent of the Senate into the hell fires from where it originally came and from where it can be quickly forgotten and not lamented. The masses will applaud with tears of joy flowing unrestrained from their eyes."

Cowen decided that this pearl of romanticism from Whitlam was an opportunity to round off this issue and move on.

"Now that Gough has raised the matter of a speech he proposes to make in burying the Senate, can I for a moment add a thought on the impact of great speeches that he has made from time to time.

"His finest was most probably the one he made at the Blacktown Civic Centre in November, 1972, when he launched the election campaign that made him Prime Minister a few short weeks later.

Gough, you named the speech – *IT'S TIME*.

At one dramatic point in it, you proclaimed,

Our program has three great aims –

To promote quality

To involve the people of Australia in the decision-making processes of our land

To liberate the talents and uplift the horizons of the Australian people

"Can I suggest that we keep those three points in mind as we proceed with our discussion? They are goals worth pursuing."

Their chosen luncheon dishes arrived at that moment.

This did not stop Gough from reaching out to shake hands with Zelman and making a playful utterance that was very close to the truth.

"It could be Zelman that my inspired words on that evening will be remembered long after my historic deeds, both good and bad, have been forgotten. At the very least, I hope I won't have the same misfortune as King Charles 1, solely remembered for losing his head."

Main

Having mutually agreed to dispense with the tempting entrees on offer, the trio had ordered healthily large servings of Mains.

Gough had chosen a fine steak of 500 grams, double the size of steaks that most club members were eating that day.

"Just like the one I ate for lunch at the Lodge on the day that Kerr sacked me. It was quite an unforgettable meal really. With every chew of every bite, I ground Kerr into oblivion."

Malcolm chose lamb, in tender strips.

"Comes from the land we call 'Australia Felix', right where I live. It's actually better than New Zealand lamb. This is a huge call, but truthful nevertheless. The All Blacks always win at Rugby Union, so we are entitled to claim superiority above Canterbury lamb."

Zelman made a much healthier choice. He had a Smoked Salmon Caesar Salad and refrained from commenting on its virtues.

They had agreed to share a fine bottle of Red from a Clare Valley vineyard that had been founded by an Order of Monks.

"It's a delightful place called Seven Hills after the seven hills of Rome. This vintage from their excellent vineyard where the grapes are constantly in God's care will keep us in an appropriately holy frame of mind," expounded Gough, who had carefully chosen it.

"Monks have ever so much more discipline than our hopeless Senate plus a depth of integrity which is in total contrast to that which was absent from the miserable soul of that infidel John Kerr. Their religious order only ever burnt people at the stake, never ever crucifying them in the excruciatingly painful manner that Kerr disposed of me."

Sins of the Fathers

He was now in full flight and enjoying himself immensely. Zelman and Malcolm chose not to deprive of the pleasure of displaying his colourful skills of provocative oration.

"Let us examine the Founding Fathers a little more closely. They are rightly to be revered for their extraordinary achievement in pulling off Federation. They did it much more smoothly than the Americans managed to do under heavy fire, but they made far too many compromises in their determination to get the deal through. The truth most probably is that they had no other options at that point in history if they wanted to achieve their goals. Even so, those compromises have left us with a few significant problems that need to be sorted out sooner rather than later as our Parliaments have already spent a century procrastinating about them."

"I thought that the art of compromise was meant to be the cornerstone of politics," responded Zelman. "My understanding is that governments will seize up unless they experience daily doses of political manoeuvring even within their own parties."

"It is not possible for any semblance of compromise to be anywhere in sight whenever you have the misfortune to be dealing with someone like Malcolm. But, there is hope in sight. I am working strenuously on his conversion and I can see a ray of sunshine out there on the horizon. However, the stark reality is that whenever and wherever you study history, you find that in every era the Conservatives have been downright bloody-minded, whereas those of us on the Left almost invariably had minds that were open and expansive," complained Gough who got a well-deserved return of service from Malcolm.

After agreeing with Zelman about the quality and appropriateness of Gough's election speech, Malcolm offered a little brotherly advice to his old sparring partner, Gough.

"If it is possible for you to concentrate your mind on to hard facts, Gough, rather than your flights of radical fantasy, may we identify some of the more significant mistakes that our Founders made, either in the Constitution or in the first Acts of Parliament that they implemented. Let me start our quest to identify them.

"Choosing to ignore the very existence of aborigines was a monumental blunder. Actually, it would not be an exaggeration to refer to it as a crime.

"Another was the embedding in legislation of a policy that ensured that White Australia was the basic culture of our nationhood, an embarrassing blot on our national pride that lasted for sixty years.

"Putting the British in charge of our defence was a further error that eventually would cost us dearly.

"Likewise, was the somewhat lax wording that enabled the Senate to use excessive power in a manner that Zelman assures us was never their intention.

"They also left too much power with the states. Education, Health and Transport are national matters that need total coordination across the continent and cannot be parochial in any way. Leaving them in the hands of the states has caused massive disruption when people move from one state to live in another. In addition, it actually shifts costs between governments.

"However, as Gough has rightly pointed out, it is highly probable that, had they handled all those matters in the way we now think they should have, the Federation movement may well have died in its infancy and this continent may now still be six independent, underdeveloped nations that are bastions of small vision and the haven of isolationists."

"Those are fair comments, Malcolm," said Zelman. "However, the critical issue at the moment is for us to work out what referendums can now be held that could actually change these obvious defects.

"Let us look at each of the errors that we think the Fathers of the nation have made and consider, in the sequence that Malcolm has laid them out for us, what action can be taken to remedy them."

Indigenous Australia

Cowen placed the raw facts on the table.

"It is very possible that a new clause can be added to the Constitution formally recognising Indigenous Australians and their rights as long term occupants of the land. Worded in the right manner, it may win enough votes to pass in a referendum. In fact, I have considerable hope that it could be passed.

"Most reasonable people will, I think, finally come to believe that it is time to recognise the undeniable truth that Aborigines owned and occupied this continent for a minimum of 65,000 years before the British arrived. We really have no option but to amend the Constitution to, at the very least, acknowledge this. We all know that the monumental Mabo judgement by the High Court made it very clear that the entire concept of Terra Nullus was a huge mistake and a grave injustice. The justices said emphatically that the land had been rightly occupied by indigenous people before the white man arrived. The courts of the future will never even consider reversing that judgement. It would irresponsible for our nation not to face all the obligations inherent in this by enshrining it in the Constitution immediately.

"There are a number of ethical and moral reasons why we should do it.

"We will hold our heads in shame when we are finally forced to publicly acknowledge to the whole world that, in the first century of British occupation, our settlers shot and killed 30,000 aborigines just because they tried to defend their ancient tribal lands from white men who were illegally stealing from them. 3000 whites were killed in that forgotten war as always happens when one nation invades another and this also was a shocking waste of life. Yet we try to hide the fact that Britain invaded Australia. Let us admit it, this was an invasion.

"Additionally, those same white men irresponsibly disturbed and destroyed the wildlife that was the lifeblood of indigenous people.

"Even worse, we introduced human diseases against which Aborigines had no protection whatsoever and thousands of them died helplessly, more actually than were ever shot.

"What this means is that Indigenous Australians reacted in exactly the same way as we would do if we were now facing an invasion from say, China. As an example, we reacted in the same way to the bombing strategy that Japan implemented against us at Darwin and Broome half a century ago. We defended ourselves with the same level of righteous indignation as aborigines had done with much lesser weapons in trying to keep their ancient lands. In fact, they had only spears. It was a very unfair fight."

Fraser and Whitlam had not the slightest hesitation in affirming that it was a profound disgrace that Aborigines had been treated so shamefully and the whole issue was made more disgraceful when we did not allow them to vote in any elections until a referendum was passed in 1967 that finally empowered them to do so. Until then, they were officially non-persons, downtrodden by arrogant racism.

Gough's words were caustic.

"Before we belatedly declared them to be human beings, they had been required to enlist in our armed forces in two wars during which they served with exceptional loyalty and valour. Yet, they were treated, day after day, as second-class soldiers who were thought to be not quite human and not eligible for the same privileges and conditions as their white counterparts. So, it was inevitable that, having been considered as being not really intelligent enough to vote, they were then accorded the status of primitive guys who were quite dispensable as gun fodder in wars. To add to the insult, they were treated abominably and miserably on their return home, despite their heroism. None of them got the war pension they had so bravely earned, just some meagre welfare handouts usually given to non-citizens."

Malcolm added, "When, as a maturing nation, we finally acknowledged that the aboriginal embarrassment was not going to go away, we tried to salve our consciences by handing out lots of money to them so we could prove that we really were good guys to whom they should now show some gratitude. That hasn't worked either. The awful truth is that our welfare strategy has been a disgraceful failure. So, we must turn everything around and begin again. A referendum that finally gives complete recognition, is a start, but only a start. We need to design and competently implement a totally new form of honourable integration. I am not clear on what that strategy should be, but it must happen. There has to be a better way than what we are doing now."

Gough rose and shook Malcolm's hand.

"Best speech I have ever heard from a Liberal and I have tolerated, with extraordinary patience, much gibberish from thousands of them for far too many decades. One day, we will give serious consideration to letting you into the Labor Party. It is even possible that I may personally nominate you."

"Gough, the possibility of the Labor Party ever accepting me as a brother worthy of being admitted to their ranks is extraordinarily remote as is the possibility that I would accept. A burning disdain of Trade Unions is burnt into my soul. However, allow me to make a suggestion that has a greater probability of success.

"I would readily consider the possibility of running with you on a joint independent ticket to get us into the Senate. We would only need a couple of thousand votes to get there, particularly if we run in Tasmania. However, let us be clear from the outset. I occupy number one place on the ticket while you graciously accept the number two spot. You owe me this honour as an act of forgiveness for all the rude comments you have made about me ever since November 1975."

Gough was speechless.

Malcolm changed to serious mode.

"Being more practical, and with a view to re-creating history, we could gather together an eminent group with the influence to establish a foundation which would raise funds to build a memorial to the Forgotten War. It should tell the factual tale of a blot on our history about which most Australians don't have a clue. Only then, as a nation, will we be able to come to terms with what has been a tragedy. It would then be a short step to embedding a meaningful reconciliation into our national life."

"When do we start?" responded Gough.

White Australia

"Let me cash in on the unanimity that you fellows have finally discovered," smiled Zelman. "May I try to continue this as we move on to White Australia as it bears a close relationship to our treatment of Aborigines."

After receiving nods of approval, Cowen moved on.

"It's fair to say that the policy of White Australia no longer exists in the laws of Australia except for one or two minor safeguards. Nevertheless, an attitude of wanting to continue to be a white nation still disturbingly pervades Australian Society and support for it appears to be growing once more, after it had appeared to be in decline for a time."

Fraser took up the issue.

"I hold the same view, Zelman. It is an indisputably unpleasant fact that too many Australians yearn in their hearts for White Australia to be re-enacted. They have an almost childish fear of migrants and refugees, particularly those from Asia, Africa and the Middle East. In truth, the blacker they are the more their presence is resented. People emotionally and mistakenly claim that migrants are taking jobs from 'genuine' Australians. There is no proof whatsoever that this ever happens.

"It's important for us to recall that when married women started joining the workforce after World War II, there was widespread hysteria that they would take the jobs that young people should have. This proved to be nonsense too.

"The same critics also say that the arrival of migrants drives up house prices by creating a shortage of housing stock when it is well known that rising prices for housing are caused by property speculators, not migrants.

"There is a similar panic mode that says that foreigners who come here blow out welfare budgets, even though most of those on the dole are lazy white Australians. The clear evidence that all of this is racist nonsense is shown by research into demography and economic history which reveals that ever since the arrival of the First Fleet, clearly and consistently for over two centuries, Australia has enjoyed a major burst of prosperity whenever we have had a large intake of migrants."

"Let me go further," said Gough. "History also proves that when people marry outside of their race and their religion, their children are likely to be of higher intelligence than in 'normal marriages'. Australia's future actually depends on us becoming the most multi-cultural nation on earth. This means that we will have become the most intelligent nation. It is clearly in the national interest to encourage more migrants and refugees to come here and marry outside of their culture and religion.

"Indeed, there are economists who claim that White Australia, in actual fact, retarded our economic development. Zelman, is there anything we can do constitutionally to stop White Australia ever raising its head again?"

Cowen thought deeply, knowing there was no satisfactory long-term answer.

"No, there is not. This is because White Australia was not defined in the Constitution in the first instance. It was created by subsequent Acts of Parliament.

"But, we could have a Preamble to the Constitution that says our policy as a nation is to be multicultural. We can discuss this again later."

State Rights

So, Cowen moved on, "This brings us to the power that the Founding Fathers gave to the states.

"I hold the firm view that Australia is paying dearly because of the costs involved in giving too much power to the states.

"As Malcolm has pointed out, having six different education systems causes enormous learning disruptions for children moving around Australia and a huge cost of needless administration and planning.

"The same applies to transport. Having different gauges for our railways has been an enormous tragedy. Even worse is that those railways all run towards state capitals instead of across state borders out in rural regions so they can trade with one another. This has severely hampered regional development."

Fraser took it up.

"I can comment likewise about health. If we had its services totally nationalised, incredible savings could be made in purchasing medical equipment and medicines and having uniform standards of medical training. As it is, we now have a stupid system that reveals to us the insanity of it all. When a New South Wales ambulance crosses the border into Victoria, the patient has to be put on a Victorian trolley or all insurance is void. The reverse also applies."

Cowen continued.

"The problem at the time of Federation was that the states held taxation powers and were wealthier than the Commonwealth which was given only the revenue from import and export tariffs as its financial base. Thus, the Commonwealth was not in a financial position to say it would take over education or health or transport. It simply had no money to do so.

"As we all know, when John Curtin was our war time Prime Minister, he demanded that the Commonwealth be given taxation power so he could finance our horrendously expensive involvement in the Second World War. A referendum was passed enabling this to occur and the Commonwealth insisted on retaining that power after the war.

"Now the Commonwealth gives funding to the states so they can keep providing services, but a full take-over is needed by the Commonwealth if truly efficient national services are to operate.

"A referendum based on considerable vision will be needed to do this and an insular parochial vote will be heavily against it."

"Well, let's put that on the list of referendums, said Malcolm, "but it will be a tough one to get through because the states simply won't cooperate. They will stoutly defend their increasingly irrelevant patch."

Gough would not be left out.

"The Australian States have been traditionally opposed to anything that is nationally progressive. It is embedded in their souls because, rather than advancing, they are steeped in the aim of reclaiming their past glories. They are hell-bent on circling their wagons around their internal empires and are not interested in nation building in any shape or form.

"In my mind, states are on the same very low rung as the Senate in their uselessness to the nation. In fact, the Senate and the states are inbred to the extent that they constantly attract too many little thinkers into their ranks who can't even work coffee machines in their offices."

The Brits

While he had the floor, Gough went on. Stirring the Brits to the depth of their souls was a pastime he occasionally enjoyed. It was time to enjoy it once more.

"And I am baffled as to why Barton agreed to Australia putting its naval defence under British control. They were not primarily interested in our security, then nor now. They just wanted Australia to be a base from which they could control the South Pacific and Indian Oceans. Even that was a somewhat tenuous commitment as we discovered forty years later when the British, for all intents and purposes, abandoned us at the Fall of Singapore. Thanks to John Curtin, we then took control of our defences without their permission and improved our position enormously. Had he not done so, the Japanese would have captured New Guinea and used it as a launch point to invade us."

Zelman responded, "I think you will find that the British told Barton that they could not pass the Australian Federation Bill through their Parliament at Westminster unless the British Navy became the Australian Navy also. To the British, their Navy was 100% of their total national pride. They sang 'Rule Britannia, Britannia rules the waves. Britons never, never, never shall be slaves'. Barton did not think that Federation should fail because of an issue he thought he could have further negotiations about at a later date when he would have a good chance of winning."

Malcolm added to the inept record of British colonial rule.

"When you look at the record of the British in Australia we have to make some sharp criticisms. They signed a Treaty in New Zealand in 1840 recognising the rights of Maoris but utterly failed to complete a similar treaty in Australia with Aborigines. That really was disgraceful negligence.

"Also, allowing each state to build railways that had different rail gauges was a hugely costly blunder. But, we prosper despite their legacy.

"Be this as it may, we can now make all the constitutional changes that we want without needing the Queen's approval. She is a figurehead only, but a revered one who has just one power. She can decline to approve our choice of Governor General."

So, it was that there was a unanimity of minds.

They affirmed that they would use whatever influence they had still retained to convince the Howard Government and its successors that they should bring about a wide range of constitutional changes that were now necessary after a century of Federation. A new era had arrived and they agreed that they should use it was possible to correct the anomalies they had just discussed so as to achieve racial and economic equality in Australia and enable a huge improvement in the cost and efficiency of community services by giving the Commonwealth more power to act on national matters.

Fraser volunteered to seek a meeting with the Prime Minister as soon as he could organise it to discuss what referendums he thought may have a chance of getting up and seek his advice on how to proceed.

It was time to have amendments to the Constitution placed at the top of the national agenda.

Coffee

In deference to their health, the three eminent Australians declined the temptation of dessert and settled for coffee.

Nevertheless, they added the luxury of an excellent Cognac that the Club Manager offered to them gratis. It would play a key role in keeping the conversation flowing in vibrant fashion. Gough had tactfully suggested to the Manager that Cognac was their liqueur of choice so long as he had a spare bottle that was of a quality above that to which the peasants may aspire. He informed the Manager that he knew with certainty that its influence had been a major factor in causing the French Revolution to break out and he was convinced that Australia needed something similar to happen.

In truth, he needed this revolt to occur as quickly as his advancing years would enable him to organise it.

The Former Chief Justice

There was a knock on the door.

Gough responded instantly.

"Enter all comrades who come in peace."

Sir Garfield Barwick appeared.

Gough's demeanour rapidly became far less peaceful.

The former Chief Justice had been a formidable political and personal foe for a long time.

Malcolm arose and swiftly walked forward to greet Barwick.

"What brings you to the club today, Garfield?"

"Dining with old friends. The Club Manager told me you were here, so I decided to drop by to convey New Year greetings."

Barwick moved forward to greet the others. Zelman first, then Gough.

Whitlam clearly was not enamoured with the prospect of having his despised adversary interrupt a luncheon which he was enjoying immensely. They had disliked one another for at least twenty years prior to the Kerr coup of 1975. Due to Barwick's involvement in that as a behind the scenes adviser to Kerr, Gough's attitude to Barwick had descended into the depths from which there was little hope of rising.

Taking a deep breath, the old warrior drew himself to his full height and greeted Barwick with cold courtesy.

"At last, we meet on neutral ground," he said with heavily strained politeness.

Barwick responded in a voice that conveyed goodwill.

"Gough, all of our future skirmishes will, you can be assured, be fought on neutral ground. As for today, I heard a whisper that you are celebrating the Centenary of Federation so I thought I would interrupt briefly and suggest that I share a toast with you to the Founding Fathers."

"We will happily share that privilege with you Garfield," responded Malcolm.

"Actually," said Gough, "we have been reviewing how the Kerr Coup which you helped to organise very nearly undid the work of the Founding Fathers."

"I am sure you are aware, Gough, that we will continue to disagree on that tenuous observation," was Barwick's sharp reply.

Zelman Cowen intervened, just as decisively, "I made two points in our earlier discussions here today Garfield. Malcolm and Gough will not mind if I repeat them.

"I stated my conviction that Kerr did have the reserve powers to dismiss Gough, but he should never have used those powers on the grounds that he did. The Founding Fathers gave the Senate the right to reject Money Bills, but never to deny a government the basic supply needed to operate."

Garfield was aghast that, even though he had been Australia's longest serving Chief Justice, the nation's most eminent constitutional lawyer was now questioning his judgement.

"Zelman, you were aware as I was, that we had an inoperable Parliament that was locked in a life and death struggle. Kerr had to do something at that very moment to resolve the impasse."

"True," agreed Zelman. "He should have used his reserve powers to ignore Gough's advice and dissolve both Houses of Parliament, then calling an election, with Gough remaining as Prime Minister. He should then have instructed Malcolm to allow Supply while this took place. After all, it was an election that Malcolm wanted to take place quickly, so he would have agreed."

Malcolm intervened respectfully.

"In hindsight, this would have been the better way to handle the situation, but we cannot overlook an obvious fact that I mentioned earlier in our luncheon discussion. Kerr was afraid that Gough would sack him. He got in first."

Barwick directed a pertinent question to Whitlam.

"Would you have sacked him if he had done what Zelman had suggested?"

"It would have been out of character for me not to have considered it seriously. Even so, I doubt that Her Majesty would have gone along with it. After all, I would only have had caretaker powers at that point so my options were limited."

Whitlam still held the floor.

"Your behaviour did you no honour, Garfield. As Chief Justice, you had no right to give advice to the Governor General without my knowledge. It was a clear breach of established protocol. Your actions may well have led to a legal challenge would have come before the Court of which you were Chief Justice and this would have severely compromised you. Your fellow Justice, Anthony Mason, would have been in a similar situation. I am very aware that he also gave advice to Kerr."

"I did not offer him advice that compromised me. He deliberately sought it from me because he had no faith in you."

"Well, I guess that the original blame lies with me," mused Gough. "I appointed the idiot in the first place. The most stupid thing I ever did in my life. Having said this, let me also say that I was never ever disrespectful of him. I gave him no concerns about his future. Nor did he ever offer me any advice on any matter as a Governor General has the right to do at any time. He was silent until the day of the coup. He did not ever raise with me the horrendous problem that I got into with that fake Iraq investor Khemlani."

Malcolm added a thought.

"Gough, a crucial factor that day was that I understood the psychology of Kerr far more clearly than you did. I knew that he would act decisively. You were certain that he would not."

Whitlam was indignant.

"For God's sake, Malcolm. I was his Prime Minister. I was not his psychiatrist."

Fraser went on somewhat mournfully.

"Now that we are able to look at it objectively after 25 years of collective political wisdom, it is fair to say that, in the hot political atmosphere of those heady days, we all did things that we probably should have done differently. The issue is this. How badly did we damage the Constitution?"

Gough waded in at full bore.

"We may or may not have actually damaged the Constitution but we did stretch its credibility. A situation was created where Parliament gave the Senate powers that it was never intended to have and we had a Governor General who allowed it to happen. As a direct result, it is now the most irresponsible body on earth and it is not even elected democratically."

Barwick was now firmly in denial mode.

"I don't believe that Kerr's action in 1975 had anything to do with that trend. The Senate had been flexing its muscles for a long time," he said with some indignation.

Gough would have none of it.

"You are romancing. The Senate overstepped the mark that day and has been further overstepping it ever since. As you did personally. When Kerr called you for legal advice, strict protocol demanded that you should have referred him to the Attorney General for whatever advice he needed.

"And may I say with all the goodwill I can muster that the Founding Fathers would never have invited you to dinner to seek your advice in the manner that Kerr did with you."

"My apologies," responded Barwick who had wanted quite genuinely to mend fences.

"I think it best that I should take my leave. As I do, can I leave you with a constructive thought. If ever a prime minister wants to hold a referendum to amend the Constitution so that it starkly defines the powers of the Senate, I will regard it as a privilege if I could be invited to join a team with the three of you to advise him on the best means of doing it."

"One moment," intervened Peacemaker Zelman Cowen.

"Before you go, let us take up your original suggestion and together toast the Founding Fathers. We owe our heritage to them. As we drink, let us declare peace among ourselves. A quarter of a century is far too long to bear grudges."

He found a spare wine glass in one of the cupboards and poured Barwick a liberal mouthful of Cognac.

"To the Founding Fathers.

Cheers."

Then handshakes.

Gough and Garfield even managed restrained smiles.

Barwick made a dignified departure, calling out as he left,

"My predecessor 'Slippery Sam' Griffith would have enjoyed being around in 1975. He had a special talent that enabled him to get involved in politics without ever appearing to do so. I could have appointed him as my mentor."

The temperature of the room lowered considerably.

Republic

The departure of Barwick enabled Zelman to steer the debate to the issue of Australia becoming a Republic as a prime step in constitutional reform.

"Can we ponder for a moment the history of the Republican Movement in Australia. The Eureka Stockade was the first significant attempt by colonial Australians to be rid of the British.

"On reflection, it is a tragedy that it failed. A victory out there at Ballarat would have sent a stark message to Westminster that Americans were not the only ones who could revolt. And there were solid reasons to revolt. Its success would have ushered in self-government for Victoria much sooner and would also have caused the persistent, brutal and unlawful persecution of the Irish in Victoria to cease. To describe their treatment as grossly inhuman is a huge understatement. It was an awful blot on Britain's colonial administration.

"Soon afterwards, the spirit of Eureka inspired Henry Parkes and John Dunmore Lang to begin a genuine Republican Movement in New South Wales. They were an unlikely combination.

"Parkes was a cunning old political rascal and Lang was a devout clergyman who was also a passionate reformer. They wanted their state to follow the example of the United States in leaving the British Empire as they greatly admired what the Americans had achieved against the superior fire power of the British. To their disappointment, their vision of a Republic of New South Wales gradually lost steam as the drive for Federation gathered momentum.

"Around the same time the continuity of British domination caused a significant number of Australians to leave our shores and start a new life in South America. They took up land in Paraguay and declared it to be the Republic that Britain had refused to grant them in Australia. They named it Utopia. It failed after a couple of decades because they could not agree on how Utopia should be governed.

"All of these republican sentiments considerably stirred the pot in London and gradually became a matter of watchful concern in both Whitehall and Westminster. The mandarins there were keeping a close eye on the situation. As a result, there was no way that Westminster would ever be disposed to give the Founding Fathers the right to make any provision in an Australian Constitution that would enable the creation of a Republic by any means whatsoever at any time in the future. This tells us that the British had learned nothing from their American debacle.

"This is an example of the typically indignant British hysteria that made them feel that civilization itself would collapse if the British Empire should fall away. This political blind spot is emphasised by the reality that, 47 years after the Australian Federation came into being, the British had to be dragged kicking and screaming to give India and Pakistan the right to cease being colonies and become Republics all in one enormous revolutionary initiative led by Mahatma Gandhi.

"They showed an extraordinary lack of any sense of understanding that the Indians and Pakistanis possessed fundamental human rights. In their blinkered view, Britons were the premier race of the world and the preservation of their status was a supreme priority. The Indian sub-continent was the Jewel of that Empire, the cornerstone of it. Unbelievably, the British believed that the 'primitive' people they had illegally ruled and constantly plundered for three and a half centuries were being deluded by mischief makers into thinking that there were no advantages in remaining part of the greatest Empire that humanity had ever witnessed."

Fraser politely interrupted.

"Zelman, in my time as Prime Minister, I took part in several Commonwealth Conferences. At the very first one that I attended, I soon became aware that more than half of the British Commonwealth of Nations had changed their Constitutions to become Republics. Nevertheless, it was quite obvious that they continued to have a great rapport with Queen Elizabeth and Prince Charles. Both are still invited to visit them regularly as revered mentors, especially Elizabeth whom they regard as a very special person. Which, of course, she is."

It was Whitlam's turn.

"Meanwhile, here in Australia, we continue to drag our feet in mortal fear of being left alone in a wicked world without being tied to Mother England's apron strings. This is incredible when all her upper crust privileges belong to an era that is now past. God will have let us down badly if He ever allows British class distinction to be reinstated. The connection was never worth having in the first place."

Cowen attempted to bring it all together.

"It's time we tried once more to take positive and carefully planned steps to make Australia a Republic while remaining within the British Commonwealth of Nations.

"This must happen despite the failed attempt that Malcolm Turnbull led back in 1999. It was lost for one reason only. The Republicans were split over the issue of whether the President should be elected by the people or the Parliament.

"Added to this was a fundamental weakness in the campaign itself. It was predominantly based around the powerful personality of Turnbull. He was utterly committed to the cause, but was cleverly out-manoeuvred by that crafty old politician John Howard when the drafting of the referendum questions was determined. Turnbull then failed to develop a large enough power base of influential community support that would gather the required votes. It was not a movement of the people. It was his movement.

"The opportunity that we now have is that once we vote to become a Republic, we will then be able to get serious about genuine reforms to the Senate and the power of the states. The success of the Republic will become a symbol for an aura of change that will gain momentum."

Gough added, "This time, we will need two separate referendums in order to make the creation of a Republic achievable.

"The first must be to give the Australian people the right to vote Yes or No on the principle of becoming a Republic while promising them that, if they vote Yes, there will be another referendum on how the President of the Republic will be chosen. Only if Yes prevails in the first referendum, will there be another vote on the matter.

"This second vote will be to decide whether the President shall be elected by a direct vote of the people or be appointed by a joint sitting of both Houses of Parliament. In each case, the exact wording of the changed clause in the Constitution must be printed on the ballot paper so there will be no need to have a third vote to approve the wording of the change."

All three sincerely and enthusiastically agreed that the advent of a Republic was desirable as soon as possible, although it became necessary for Malcolm to restrain Gough from launching into yet another tirade about what infidels all royalists were. For once, Gough took Malcolm's advice and stopped midstream. This was a rare event in Gough's life.

Zelman had a thought to add.

"At some point, we should investigate whether or not it is absolutely necessary to use the words Republic and President, which carry the image of radical change. It could be that all that is necessary is to remove all reference to the British Crown and retain the words Commonwealth and Governor General. It could make it all a lot simpler."

Malcolm continued the debate.

"We should certainly look at that idea, Zelman, but for the purposes of our debate today, could I raise another matter.

"What do we think personally about the election process to choose a President? Do we leave it to the Parliament to choose or do we let the people decide?"

All three expressed the view that it was best for Parliament to choose.

Gough made it clear that he was utterly opposed to even thinking about a president who was directly elected by the people, but Zelman summed it up best.

"I am an unshakeable believer in democracy and will always champion the voice of the people. But, in this case, if voters are given the right of choice, this will result in the election of a political president. To become the winning candidate, that person will have to be a very skilled politician.

"This will result in Australia having a president who believed that he or she had a mandate directly from the people to influence the affairs of the nation. This would place the President in a position of being in opposition to the mandate that the Prime Minister already will have been given.

"To be elected as President in a public ballot, all candidates would have no option but to make commitments as to what they will do for Australia when they become President. No one will be able to win by saying, 'I am a good guy, please elect me.' This direct election process would cause major political standoffs between the President and the Prime Minister. This will serve no good purpose."

Gough agreed.

"Every man and his dog will nominate to have a go at being President of Australia. We will have a voting paper that is a kilometre long. To stop this, there would be have to be strong qualifications that are required to be met before you can nominate."

"Well," responded Malcolm, "it may be wise to look at an improvement to the means whereby Parliament chooses the President.

"It may be a better idea to have a process whereby voters can nominate people whom they think would make a good President. There could be a requirement whereby a nominee must have the signatures of a minimum number of voters on a petition before his or her nomination could be placed before the Parliament for participation in their vote. There can be an added proviso that no Member or Senator can nominate a candidate from the floor of the Parliament without the prior backing of that same minimum number of signatures. This means that if the Prime Minister or any MP has anyone in mind to be President, he or she will have to collect the required signatures in the same manner as any voter is required to do."

"That could work, Malcolm," said Gough. "It means that politicians can only vote on those names submitted either by themselves or the people of Australia, each with the backing of a considerable number of voters. A figure of 25000 should suffice. Getting so many signatures would be a democratic achievement in itself."

Zelman added an extra safeguard, "To make the selection hurdles a lot higher, it can be declared that a two thirds majority at a joint sitting of both Houses of Parliament is needed for the President to be selected. This would make it exceptionally difficult for any political party to have its nominee elected without gaining bipartisan support."

All three went along positively with all of the above.

The prospect of it being achieved was quite appealing. The politics of it all were achievable given quality leadership from our Parliament.

Who Is Eligible to Sit in Parliament?

Zelman raised an interesting issue.

"I am of the opinion that many of the people who have been elected to Parliament since it was founded in 1901 have not been eligible to take their places.

"When the Founding Fathers wrote the constitution, they recorded in it that no one could be elected to Parliament if they had an allegiance to another nation.

"There was a simple reason for this. When the Constitutional Conventions were being held, they were all British citizens, living as they did in six British Colonies on the one continent. Because of this they wanted to achieve two goals.

"Firstly, they wanted all citizens to cease being British and become Australians. The initial step with this was to ensure that all Parliamentarians were required to do so.

"Secondly, they did not want any foreigners in the Parliament. However, they did not regard people of British descent who lived anywhere in the British Empire as being foreigners, unless they happened to be non-whites, such as aborigines. British citizens were family, but Germans, Dutch, French, Italians etc. were definitely beyond the ranks of family. So, if anyone came from a non-British nation, they were required to renounce their citizenship and become Australians if they wanted to run for Parliament.

"So, these aims were written into the Constitution. But, in practice thereafter, Parliament turned a blind eye to British people who did not become Australians and ignored the fact that a few foreigners who were good guys actually got elected.

"The most famous example of this was Chris Watson. He was born in Chile and educated in New Zealand, but he became our third Prime Minister without ever becoming an Australian citizen. He simply believed that he 'belonged'.

"Even more strange is that the strict wording of the Constitution has never been enforced. This has resulted in many people with dual citizenship having been elected to Parliament.

"One day, someone will make a huge political issue of this and the High Court may be called upon to dismiss some MP's and Senators."

Both Malcolm and Gough expressed surprise.

Gough responded first.

"It seems to me that the Constitution should be changed to say that anyone who holds an Australian Passport is eligible to election to Parliament."

"This is a sensibly simple solution, Gough," said Malcolm. "People who hold dual citizenship may be quite reluctant to give up their non-Australian passports. It is interesting that the United States insists that only those born in America can run for President. But they don't ask if they have, by birth, a right to be a citizen of another nation."

Zelman had the final word.

"Can I re-emphasise my point? One day some powerful people will be highly embarrassed by this constitutional requirement when their political enemies deliberately strive to catch them out."

Changing the Constitution

It was time to get other legal hurdles on to the table.

Zelman commented on the puzzling matter of the extraordinary difficulty that Australians have persistently had in approving referendums for any changes to the Constitution relating to any subject whatsoever.

"Only one fifth of all proposed Constitutional changes have been passed by voters over an entire century. There have been 19 referendums in which 44 proposals for change have been put before the Australian people and only 8 of those proposals achieved a successful result. 36 have failed. We need to pause for a moment to examine why this has been so. In moving towards the organisation of new Referendums, we must not repeat the mistakes of the past."

As usual, Gough had a solution.

"The predominant problem that has been encountered in bringing about constitutional change has been that most of the proposed amendments have been put forward either by governments or an elite group of politicians. Very few have ever had their genesis in the minds of activists out among the voting public where an effective community organisation has had a solid enough power base which could assemble sufficient numbers who would demand action on a referendum and effectively campaign to achieve it. There is not even a clear legal path set out in the constitution that enables people to request a referendum for change. There have been only one out of 44 proposals to my knowledge that actually had a private citizen as the figurehead who campaigned fervently for its adoption.

"We must remind ourselves that, a century ago, the concept of Federation was labouring heavily as the result of immense voter apathy until a patriot by the name of John Quick turned it into a citizen's movement at Corowa in 1893. It seems to me that, if we want to get anywhere with the winning of referendums, we must now start a powerful movement called something like Citizens for Constitutional Change that can be a major force for reform in the 21st century. There are a number of small groups in existence, but they have insufficient clout."

Fraser could not resist another playful slap on the wrists for Gough.

"The problem is that you and I are politicians, Gough, and we were controversial ones who have accumulated a fair degree of voter anger. We can't start such a movement. We will be blacklisted."

"Oh, my goodness, Malcolm, we are surely, at the very least, revered emeritus statesmen who abide as close to heaven as you can possibly get without being a clone of St Peter. Even so, I must humble myself for a short moment and take your point. We do carry accumulated baggage and we now have no alternative but to draft young Zelman into the job. He has managed to stay above politics for most of his life. Or at least he appears to have done so, but we can easily check this out by phoning a few Rabbis."

Zelman let Gough's remark go through to the 'Keeper' and had the last word on this challenging topic.

"I have for some time belonged to a group of eminent lawyers who meet regularly to discuss constitutional changes and consider the strategy that will be required to have them approved. But, we need to expand our endeavours beyond the realm of lawyers to involve other professions and community leaders. Our base for both thought and influence is far too narrow at the moment.

"While we are doing this, it is of interest to note that the first project our group is working on is to have Indigenous Australians clearly acknowledged at the very beginning of the Constitution as the original owners of the land, then move on to the creation of the Republic once more. As the three of us have already agreed, we really can't become a Republic without firstly fixing the terrible wrong we have inflicted on First Australians both in terms of their heritage and their humanity and their civil rights."

Malcolm and Gough cheered this with their last sip of Cognac.

Zelman went further.

"Whenever we think of Constitutional change, we must commence from the point where the Founding Fathers started. They revered Parliamentary Government and firmly believed that the British Crown represented the upholding of the law. They also believed that the power of the British Empire was important to maintaining the stability of the world.

"Many prime ministers were unshakeable in continuing that tradition. Fisher, Bruce and Lyons are examples of that frame of mind, but Menzies was the greatest. He was British to the bootheels.

"However, I think that most Australians do not now see the Britain as the cornerstone of the world. We believe that if we are ever threatened, it will be the United States that comes to save us. But, solid Parliamentary Government and the rule of law are still regarded as being fundamental to our future. All changes to the Constitution must reflect this."

Then, Malcolm chose to make a further observation.

"Agreed, Zelman. But, let us remember that most referendums have failed, not because the subject was unworthy or was a violation of the work of the Founding Fathers, but because opponents of change have always raised peripheral issues that muddied the water, confused the voters and put fear in their minds. Few have been rejected on their merits alone. These unfortunate political tactics will, regrettably, continue while people who have no qualifications other than political cunning are endorsed by political parties as their candidates.

"We can but weep. Even so, let's move on to the next agenda item that Zelman wants to test us with."

The Search for a Preamble

Cowen took up the invitation.

"John Howard has for some time been strongly advocating the sound idea that there should be a Preamble to the Constitution that sets out a philosophy for an Australian way of life. I think he will have more success if it is a code of values that most Australians can feel is an essential for our future as a nation. But, this will be hard to achieve. Nevertheless, if it is to be placed at the forefront of the Constitution, it must include a statement of Indigenous ownership."

Gough had a thought on it.

"John Dunmore Lang tried to prepare such a statement of our values 150 years ago, at the same time as he tried to make New South Wales a Republic. The problem he faced was that multiple religious groups fought bitterly over what their faithful members did or didn't or should believe. He could not find common ground even among his friends."

"Alfred Deakin tried also, with the help of a Tasmanian MLA and Clergyman named Bolton Stafford Bird. They hit the same hurdle," said Malcolm. "All of those efforts are clear evidence of democracy at its most painful worst."

"Does any record exist of the wording they suggested?" enquired Zelman.

"None that I know of," responded Malcolm.

Gough agreed.

Cowen suggested that they spend a few moments considering what the main elements of the wording of a preamble could be.

Whitlam was the first off the mark.

"Instead of recognising First Australians in the main body of the Constitution where it would create a number of subsequent legal difficulties, it will be more acceptable to voters to have them acknowledged in a Preamble, highlighted right in the opening line where no one can miss it. Their long history and culture, as well as their original ownership of the land, can be openly and honestly recorded as a powerful statement of fact."

It was Fraser's turn.

"No problems whatsoever with that, Gough. Let's move on from there to address the manner in which convicts have been forgotten. We must acknowledge the sweat and toil of those cruelly treated human beings. Without their compelling desire to get rid of them permanently, the British may never have decided to send settlers here. The nation of Australia would not exist but for a need for a faraway home for the small-time criminals of England who stole a bed or two."

Zelman next.

"Acknowledgement should be made of the fact that the first non-indigenous religion to be practiced here was Christianity. It was followed by the Jewish faith, then Muslims, Hindus and Buddhists. But, it must also be acknowledged that the first religion was aboriginal spirituality. This means that we can state that we are a religious nation that welcomes people of every faith as friends and neighbours."

Gough.

"This brings us then to race and culture. My understanding is there are now over 100 nationalities represented here in our nation. We must state emphatically that we are happily a multi-cultural society that welcomes all who come here with a clear intention to live in peace and will live out that intention.

"I recognise that some people don't like the word multicultural for a variety of odd reasons. Even so, the fact is that our country of Australia is a national family of all colours and creeds. Generally speaking, they seem to live side by side in harmony and at peace with one another while observing the basic principles of our Constitution. I can't think of a better description than multi-cultural unless someone comes up with words that describe our unique culture."

Malcolm.

"The matter of economic philosophy and practice now arises and cannot be excluded. Clearly, we must avoid words like capitalist, communist, socialist etc. However, it is imperative that we indicate that we foster a market place which operates on a basis of honesty, responsibility and justice on a level playing field where there is equality of opportunity and a constant striving to narrow the gap between rich and poor."

Gough again.

"It must finish with appropriate words about the quality of society. Community service, generosity and goodwill must be embedded as the basic assets of a good society that we strive to foster."

Zelman attempted to round it off.

"These thoughts are not a bad start. A talented word-smith is needed to work on knocking this into a concise collection of powerful words that will inspire the nation. We can all give some thought to possible writers and agree on the right person to come up with an initial draft. Then, we can get one of our eminent newspapers to foster a public debate on it even though we may well hit the same brick wall as Bird and Deakin."

As could be anticipated, Gough had the last word.

"Ah, comrades, I think it is approaching the time for all of us to acknowledge our age and retire to a well-deserved afternoon nap. May I say thank you for sharing a wonderful luncheon with me. Our discussion on a noble preamble to our Constitution is a fine way to conclude our vibrant encounter.

"God bless Australia and its Founding Fathers. They gave us a fine platform from which a great nation has been able to emerge to an honoured position of world leadership."

Farewell

They prepared to go their separate ways.

There was agreement that they should continue their dialogue by dining together from time to time for a convivial lunch over which they would report progress on their individual efforts to advance Australia and then plan to keep kicking more goals for a progressive nation while they all had life and strength.

Zelman Cowen had some parting words to which his friends warmly applauded.

"There are many things wrong with Australia, but there is much more that is right about it.

"What is certain is that we have advanced a long way from the brutal convict colony that was our tragic starting point, and the suppression of Aborigines that was an inevitable subsequence of the culture of colonial aggression. That unsavoury beginning has, for a long time, maintained a powerful influence over our state of mind in reflecting why we are Australians. We have gone to extremes to cover it up.

"I am sure that the three of us will agree that, as a nation, we have an opportunity to bring about the reforms that will make us a model example of enlightened government for the whole world to follow. We will all want to help start the ball rolling in the right direction before our days are done. With some sense of urgency and with genuine humility, we will acknowledge that to do anything less will be a betrayal of our national heritage which is now very different from its British origins. We are clearly a nation which has been moulded by many cultures, growing more so every day, and becoming a more mature society as a result."

Gough felt a need to add appropriate words.

"Our days are nowhere near done, Zelman. We can proceed carefully more so than rushing. I was born into a family with genes that reek of longevity and immortality which means that I have youth on my side and I express the hope that both of you will enjoy similar assets of ageing."

Malcolm decided to enter a game of one-upmanship.

"One of my goals in life is to live longer than you, Gough. I value our newly found friendship but my soul savours one final sweet victory."

"Bless you, comrade, bless you. But, let not your heart be troubled if you fail to achieve this goal."

With those well-meaning words, Gough Whitlam lead the way to the front door of the club.

As they walked down the grand staircase, Gough paused and whispered quietly to Malcolm.

"Give my love to Tamie, I hold her in the greatest affection."

"I can instantly convey to you her heartfelt reply. It will be that she responds with the same affection. She regards you as a trusted confidant, grateful for the wise counsel and pragmatic help that you gave us when we were hit personally by the disaster that struck our investment in Lloyds of London."

Zelman managed to hear the whispers and felt a warm glow. Politics had not totally degraded the virtue of human affection.

The Historian

As they walked towards the door of the club, Manning Clark strolled through it.

The great historian greeted them warmly.

"Why are you all leaving just as I am arriving? We should toast the New Year."

Malcolm chastised him for not appearing earlier.

"We could have used your presence and your talent for words in a debate we have had about our nation's Founding Fathers and the modern relevance of the Constitution they drew up and that has survived for a century."

Clark clearly looked disappointed.

"You absolutely needed me there. The Founding Fathers were determined visionaries who had all the flaws of humanity at large, but they pulled off a wonderful achievement. Quite unparalleled in the colonial history of the planet. They even contrived to ignore aborigines and got away with it at the time. If they tried it right now they would be crucified."

Gough decided to turn on some theatrics about Barwick.

"We just toasted the New Year with former Chief Justice Barwick and I chastised him, somewhat gently, for his unsavoury relationship with Governor General Kerr of fond memory."

"You only chastised him. Goodness me, Gough, you are becoming quite benign in your old age. Just a few years back, you would have murdered him."

"Ah," lamented Gough, "further evidence of my many human frailties?"

"Did you accuse him once more of being involved in a plot by the American CIA to get rid of you? I actually did some historical research on that possibility when you originally accused him of it. To my profound disappointment, I could not find any hard evidence. Just a flow of quite logical rumours, but then nothing more than rumours. It was all based on a dinner Barwick had attended in America that was hosted by the CIA Director when he was Minister of Foreign Affairs before he was appointed to the High Court. He did maintain some friendships in that area as the result of that dinner, but it appears to have all been quite honourable and of little subsequent value."

"With some considerable restraint, I thought better of raising it today," mused Gough, "but I am certain that, in a couple of thousand years, some learned archaeologists will dig up a canister with computer data inside it that proves me right. It will become as famous a discovery as the Dead Sea Scrolls."

"That's what we might loosely refer to an historical fantasy, Gough, interesting and highly readable, but fascinatingly unlikely. However, this reminds me to remind you that many judges in the history of Australia have strayed from the paths of righteousness far too often.

"Let's take the revered Founding Father, Samuel Griffith, as a prime example. He openly campaigned in favour of a Yes vote in the Queensland Referendum on Federation just over a century ago. His fellow judges advised him against it and his Premier did likewise. But, he went ahead anyway. The cunning old bastard was actually campaigning for the job as the nation's first Chief Justice. He got there, so I suppose that the end justifies the means."

Malcolm had the last word, waving away Gough's intended retort.

"Interesting thoughts Manning especially as Barwick did comment on Griffith as he was leaving. But, we really must go. Zelman and I have planes to catch and Gough is craving for an afternoon nap.

"You know I really should be volubly angry with you because you ardently backed Gough when I staged my coup in 1975. I lie awake at night worrying about what you will write about it when you pen your version of the history of that epic day."

"Had no other option, Malcolm. You and Kerr broke the law, but you won so, again, the end justifies the means. The important thing at the end of the day is that you and Gough are now on friendly terms. This means you have risen in stature. Travel safely."

"Thank you," replied Zelman.

"Can I ask you as an historian how you think that your successors as historians will view the Founding Fathers a century from now?"

"Most historians get more critical about people and events with the passing of time and the discovery of more evidence of past history, but I have the feeling that the Barton team will continue to get a genuine tick of approval. And that will be well deserved.

"They were the right men in the right place at the right time."

"And what of the Dismissal of 1975?"

"This is interesting. Kerr will never be forgotten, nor forgiven. His stupid coup has gained himself a permanent place in history that he does not even remotely deserve. Had the political deadlock of 1975 not occurred, he would have served out his term of office and then been quickly forgotten. He had been a very ordinary person and a totally inadequate Governor General.

"Because of the coup, he will be talked about forever. Ned Kelly has been treated in the same way. He becomes a greater hero of the oppressed Irish as the years pass. In another century, he may well be listed a saint.

Shalom."

Homeward Bound

Ponsonby

Gough had arranged for a Commonwealth car to be waiting for him outside the club in Macquarie Street ready to drive him to his home and his beloved Margaret.

Such a car was a lifetime entitlement of former prime ministers, much more upmarket and speedier than the horse drawn carriages provided for the Founding Fathers.

His plan was to rest for a while before he and Margaret hosted their family for a New Year's Day barbecue dinner. There, he would enjoy himself immensely as he held forth on the state of the world while displaying what he constantly touted as being his great skills as a gourmet cook. His stature in this regard was still a matter of unresolved family debate.

His regular driver was a middle-aged Englishman who had migrated to Australia only in the last few years with a plan to settle in, understand Australia and gain new friends before spending his retirement years in this fair land.

Because he was an Englishman, Gough had nicknamed him Ponsonby without ever asking him what his name actually was.

"Ponsonby, old chap, as a loyal Pom who has absolutely and unquestionably loyal devotion to the British Crown, what will be your personal reaction when Australia becomes a Republic. Will you run home to Old Blighty cursing the infidels who brought about this outrage? Will you stand outside Buckingham Palace waving a flag every morning or will you stay here to witness the former glory of the British Empire slowly fritter away?"

"Firstly, Mr Whitlam, I will be most disappointed if this happens, but I won't weep and wail and mourn. Australia and England are many kilometres apart at the opposite ends of the earth, so it is inevitable that time will cause the bonds to gradually weaken until they exist no more.

"At the same time, I assume that the trading links that Australia has forged with India, China, Japan and Indonesia will grow steadily as the years pass. Most likely, it will be a new world out here, quite foreign to all I love about England, but I will have to adapt to it or I will back myself into an unfortunate corner where my final years will be unhappy ones.

"Nevertheless, I will continue to talk of and treasure the basic values of old England that I grew up with and still cherish so that everyone around me will be quietly reminded of the proud heritage from which I came."

"Ponsonby, my fine comrade, that fine speech has been quite Churchillian. You have stirred me to fight on the beaches as I foster among my fellow Australians an attitude of national pride similar to the one you have just displayed to me. Well done, old chap. I solemnly pledge never to call you a bloody Pommy whinger ever again."

Gough dozed off with peace in his soul while Ponsonby loyally conveyed him safely home with the traditional reliability of one of the Queen's men.

Old Soldiers Never Die

Malcolm and Zelman shared a Commonwealth car to Sydney Airport for their late afternoon flights home to Melbourne. Governor generals, like prime ministers, past and present, have an entitlement to the privilege of free chauffeur-driven vehicles to any reasonable destination.

Malcolm commented on what an interesting, amiable and productive lunch it had been and what delightful form Gough had been in.

"He is ageing in a most benign fashion and his entertainment value is enormous. It is true to say that, with the exception of the comments he will forever make about John Kerr, his wit is now directed at creating goodwill rather than the old rapier-like aggression for which he was famous, often infamous."

Zelman was in agreement that this was a pleasant description of the atmosphere that had abounded, then added,

"While we make our way to the airport, can we continue our crusade as reformers the way that old soldiers are supposed to do. I would like to take up the matter of referendums again?

"We need to amend the constitution to set out a clearer pathway for rank and file Australians to be able to petition the parliament to call a referendum on issues that meet criteria for legitimate changes. Right now, this power lies with the Parliament alone.

"I am certain that a referendum on changing the constitution to enable citizens to do this will easily win a nationwide vote. This action will have a side benefit. It will encourage people to put forward constitutional changes rather than just complain about a lack of democracy."

There was a murmur of approval from Malcolm as he added, "Agreed, Zelman. Well, worth putting on our bucket list."

Cowen continued, "Now, can I return to the huge challenges relating to Aborigines whom we are now encouraged to describe as First Australians. As an aside, can I comment that the Oxford Dictionary describes an aboriginal as 'having lived in a place since earliest known times'. This definition describes the situation precisely whereas the British Government only decided in 1824 to call the continent Australia and its residents only became Australians at Federation in 1901. Prior to that they were Victorians or Tasmanians etc. This means that the title of First Australians is not quite accurate. They deserve a title not inflicted on them by the British. Be this as it may, there are some related matters that I would like to discuss."

And Fraser responded, "Certainly. If you had not raised it, I was planning to."

Zelman took a deep breath.

"Can we go back to the earliest days of the arrival of Aborigines on this continent? The Founding Fathers did not have any knowledge that indigenous people arrived here from Asia 65000 years ago. Back in 1901, anthropologists had not yet reached a point in their science where they could accurately pinpoint the era when it happened. They just knew that it was a long time ago.

"There was no appreciation then of how long it took for those immigrants to gradually cover the whole continent and then cross Bass Strait to populate Tasmania at a time when the sea level was much lower than it is now.

"The indisputable fact is that, when James Cook arrived in 1770, he could not find any buildings and presumed that it was unoccupied except for a few nomadic people who gave the appearance of being quite primitive. When Arthur Phillip arrived two centuries ago, he had no intention of occupying the entire continent.

"As we discussed at lunch, his commission from King George was to establish a penal settlement and occupy enough of the region around Botany Bay to make it self-sustaining. About one percent of the continent would have provided sufficient space in his view. When he sailed for home, he had no idea that his settlement would expand much further than this and deprive aborigines of the pastures that were their finest and most plentiful food sources.

"Matters just slowly evolved and encroachment became persistent. So, the Founding Fathers inherited a problem that was not of their own making so they had solved the issue by ignoring it. Aborigines were left out of the Constitution. We now know that Federation would not have happened had an attempt been made to include them as citizens in the new nation. The Constitution would have been voted down by a huge margin.

"So, where do we go from here? You and Gough and I and influential friends must work persistently to have our indigenous citizens recognised in the Constitution a century after they should have been. It is almost inevitable that a future prime minister will be compelled to take it up and get it approved by the people, so we must now lay the foundations of it.

"However, constitutional recognition will not be enough. It is about one tenth of the issues involved in integrating white and black Australians into a great society. Aborigines want more than this as do many non-indigenous Australians. We are now at a time in our history when we have to make rapid progress that will lead to the achievement of the remaining 90% of the task."

"Zelman, you have highlighted an issue which is a gaping sore in the life of Australia since Arthur Phillip arrived at Botany Bay. We have treated Aborigines as sub human since that awesome day in 1788 when the First Fleet made landfall. Then we made the totally irrational mistake of trying to buy their souls with money as this made us feel better about the way we had mistreated them. This appalling naïve strategy has failed miserably, which it was always destined to do. It is now a matter of constantly nagging controversy and I share the guilt for this as I was a fellow traveller who perpetuated this deplorable policy when I was Prime Minister.

"But, the question is this. What can we do about it in a way that will enable us to implement a gradual change of heart over as many years as it takes so that we can bring as many of the population as possible along the path together? We must not seek any short-term solutions that are not just another way of kicking the can down the road."

Zelman had a view on this.

"After achieving the first step of constitutional recognition, we could then seek to agree on a Treaty, not unlike New Zealand's Treaty of Waitangi, that recognises joint ownership of the continent without any financial or material compensation being involved whatsoever. It must just be stated as a fact of history and a recognition of honesty.

"What such a Treaty can agree upon is to have a merger of the finest traditions and beliefs of both cultures and heritages. This will then open the door to economic and social partnerships that will enable joint ventures to occur in a wide range of projects that are not only the ideas of Whites but will create employment, education, recreation and a perpetuation of both indigenous and western culture. There must be no attempt to turn aborigines into white men or to make whites feel permanently guilty."

"Your vision is worth pursuing, Zelman. In retrospect, it is regrettable that it was not done at the same time as New Zealand signed its treaty with Maoris in 1840. Knowing how successful that was, the British Government should have moved immediately to achieve exactly the same Treaty here. It was a huge blunder, but they made many, like allowing states to have different railway gauges. They were not a top-quality colonial administration. Far from it. Nevertheless, it is reasonable to assume that the French, Spanish and Dutch would have been worse.

"This brings us to the unavoidable question, who is the leader to bring this all about right now?"

"Malcolm, I lie awake at night seeking an answer to this question as, without the slightest shadow of a doubt, changes as momentous as this will come into being only if an extraordinary leader can be found from beyond the ranks of current politicians who must be willing to take an enormous amount of flak before a satisfactory result is achieved," lamented Zelman.

Fraser raised a possible solution that could evoke a fair degree of controversy.

"Strange as this solution may seem to be, coming from an old Liberal Party Prime Minister who was a considerable political enemy of Paul Keating, may I suggest that the solution is to appoint someone of the calibre of Keating to make it happen, if not Keating himself. For all his faults, as well as his penchant to get a lot of people offside, he was an achiever with a vision of considerable magnitude in taking on controversial challenges. He loved battles against all that is traditional.

"In this instance, I am reminded of the magnificent vision he expressed when delivering his famous Redfern speech, perhaps the best ever made by an Australian Prime Minister about the relationship of the nation to its Aborigines."

"Your suggestion is controversial, Malcolm, but it is worth pursuing. Perhaps we can ask him to lead a team of younger Australians who have varying cultural backgrounds and who have a spirit of revolution in their souls and a sharing of the incredible passion with which he approaches issues that he believes in. He can be their chief mentor and motivator while they choose an involve the right person as their new leader.

"However, before enlisting this young team into such a fine intergenerational partnership, the first task will be to find an aborigine of stature who is of similar mind to Keating, or his alternate, who would join the team and play a leading role. This will be a tough task as there are fine aboriginal leaders out there, but, usually, they are not universally loved by their own people for tribal reasons and will have a battle to be accepted as their spokesperson. But, the right person must be found."

"Where then can we start?" enquired Malcolm. "I guess that the right point for a beginning would be to chat with the Prime Minister as I already plan to do on other matters, and move on from there as nothing can really happen in Australia unless the Prime Minister of the day takes it up. I am fairly certain that John Howard will express the view that, as Aborigines are Australian citizens, it may not be legally possible to acknowledge them in a Treaty as this would give them a status which is different to other Australians. It will be a valid comment for him to make. I will seek his advice on how to overcome this hurdle through a legitimate variation of a Treaty.

"I will call you to let you know how I get on. We can then chat about what our next step will be. However, we must not let this important matter drift. If John Howard indicates that he does not want to take it up or is reluctant to involve Keating, or anyone similar to Keating, then we will have a major problem to resolve. We will best handle it by getting together to start our thinking processes again."

Zelman had a suggestion.

"Another starting point could be to meet with leaders of the Jewish community. I am certain that they will want to become involved. They feel that aborigines are now suffering the same persecution as they have experienced worldwide for at least 2000 years. They have a burning passion to remove injustice."

Malcolm had a final thought that could cause some alarm among those who still crave for a White Australia.

"I hold the view that justice will not be done for Indigenous Australians until we acknowledge that the Founding Father was, in genuine fact, not Edmund Barton, nor Arthur Phillip, nor James Cook, but Mungo Man. Anthropologists track him back 40,000 years. Until someone finds an earlier one, he has the greatest right the title of Founding Father."

Life Was Not Meant to Be Easy

"That's life," was Zelman's intended parting comment. "It is all about starting again. As you so famously said, 'Life was not meant to be easy' and it isn't."

This just stimulated another response from Malcolm.

"It is interesting that you say this, Zelman. That sentence was not an original thought of mine although I would be honoured to claim that it was. In that particular speech, I was actually quoting Arnold Toynbee. He said that, throughout history, all nations have been confronted by a never-ending series of challenges. Whether they survive or fall by the wayside depends on the manner and character of their response. In his view, life would never ever be easy. I simply agreed with his viewpoint. It is utterly correct."

"You know, Malcolm, I am baffled by the fact that voters always expect their governments to protect them from the inevitable challenges that life will always throw at us, irrespective of who holds power at Parliament. So, they get angry when their politicians don't see those challenges coming and they vote them out in a brutally unceremonious fashion."

"Just proves Arnold Toynbee's point, Zelman. There is a general decline in respect for politicians and it has become a sport to punish them.

"Emphatically, this means that life is not meant to be easy now and will get less easy as time marches on."

"Your comment," said Zelman, "highlights another thought in mind that adds to the thought that your life has never been easy.

"At the time in time when Kerr sacked Gough, it is fair to say that many Australians felt that Gough thoroughly deserved his treatment because they felt that he had grown to be public enemy number one.

"But, as the years have relentlessly passed, Gough became a legend and most got to believe that he had been badly treated.

"This being so, you were elevated in the public mind as much more of a bad boy than Gough because many were disenchanted and disappointed by your years as prime minister.

"Gough has quietly revelled in this. He is of the view that history will prove that you had actually done him a favour by staging his spectacular downfall."

"Correct again, Zelman. You have defined the situation with words that bear a solid ring of truth. More people will attend Gough's funeral than will turn up at mine."

The Anonymous Barton

After yet again expressing goodwill and gratitude for the day they had enjoyed, Malcolm and Zelman parted at Sydney Airport with anticipation that their twilight years may achieve some worthwhile goals. Clear in their minds was the thought that these goals were not just worthwhile, they had an air of urgency about them.

They were travelling on different airlines and went to the private lounges that were made available to distinguished travellers.

Gough was already asleep at home.

Together, they had done some constructive planning and it is highly possible that the Founding Fathers would have given a tick of approval for their good intentions.

History records that the three of them did valiantly attempt to use whatever influence they had in their final years to improve the Australian Constitution despite the fact that they were very aware that their effective political clout no longer existed, even though they held a not inconsiderable amount of community respect and goodwill.

Nevertheless, they intended to leave a clear trail for others to follow as the destiny of Australia is a work in continual progress.

Their concern was that those Australians who have read of the life and times of Edmund Barton may well say that we now, lamentably, lack a leader of his stature. This view of a dearth of leadership will be shared by an ever-growing number of Australians who have never heard of Barton, but are unconsciously seeking someone like him.

Even so, they knew that any unbiased, but critical review of his life at any point during the century or more after Federation, would determine that the judgement of history will be that Barton was the right choice to lead the momentous times in which he lived. In the same manner, Mungo Man was most probably the right pioneer for his time.

It was beyond argument that Barton had an acutely sensitive constitutional brain and superb negotiating skills that brought warring parties together to make decisions. Significantly and fortunately, he had an understated determination to get the results that he achieved in a manner that was quiet, but unstoppable. That he managed to gather all of the Founding Fathers at the starting gate for the deadline of 1 January, 1901, with only a day to spare, was nothing short of a miracle.

It is a national disgrace that so few Australians even know his name and have no evident desire to find out. He remains an anonymous giant who led a rare breed of nation builders who may never become legendary household names.

A century later, the three wise men who had honoured him at their luncheon held no doubts that somewhere, somehow, his successor will step forward to change the course of the nation's history.

She will be warmly welcomed.

Book Three
Epilogue

The Challenge

119 years have passed since the momentous days of 1901 when the Australian nation was born with enormous hope and enthusiasm.

Any reading of the history of nations across the entire planet reveals that the creation of Australia and its subsequent record of progressive government, must be rated high on the ladder of notable political achievements of international significance.

The huge question now is this.

Where does Australia go from here in a world that is changed daily by the rapid advance of technology, reformations in ideology and religion, plus the impact on the economy and social structure of a rapidly ageing population that will cause huge adjustments to be made in the way that Australians live and move and have their being?

It will be obvious to most unbiased observers that three key challenges to our nation lie ahead of us.

They must be faced and achieved as they are unavoidable.

One is constitutional change – constant and often and enlightened.

Another is the creation of an economic and social fabric that is based on equality of opportunity. It must give every Australian the chance to enjoy a good life. This will involve reducing the huge financial and social gap between rich and poor, thereby providing everyone with a reasonable chance of achieving their aspirations. It should be possible for this to be done in a way which will gain sustainable peace and prosperity for the maximum number of Australians who face challenging situations every day.

The third is the development of a compassionate society where the old Aussie concept of mateship, which flourished at the time of Federation, is revived, reviewed and upgraded. In the pioneering years, Australia was one of the most caring nation on earth. We can achieve this stature again by fostering genuine community partnerships in which even the poorest and most humble can make a contribution to society even if it ranks with the widow's mite.

All three are worth a huge input of skills, energy and commitment to which every Australian can and should have the opportunity to make their mark.

As Mark Twain once uttered memorably, "There comes a time when every person has to ask themselves a simple basic question, Why am I here?"

This leads us to consider what, in later life, was the fate of the ten Founding Fathers who were gracious enough to attend my dreamtime dinner and take us on a fascinating walk through the birth of a nation?

They didn't fade away, but their greatest days had been those when they played their magnificent role of making a Federation of Australian States actually happen. Nevertheless, their twilight years were intriguing and so it is worth a few moments to take a look at their paths to eternity during which most of them continued to make an impact on the nation.

They are listed in alphabetical order so as not to display any favouritism.

This choice of listing quite naturally ensures that Australia's first Prime Minister and Founding Father heads the list, an honour that is utterly appropriate and valiantly earned.

Barton

Served as a Justice of the High Court of Australia for seventeen years after he resigned as Prime Minister in 1903 until his death in 1920. He was very disappointed that he was not appointed Chief Justice when Griffith died in 1919, but, Prime Minister Billy Hughes, who had been elected to the First Parliament of 1901 as a Labour MP and a regular critic of Barton's performance at that time, made a political choice by appointing Sir Adrian Knox from outside the Court. Objectively, it could have been Barton's age and declining health that were the deciding factors in not offering him this prestigious honour. In hindsight, this was wise, because he would have served for less than a year as the leader of the Court.

He goes down in history as the only Prime Minister of Australia ever to be appointed as a Justice of the High Court.

More importantly, history will never overlook the fact that he was the prime leader of a group of incredible equals in the quest for Federation, addressing over 300 meetings covering all states to ensure Yes votes in all the referendums. He chaired the debate on 286 proposed amendments to the Constitution at the final Convention, then led the delegation to London to gain approval from the Imperial Parliament to create a nation.

He followed this by successfully leading Australia's first Parliament where its government had to proceed into unchartered waters every day as they established all of the legislative procedures that were needed to have a Parliament that actually worked and produced results. This incredible work still provides the basis on which the Australian Parliament operates effectively to this day.

Some historians rate the contribution to Federation of Griffith and Deakin as having been far more important than that of Barton. But, this would be a huge misreading of history. Deakin and Griffith were giants of our history who were visionary motivators and essential members of the Federation team, but Barton was the one who negotiated all the fine details with so many difficult and pedantic people whose votes were vital. He made it all possible.

A major defect of his personal life was that he was an appalling organiser of the finances of his own family and spent much of his life struggling to pay his bills (not unlike Henry Parkes). On a couple of occasions, his friends had to 'pass around the hat' to keep him afloat. He did not ever overcome this lack of financial discipline and, at his death, he left his wife, Jeannie, in a difficult financial position which she overcame with frugality and dignity.

Despite this strange character flaw in such a talented person, many accolades were bestowed upon him throughout his public life and these softened the embarrassment of his financial distress and his failure to be appointed as Chief Justice of the High Court of Australia.

He received Honorary Doctorates from both Oxford and Cambridge Universities, a dual honour that has been bestowed upon few as most have received accolades from just one of those illustrious academic institutions, but rarely from both.

Twelve prestigious London Clubs granted him Honorary Memberships. No other Australian has ever achieved this quite stunning honour.

King Edward VII made him a Knight of the Realm and he was appointed to membership of the Privy Council in London, the ultimate law-making body of the Empire at the time.

Around the same period, the Emperor of Japan appointed him to the Order of the Rising Sun, as a sign of goodwill between nations.

The Pope granted him a personal and private audience, as well as an engraved medallion as a memento of the occasion, the first ever given to an Australian Prime Minister. This provoked 30,000 bigoted Australian Protestants to sign a petition of protest that scurrilously attacked him and declared him to be a papist, an act that would appal most Christians today. Indeed, such a petition would now barely get a single signature.

He died at Medlow Bath, west of Sydney, just short of his 71st birthday, and was buried at South Head Cemetery after a State Service in St Andrews Cathedral in Sydney. He was survived by his beloved Jeannie, four sons and two daughters.

Chief Justice Sir Adrian Knox said of him, "It has been given to few men to inspire as he did."

Well said.

Bird

Maintained his long involvement in the politics of Tasmania, remaining a Member of its Legislative Council, including a term as Leader of the Opposition, until 1923, one year prior to his death on Bruny Island, just south of Hobart.

In 1920, he was awarded a CMG by His Majesty, King George V, for his outstanding services to Australia, particularly through his staunch advocacy of Federation and his committed contribution to Tasmania in politics and religion.

He remained a revered Congregational Minister until the end of his days, his thoughtful sermons always drawing a full house.

He did not ever retreat from his dream of having the Constitution that included a Preamble which set out a code of ethics and values as a cornerstone of the nation's reason for being. Sadly, and to his great disappointment, his sincere entreaties evoked little action from the leaders of the nation. It was always put in the 'too hard' basket.

It would have delighted him to know that John Howard seriously raised the matter during his term as Prime Minister a century later. He suffered the same fate as Bird and Deakin had done.

It remains a work in progress. If it ever happens, it will be a lasting memorial to Bolton Stafford Bird, a fine and decent man.

Deakin

By the time of the 1911 Dinner, Deakin's parliamentary career and his political power were already in decline. He was well aware of it personally, but did not ever acknowledge it publicly.

When his third prime ministership ended in 1910, he steadily grew weary of his subsequent role as Leader of the Opposition to the point where it began to bore him. His lack of power frustrated him and so he resigned from Parliament with huge regret, but positive memories, in 1913.

His health then deteriorated steadily, with his memory declining at greater speed than his body. Dementia set in and progressively began to diminish his talented ability to negotiate and deprive him of his formidable skills as a public speaker.

He died at his South Yarra home in October, 1919, only a few months apart from the passing of Griffith and Barton. He was only 63. His wife, Pattie, and three daughters survived him. It had been a long and happy marriage. The strength of his family had been a powerful element of his life.

Many historians rate him as the finest orator ever to grace the Australian Parliament, ranking him ahead of master speechmakers such as Menzies and Whitlam. They are most probably correct in making this assessment, giants though both Whitlam and Menzies were.

Given this huge talent, it is of interest to note that among his private papers that were read after his death, he noted that whenever he made an important speech his heart beat rapidly, his throat became extraordinarily dry and his hands shook.

He is buried at the St Kilda Cemetery with a humble tombstone that simply records his name and the date of his death. There is no mention that he was Prime Minister of Australia. Yet, on the day of his funeral, crowds packed both sides of the streets all the way from the Melbourne CBD to St Kilda Cemetery. It was along this road that he rode his bicycle to Parliament and back on every day that it was sitting.

There is much that is not recorded about him.

One important fact is that Queen Victoria awarded him a knighthood at age 30 which he declined. King Edward V11 offered him a place on the Privy Council, the greatest honour that can be granted to a lawyer and he declined that too. His life had been based around achievements, not accolades, so he remained the Honourable Alfred Deakin. This described him well.

His frugal lifestyle is another. Of the three delegates to the Federation negotiations at Westminster in 1900, Deakin refunded half of his allocated travel allowance. Barton and Kingston overspent theirs and had to be paid supplements.

Australia did not forget him.

In Melbourne, one of Australia's finest universities is named after him, as is a Federal Electorate and a suburb of Canberra.

What is absolutely extraordinary is that the modern Liberal Party regards him as their founder even though they now disown what can be defined as his left-wing ideology, when in reality it simply was common sense. It may be timely in political terms, if they narrow the gap between their current ideology and that of the great man who was their Founding Father. He was, by any objective viewpoint, a progressive conservative with a huge social conscience.

He had other skills that all parliamentarians of whatever political colour could follow.

He was a superb negotiator whose talents caused many controversial Bills to gain passage through the Parliament. He also had a guile that enabled him to sniff the political breezes and head off crises before they got wind in their sails.

Indeed, his life story should be made compulsory reading for every political candidate who runs for a place in any Parliament.

An interesting sidepiece to his journey through life is that, throughout his time in Federal Parliament, even when he was Prime Minister, he wrote regular, highly acclaimed articles for a London newspaper, *The Morning Post*, using an assumed name. To prove to himself that he was a genuinely objective journalist, he quite often criticised his own government, but privately regarded this as part of his thinking processes in trying to be a better servant of the people. None of his parliamentary colleagues were aware of this until after his death.

He was an ardent spiritualist for all of his life and so it is worthy of note that he died still holding the firm view that his personal power came from a source beyond himself. He spent his lifetime on a search to more fully understand the depths and limits of that power and passionately harness it. This spiritual journey was the vibrant element that made his life such an extraordinary success. It was the driving force that placed him on a level above others.

Bolton Stafford Bird and Deakin were closer spiritually than critics of religion could ever have imagined. Bird identified his spiritual power as God. To Deakin, it was a Great Spirit without whose presence he was an inadequate person.

This is emphasised in the Deakin diaries which he maintained in detail throughout his life. In them, various historians have found comments such as,

O God, show me the way.

O God, give me the strength.

My duties are not beyond my desire or aspiration but, without God, are beyond my capacity.

This tells us is that it cannot be denied that *Affable Alfred* was a most extraordinary person whose name will forever rank among the greatest of Australians.

Fisher

Like Deakin, he was Prime Minister three times, gaining a well-earned reputation as a reformer.

History particularly remembers him for the key words of his speech when, during his third term as Prime Minister in August of 1914, he declared that because Britain was at war with Germany, Australia was automatically at war with them also. Historians never cease reminding us of his words, "We will defend Britain to the last man and the last shilling."

After finally losing office in 1915, as the result of a coup by Billy Hughes, he became High Commissioner to London.

Shortly after his arrival, he was invited to pay an official visit to the land of his birth, Scotland. There he received a hero's welcome. They lauded him as a young Scottish lad who started work in one of their coal mines at the age of 10 and rose from the grime and poverty of those primitive mines to reach great heights by being elected as Prime Minister of one of Britain's finest Dominions. They also noted that he had been Secretary of one of their local miners' unions at age 17, the youngest ever in the history of Scottish mining, obviously, a future leader.

His term in London ceased abruptly when he disagreed with Prime Minister Hughes over Australia's strategy at the 1919 Versailles Peace Conference just after the end of World War I. He believed that, in the long term, nothing would be gained by hammering Germany into oblivion. Subsequent history proved that he was correct.

This was an unsatisfactory and disappointing end to a great career which began when he was elected to the Queensland Parliament in 1893, then moving to the Federal Parliament in 1901.

The people of Western Australia particularly remembered him fondly when, in his first term as Prime Minister, he was responsible for authorising the construction of the Transcontinental Railway across the Nullarbor which transformed their ability to travel to and trade with the other states. He persistently kept its construction on schedule, while John Forrest was his strongest ally in achieving its completion.

After a brief return to Australia in 1921, and a failed attempt to be endorsed by his party for a return to Federal Parliament, he finally accepted that his days in politics were over.

Dispirited, he returned to Britain in 1922. There, he purchased a home in London and lived in that city until his death in 1928.

Like Deakin, he had severe dementia and spent his final years sitting in a chair and staring at a wall, almost totally unaware of his surroundings and the company of those who loved him. His wife, Margaret, with whom he had six children, tenderly cared for him with extraordinary devotion.

It was a tragic finale for a man who was an inspiring example of what a human being can achieve if he or she has the willpower to overcome the horrendous obstacles of poverty and reach for the stars.

This quiet, honest, warm-hearted man was buried at Hampstead Cemetery in London and, at his funeral, the eulogy declared him to be 'honest and trustworthy, with great wit, oratory and a brilliant mind'.

In 1930, Ramsey Macdonald, the first Labour Prime Minister of Britain, unveiled a granite obelisk above his grave. Overcome with emotion, he declared that Fisher had been a great servant of the British Empire and a statesman far more than a prime minister.

An electorate of the Federal Parliament is named after him.

All pensioners in Australia should remember with gratitude both him and Deakin as the founders of the Age Pension. Although in different parties, they joined together in a bipartisan alliance to ensure that the Pension was implemented in 1908 and continues to this day.

Forrest

A proud son of upright Scottish immigrants, he should have been chosen as Prime Minister in 1912 when Joseph Cook dramatically and surprisingly defeated him by a single vote for the leadership of his Party. He had confidently expected the support of Alfred Deakin who, unexpectedly, changed his mind at the last minute. Seven years later, he unsuccessfully challenged Billy Hughes for the leadership, thus ending his cherished dream of becoming Prime Minister of Australia.

On each occasion, he lost mainly because of personality issues. He had very little sense of humour and had a frequent tendency to brow beat his political opponents in debate. He also didn't look the part. He weighed 120 kilos.

He died in September, 1918, on a cruise liner off the coast of Africa on his way to London for specialist treatment for a brain tumour which Australian doctors had told him was terminal.

Another purpose of his London visit was to be installed into the House of Lords as Lord Forrest of Bunbury, an honour that was announced by the King before Forrest's illness became known.

He was buried in Sierra Leone, but his body was, eventually, brought back to Australia for burial in Perth.

The Forrest pioneering legacy lives on.

His great grand-nephew is the noted Pilbara iron ore miner and philanthropist, Andrew 'Twiggy' Forrest.

He died unaware that a powerful movement was being organised for his beloved Western Australia to secede from the Commonwealth of Australia. In the mind of the perpetrators, Eastern Australia was blatantly ignoring them. It took them a long time to get organised, but a referendum was finally held in 1933. After a bitter campaign, it was soundly defeated, thus vindicating Forrest's original decision to back Federation in the days when he was the state's first Premier.

He has footnotes in history other than for politics.

During the years prior to Western Australia becoming a self-governing colony, he led a search party from Perth looking for the lost explorer Ludwig Leichardt who was thought to have died in the far north-western deserts of Western Australia. Like all other search parties for Leichardt, who had set out from Brisbane to cross the continent, he failed to find any trace of him.

He was also the first explorer to cross the Nullarbor from west to east, following the same route that Edward John Eyre had done in the reverse direction thirty years earlier. Whereas Eyre had almost perished, Forrest arrived in good shape. In honour of this journey, the tiny village of Forrest on the trans-continental railway is so named because he had camped there for a few days' rest.

The Lord Forrest Hotel in Bunbury, the largest hotel in town, has many photographs of him on its walls. Bunbury was the electorate he represented in both the State and Federal Parliaments during his entire career in politics.

Many Western Australians regard him as the finest politician in their history but it can be argued that John Curtin, Australia's Prime Minister in the Second World War, and the only Western Australian ever to become Prime Minister of Australia deserves this honour.

Griffith

The distinguished lawyer continued to serve the nation as Chief Justice of Australia until a few months before his death at 'Merthyr', his splendid Brisbane home named after his birthplace in Wales, in 1919.

He had served sixteen years in that high office during much of which he was in declining health, but stubbornly refused to make way for Barton who faithfully covered for him whenever he was unable to attend to his duties at the Court, which was often.

During his term at the High Court, he made several visits to London to sit on the Privy Council and on all of those journeys, he would visit Italy, a nation with a history and culture that fascinated him. He had first visited there in his student days.

He was Premier of Queensland twice during the period from 1883 to 1893, then Chief Justice of the Queensland Supreme Court, a position he held for a decade.

He created controversy when he openly campaigned for a Yes vote in Queensland's Federation Referendum. Many felt that as Chief Justice he should have remained neutral. Others accused him of campaigning because he wanted to be made Chief Justice of the soon to be established High Court and felt that he must earn the position by creating goodwill among the leaders of Federation. Available evidence suggests that they were correct.

He also continued to expand the legend of 'Slippery Sam', being instrumental in ensuring that Barton did not succeed him as Chief Justice. He always held an almost childish jealousy of Barton's popularity with the average

Aussie, and even tried, but failed, to stop Barton being made Acting Chief Justice during his many absences.

He was born in Wales in 1845, the son of a Congregational Minister, and was knighted twice by Queen Victoria who admitted him to two different Royal Orders.

He is buried in Brisbane's Toowong Cemetery.

A fine university in Brisbane bears his name as does a Federal Electorate in Queensland and a suburb in Canberra.

The Australian Constitution is his permanent memorial as he had an enormous influence on its preparation and, during his time as Chief Justice, he stoutly defended the principle of State Rights that he had enshrined in it in his efforts to protect his home State of Queensland. Many criticised him for his stance, but he was unwavering in his defence of it, arguing that his attitude would change only when a referendum was approved that changed the Constitution.

In actual fact, he frequently advocated that the existing states should break up into smaller ones.

Kingston

(For the sole purpose of having Kingston attend the dinner of the Founding Fathers, I have taken a huge liberty by choosing to ignore the fact that he died suddenly of a stroke in 1908. As he was such a giant of Federation, he could not be left out of the story. This caused me to make the difficult decision that it was an absolute necessity to have him present at Barton's dinner at the Melbourne Club. I have taken the same liberty with David Syme of the Melbourne Age who died in the same year.)

Always a figure of continuous controversy because of his determined support of all causes that were revolutionary or would be certain to shock the establishment, Kingston was a powerful and decisive leader who was a radical liberal in the most extreme sense of the word, having little tolerance of conservatives.

He will always be remembered in Australian folklore as the first Australian State Premier to legislate for women to have the right to vote, actually second in the world to New Zealand. He also was the first to pass legislation to allow them to stand as candidates in parliamentary elections, actions that shocked those of British heritage who intensely despised suffragettes.

His private life at the time was anything but private, being regarded as quite scandalous, although future generations would probably have turned a blind eye to it.

His wife, Lucy, became an invalid early in their married life and encouraged him to father a son with another woman and then adopted the son. Kingston took this extraordinary act of marital approval as giving him permanent authority to continue to father children in this manner. He is officially known to have fathered six illegitimate children and there was considerable suspicion that he actually fathered more, but he did a superb job of covering up the evidence.

For this infamous record, he was permanently ostracised by Adelaide's 'high society' who did not ever try to conceal their contempt for him. Nevertheless, he did not ever try to hide his contempt for them either. What was even more mind boggling, was that the 'ordinary' voters of South Australia kept re-electing him with larger majorities to the absolute astonishment of his political rivals. To this day, no one can explain how this political aberration occurred.

Queen Victoria offered him a knighthood in 1897 which he declined, much to the distress of his invalid wife who by that time had also become highly eccentric. He refused because he totally despised the aristocracy of England. By accepting the honour that the Queen had offered, it would have meant that he had to fraternise with the upper crust of society, a prospect that he utterly detested.

In an extraordinary event, over a century later in 2008, two people obtained a court order to have Kingston's body exhumed in order to prove that they were descendants of his illegitimate children. The DNA findings were not published and the matter was dropped. One can only wonder why anyone bothered to take such an extreme action as the matter was of little public interest and there were no financial inheritances to contest. He did not die a wealthy man. Perhaps it is a tribute to Kingston's place in Australia's history that people still want to prove that they are related to him.

He has been buried twice at the West Terrace Cemetery in Adelaide.

Lucy survived him, but she was physically and mentally ill for the remainder of her days.

The sporting community will be pleased to note that he was one of a small group of pioneers who founded Australian Rules Football in South Australia. So, it is important for the Adelaide Crows and Port Adelaide to claim to be part of the family of one of the founders of the nation.

Lyne

Despite contesting the leadership of his Party several times, he failed, like Forrest to achieve his goal of having the honour of being Prime Minister of Australia. The closest he ever came to achieving it was when Hopetoun tried to give it to him on a platter in 1901.

His constant rejection by his political colleagues appeared to be the result of him ceaselessly playing personal politics so as to gain titles rather than achieve actual results by legislating good policy. It did not help that he was by nature narrow-minded and parochial, generally failing to see the big picture. Nevertheless, he overcame those political impediments to be regarded as a giant of New South Wales and Australian politics for thirty years and deserved the knighthood he received in 1900.

He had led an interesting life.

Born in Tasmania and living at Ross in its Central Highlands for twenty years, he moved to North Queensland which had been described to him as the frontier where fortunes could be made. He quickly came to the opinion that it was not and so he returned south to take up land near Albury in New South Wales before acquiring more land at Goulburn.

He consistently opposed Federation, even though he represented New South Wales at the 1897 Constitutional Convention. He believed that Federation would downgrade both the prosperity and stature of his great state, but readily accepted Barton's offer to become Minister for Home Affairs in the first Government. It was a step up the promotional ladder.

In this role, he sponsored and passed the legislation which enabled women to vote in Federal Elections. His colleagues were warm in their praise as were most of the female population of Australia. Lyne regarded it as his political epitaph.

His highest office thereafter was to become Treasurer. For baffling reasons, Deakin chose to take him to London as Australia's second delegate to the Colonial Conference there in 1907. No one could really understand why, given that they were bitter political opponents. Perhaps Deakin made an attempt to mend fences at that moment, but it did not last.

Lyne continued to make it obvious that he was more a politician than a statesman and was resistant to changing his rigid views of life. He finally had a massive fallout with Deakin who called him 'a crude, sleek, blundering, short-sighted, backblocks politician'. This is hardly an ideal character reference to impress historians.

Nevertheless, he was a typical Australian bushman with a great sense of mateship for those who lived in the bush. Especially, he was noted for his personal generosity to good causes, particularly the downtrodden. To his friends, this virtue always seemed to be totally out of character.

He married twice and died at his city home at Double Bay in Sydney in 1913, a few months after losing his seat in Federal Parliament at a General Election.

He is buried at South Head Cemetery, not far from Barton's grave. Some say that they rest uneasily together.

The Federal Electorate of Lyne, based around Taree in New South Wales, is named in his honour, as is the Canberra suburb of Lyneham.

He had gone within an ace of having a place in history as Australia's first leader.

Reid

Deciding that he had no realistic prospect of becoming Prime Minister for a second time, London beckoned George Reid. So, he left Parliament to accept appointment as Australian High Commissioner there until he was replaced by Fisher. He served with distinction as an astute diplomat, a great host and a superb raconteur, becoming a celebrated identity on the social circuit.

(He actually took up his appointment in 1910, but, for the purpose of including him in this book, I have delayed his departure so he could attend the dinner.)

After Fisher's arrival as his replacement, he made a decision to remain on in London as he was enjoying his life there immensely. As a British Australian, he was eligible to run for a seat in the British Parliament and so he immediately sought election to the House of Commons at Westminster and won, holding his seat for several terms and becoming a figure of considerable influence around the Parliament. It was a fitting conclusion to a colourful career in politics.

He had the distinction of being the only person in the history of Australia to have won election to three Parliaments – State, Federal and British.

He had been a powerhouse in the NSW Parliament before Federation, rising to be one of its most famous Premiers. His greatest political sin was that he played political games with Federation for far too long for the simple reason that he used the issue to undermine his political opponents, especially Henry Parkes, usually focusing on totally unrelated issues in doing so. His position on Federation changed so many times that he earned the title of 'Yes/No Reid' but, when the final crunch came in the second Referendum, he made sure that it was won. Had he taken the reverse decision; Federation would not have taken place at that time.

Some historians say that his attitude to Federation was irresponsible. He would say that he handled the politics of the day quite astutely so as to gain as many other benefits as possible for New South Wales at the same time as achieving Federation. In fact, it is reasonable to state that it was his political actions in 1897 that renewed the serious involvement of New South Wales in negotiations for Federation.

The nation noted him fondly for his huge moustache, his excessively corpulent frame and for his irrepressibly dry humour, a talent which this book has endeavoured to convey.

The fondest memory of him is his famous, often quoted, confrontation with a humorous interjector during an election campaign rally.

Noting Reid's substantial gut, the voter called out, "What are you going to call it, George?"

Reid's instant response was, "If it is a girl, I will name her Victoria after our beloved Queen. If it is a boy, I will name it after myself. If, as I suspect, it's all piss and wind, I will name it after you."

Watson

Outlived them all by surviving until 1941.

After his very short term of four months as Prime Minister in 1904, his political power gradually declined and he was soon replaced by Fisher as leader of the Labor Party. His career was then somewhat dormant until he left Parliament in 1910, but he remained very active in the Trade Union movement, then, and after.

At the same time, he commenced a new life as a company director.

One of the companies that he joined was the major oil company, Ampol, for which he became Chairman. Others were the National Roads and Motorists Association (NRMA), Yellow Cabs and the Sydney Cricket Ground Trust.

He wanted to have a foot in three camps – Business, Unions and Politics – so he could be a positive agent to bring them together in developing Australia.

After leaving Parliament, he continued to be elected as a delegate to ALP Conferences, but was expelled from the Party in 1916 for actively campaigning in favour of conscription for the Great War. His firm belief was that those who had volunteered for war service must be backed by their fellow countrymen to the fullest extent. The Labor Party was, quite trenchantly, of the opposite view. They dispensed the supreme political punishment upon him for voting according to his conscience.

His political assassin within the ALP was Billy Hughes who also despatched Andrew Fisher.

At his funeral, two of his pall bearers were former Prime Ministers, Sir Joseph Cook and John Curtin from opposite sides of Parliament.

At that time, and for the first time in its history, the Federal Labor Caucus passed a motion of condolence and regret, a fine tribute to a man whom they had callously removed from their ranks. They had the good grace to refer to him as a capable and dignified man who had strength of character and sound judgement.

Watson had already scored another first.

He had the distinction of being the only Prime Minister of Australia to have been born in South America. His parents had lived in Chile for some years before migrating to New Zealand and then coming to settle in Australia.

Astonishingly, he did not ever become an Australian citizen.

Some now claim that this made him ineligible to become prime minister and that this fact should belatedly be recorded in a posthumous censure motion.

They were absolutely correct about his ineligibility, but, 115 years later, no sensible parliamentarian could care less about it.

So, we move on.

But, before we do, there is one more to be honourably remembered. A grand lady who must never be forgotten.

Lucinda

She sailed into legend almost by accident but it cannot be denied that she changed the course of Australian Colonial History.

If only she had ears, she could have disclosed to the nation some of the heated conversations between Barton, Griffith and Kingston as they robustly drafted the first version of the Australian Constitution.

Alas, like too many extraordinary females, *Lucinda* had a sad fate.

She was beached on Bishop Island at the mouth of the Brisbane River in 1937, after having served for years as a coal freighter on the Bremer River at Ipswich, a severe comedown from her glory days as a passenger ship of quality used only by the upper crust of the Queensland political establishment.

So, we find that 44 years after she gave birth to the Australian Constitution, she was in service no more. She is now covered over forever by mud and rocks dumped there for the expansion of the Port of Brisbane.

The good news is that she is not totally lost.

Her bar, and some of the panelling of her saloon, are on display at Parliament House, Brisbane. Someone with a great sense of history and honour performed a gallant act in saving something to perpetuate the memory a beautiful soulmate of Australia before her life ended.

Now, we must not forget the trio who dined in 2001.

The twilight years of those three reviewers of the sensational events of November, 1975, also make an intriguing footmark to history.

Cowen

Declined a second term as Governor General, having achieved his aim of calming and uniting the nation after the Kerr debacle had torn Australia apart.

Labor Party MPs and senators, who had refused to have anything to do with the Governor General while Kerr held that office, all returned to the fold when Cowen arrived on the scene. He held their deep respect throughout his term of office and, with gratitude, they called him The Healer.

Already a knight of the realm before he became Governor General, he then re-entered the world of academia as Provost of Oriel College at Oxford where, among other things, he raised a significant sum of money to restore the ancient college that had fallen into disrepair. He had a very natural talent for fund raising, having proved his skill early in his career when he was Dean of the Law School at Melbourne University. There he raised a major sum to endow and expand the school as the finest and most progressive in Australia.

While in England, he also served as Deputy Chancellor of Oxford University and Chairman of the British Press Council.

Returning to Australia some years later, he became Chairman of Fairfax Newspapers. He accepted this invitation from Conrad Black, its owner. Black was a former graduate of Oriel College who, to Cowen's great embarrassment, subsequently fell from grace and served a term in gaol in Canada.

Zelman also undertook many civic roles, including a substantial input into the Republican Movement, the founding of the University of the Sunshine Coast and the establishment of a Law School at Griffith University, honouring the Founding Father whose knowledge of the law and whose stature as a Judge he greatly respected.

He passed away in Melbourne in 2015, ending a distinguished career of public service.

An enormous crowd attended his funeral at the Melbourne Synagogue.

A distinguished life well lived and fondly remembered.

Fraser

After his crushing defeat at the hands of Bob Hawke in the election of 1983, Fraser gradually severed his links with his conservative political world. Eventually, he was asked to resign from the Liberal Party and he did so expressing the belief that it had moved so far to the right that it no longer upheld the Liberal philosophy of its founder, Sir Robert Menzies.

He found a new life as an activist for humanitarian causes that were left of centre. More accurately, his social conscience grew as he aged.

Unfortunately, he is most likely to be remembered as a tragic figure of Australian history.

He did not ever overcome his intense feelings of guilt over the very dishonourable removal of Whitlam. Had he patiently waited just six months until a legitimate election would have been called at the scheduled end of the parliamentary term, he would have won it decisively and borne no feelings of illegitimacy.

He suffered politically also from his desire to recreate the glory days of the Australia of yesterday that had been created by his idol, Menzies, who was his role model as a genuine Liberal. This dream was never realised and, as the Liberal Party moves further to the right, it won't ever be.

He died in 2016 a few years after tragically losing his beloved rural home 'Nareen', in Western Victoria.

This was caused by a collapse in his financial position as a Lloyds Name, i.e., a guarantor of Lloyds of London, an ancient and venerable financial institution that went through very dark days of mismanagement and destroyed the lives of many fine people worldwide who did not ever remotely consider the possibility that Lloyds could ever possibly fail. Most of the world believed it to have as secure a financial status as the Bank of England.

He did not deserve this tragedy. Magnificently, when it did happen Gough Whitlam was one of his closest counsellors and staunchest defenders. Fraser's wife, Tamie, in particular, hugely appreciated this.

In community life, he served with a deep commitment for many years as Chairman of the not for profit foreign aid agency, Care Australia. He especially worked with them in Africa, a continent in which he had immense personal interest that grew out of the leadership role that he undertook in gaining independence for Zimbabwe during his term as Prime Minister. He profoundly regretted that his action let loose a monster called Mugabe.

The words of his famous speech constantly rang true throughout his own life.
Life was not meant to be easy.

Whitlam

After leaving Parliament, he devoted a few years to the task of being Australia's Representative at UNESCO in Paris.

He had had enough of Australian politics after two massive election defeats at the hands of Malcolm Fraser, and, after a close involvement in many social and civic institutions beyond Parliament, he almost made it to his century dying just a few months short of it.

At his funeral in 2016, people who had previously reviled him so viciously when he was Prime Minister now gave emotional eulogies, declaring him to have been a visionary who was born before his time and lamenting that they had mistakenly ignored his talents to the detriment of Australia.

Whitlam was one of those who benefited from the long battle that Chris Watson had fought to have the Labor Party embrace talented people beyond Trade Unions. Gough was never a Trade Union man.

He was a brilliant lawyer and it was something of a miracle that he gained ascendency over so many union powerbrokers to make his way to the top job in the land. The truth is that he despised many of them for their lack of education and managed to consistently and unwisely convey this view to them. This meant that his support base was quite fragile among party members when he most needed their support during his darkest days.

He was Prime Minister for only three years. but they were momentous ones. Also of note is the fact that he was Parliamentary Leader of the ALP for more than eleven years, their longest serving leader in their century old history.

Medicare, which is now a central element of the health of Australian society, was his brainchild and it was only his superhuman efforts, combined with the relentless commitment of Bill Hayden, that saw it approved by Parliament. The Conservative Coalition who stridently opposed him, declared it to be based on communist ideology. Voters today find that ideological position to be quite incredibly stupid. Any political leader who now tries to diminish Medicare in any way will be mercilessly crucified at the polls by voters of both left and right.

He also gained parliamentary approval for historic legislation to grant women equal pay for equal work. The same Conservative Opposition that denigrated Medicare screamed again, even more loudly. They declared that this disgraceful legislation demeaned the males of the nation and would inevitably encourage irresponsible mothers to desert their families to chase lucrative jobs, thereby destroying the very fabric of a society that heavily favoured males. Their grossly immature stand is now considered by 99% of Australian women to be a supreme insult.

His dismissal by John Kerr will remain forever in Australian Legend. Vale Gough.

Barwick and Clark

(As I did with Charles Kingston and David Syme at the 1911 Dinner, I have taken a further liberty with Garfield Barwick and Manning Clark at the 2001 Luncheon. They died in the decade prior to that event, but their eminence in the history of the era gave me a compelling reason to include them both.)

Manning Clark's six volume History of Australia has had a powerful influence on the way in which the nation thinks of itself and his prolific writings have always been a source of huge controversy.

It is important for him to have a role in this book as he is regarded as one of Australia's finest historians and was a passionately vocal backer of Whitlam when Kerr struck his mortal political blow.

Garfield Barwick's long term as Chief Justice equalled the achievement on Sir Samuel Griffith a half century earlier.

Prior to that he had been elected as a Member of Federal Parliament and was appointed as Minister for External Affairs with extensive experience in dealing with the British Government. Thus, he was doubly qualified to take part in a discussion about the Constitution.

More importantly, without his backing, Kerr may not have had the courage to move on Whitlam.

These were remarkable men who left an indelible mark on Australia.

Giants of History

All of the thirteen legends who were the prime guests at either the dinner or the luncheon were giants of Australian history. Despite all their human frailties, they deserve our profound gratitude and respect.

We can proudly rank them high on a list of the elite of Australia's greatest sons.

In doing so, it will be wise to recall what Charles de Gaulle once said when asked what would happen to France when he died.

"Graveyards are filled with indispensable people."

Book Four
End Notes

Followers of the Founding Fathers

No worthwhile book has ever been written by an author working alone.

One of the joys of writing is the pleasure of having friends who become involved in your quest for excellence and contribute to its fulfilment through research and advice. You treasure the invaluable partnerships you form with them.

So, my first thoughts are my gratitude to good friends whom Australians, at the time of Federation, would have referred to as 'mates'.

Like me, they are believers in the cause of the Founding Fathers and are pleased to be involved in the pleasant task of informing modern Australians of the incredible tale of their nation building.

Graham Freudenberg, was the speech writer for Gough Whitlam for his entire time as Leader of the Opposition, then Prime Minister, then Opposition Leader again. His input has been invaluable, particularly as he is a long-time student of the Australian Constitution. He spent many hours reviewing and amending a draft of this book and more hours at two long and fascinating lunches in in which he gave me background information about the legend of Gough Whitlam and the impact of the Founding Fathers on his political career. Graham's personal history as a speechwriter for Arthur Calwell and later Bob Carr added to his immense knowledge of political history. He has added immense credibility to this book.

Graham's brother, Rex, a long standing and valued friend of mine who served with me on the Board of National Seniors Australia for a quarter of a century, introduced me to Graham and joined in our fascinating discussions. This was valuable as he is poles apart politically from his brother and he made sure that this book did not ever stray too far to the left of centre.

John Herron certainly gave the book a conservative tone. He was a Senator in the Howard Government who served as Minister for Aboriginal Affairs, then Ambassador to the Vatican. He discussed with me at length the coverage that the book gives to Indigenous issues and the powers the Founding Fathers gave to the Senate. As a devout Christian of the Roman Catholic Faith, he helped also with the wording of a Preamble that I have included in the closing pages of this book.

Significantly, he reviewed the book with **John Howard** who expressed in a personal letter to me his very clear views on the events of 1975. Howard believes that Whitlam and Fraser were the two most at fault on that infamous day, much more so than Kerr. He also pointed out the pitfalls that will be created by an Indigenous Treaty, opinions that I greatly value and took into account.

Then I moved to the left to talk with another old friend, **Stephen Loosley**, former ALP Senator for New South Wales and now a lawyer in private practice from which base he has become a very successful author of political books. His experience of politics in and out of Parliament is immense. He too has clear views on the coup of 1975, its aftermath, and the issues of Senate powers, as well as the saga of how the Founding Fathers went about creating Federation in 1901.

Ian Walker is a former ember of the Queensland Parliament and Minister in the Newman Government, having been Senior Partner in a major law firm in Brisbane before entering Parliament. Our friendship goes back a long way and he was very frank with me about issues relating to State Rights and on constitutional changes that may be necessary regarding the powers of the Senate and the creation of a Republic.

Greg Cary, a legend of Brisbane Radio, has been an enormous help. He and I chatted on air every week for more than a decade and, for this book, I sought his aid on the issues that concern 'the man in the street' about how Australia is governed and what should be done about it. Over the decades that he was on air, he interviewed countless politicians from Prime Ministers downward and expressed his views on their attitudes to all that the Founding Fathers stood for.

John Harrison of the School of Journalism at the University of Queensland encouraged me to write this book and directed me to much relevant background material, particularly as to the historic events that occurred on the *Lucinda*. He had previously helped me wholeheartedly when I first contemplated writing a book about Flynn of the Inland that I successfully published under the title of *The Man on the Twenty Dollar Notes*. In both cases, he has been a huge mentor on the art of writing and our friendship is something that I greatly value.

Ian Taylor, a retired minister of the Uniting Church in Australia, who was ordained sixty years ago, is another valued friend and ardent student of history. Above all he is a superb editor of books who has gone to great lengths to keep me on the straight and narrow with my use of the English language. Most of his ministry has been in remote regions of Australia and the Pacific Islands and he gave me a vivid account of how people in those distant places feel left out of the political processes, something that he wants future governments to do something about.

Alan Jebb and **Andrew Norton** are fellow members with me at the Aspley Uniting Church. They originally came to Australia as migrants who knew little about how Australia is governed. They accepted my invitation to read this book and ask questions about issues that puzzled them. This enabled me to fill in many gaps in the logic of the story. Both have been superbly constructive critics and their contribution has made this book for more interesting to non-political readers.

Books on the Founding Fathers

As you would expect, I enjoyed a lot of reading about the Founding Fathers and the three wise men who were part of their legacy.

Most of it came via the endless resources of Google but I particularly relished the books that have been published about the Founding Fathers, sparse though they are in number. I find it astounding that historians have ignored them to the extent that there is a great scarcity of documents that tell the Federation story from start to finish.

While I have been careful not to quote directly from any of them, let me acknowledge their fine work,

Biographies of Edmund Barton by **John Reynolds** and **Geoffrey Bolton**.

J A La Nouse book on Alfred Deakin and the splendid book by **Judith Brett** which she has called *The Enigmatic Mr Deakin*. It was written in 2019.

The biography of Samuel Griffith by **Roger Joyce**.

A really splendid account of the life of Andrew Fisher by **David Day**.

The sympathetic description of the short time in power of John Christian Watson that was written by **Ross Fitzgerald** that he called *So Great a Travesty* and a biography of John Forrest by **Frank Cowley**.

Graham Freudenberg wrote a masterly book, A Certain Grandeur, as his personal account of Gough Whitlam's time as Prime Minister.

Zelman Cowen's autobiography, *A Public Life*.

Michelle Grattan's book on Australia's Prime Ministers.

There could be more, but I have been unable to locate them.

It is unfortunate that Federation has been so undervalued by generations of writers, a fact that encouraged me to write this book.

Chats with the Greats

Fortunately, down the years, I have enjoyed personal contact with the trio whose luncheon is a significant factor of this book. Many of my comments reflect views they expressed to me.

A Great Australian

Zelman Cowen is one of the most valued friends of my life. It was an honour and a privilege for me to have worked with him in the organisation of fund-raising campaigns at the University of Queensland and at Oriel College, Oxford, as well as spending valuable hours together bringing community projects to fruition in Australia and England.

Two pages of his memoirs are devoted to describing our work as a team. I treasure those pages, as I do our many conversations while I was a guest in his home. They focussed on the strengths and weaknesses of the Australian Constitution and the politics that it has generated for more than a century.

Added to this are his strong views on the constitutional impact of the Great Dismissal of 1975 and his profound thoughts on the opportunities and responsibilities of being an Australian.

He was a very proud citizen of our land, a huge intellect, a superb legal brain and one who had very few peers in knowledge and understanding of the constitutional history of Australia.

Most of the issues that are discussed at the Centenary Luncheon at the Australian Club are based on recollections that I treasure of many long and fascinating discussions that we had on memorable occasions spent together in Brisbane, Melbourne, London and Oxford.

Many of the comments that I have made about Whitlam and Fraser have their source in his recollection of them. He was particularly fascinated by the colourful language that emanated from Whitlam. His thoughts on this are reflected in some of the flamboyant turns of phrase that I have attributed to Gough.

Giant

I met Gough Whitlam on a number of occasions, one of them being a luncheon at the Lodge during his term as prime minister when I was fund raising consultant to his project to build John Curtin House in Canberra.

Another was at Charles de Gaulle Airport in Paris during his time at UNESCO. We spoke at length while were waiting in the lounge to take flights to different destinations.

On another of our chance encounters, I spoke with him about a visit I had made to the New Hebrides when it was transferring from colonial rule to the founding of the new nation of Vanuatu. I had assisted the Presbyterian Church there to gain financial independence from its counterparts in Australia and New Zealand instead of continuing to be a missionary outpost. To my astonishment, he phoned me a few weeks later to talk about a plan that he was proposing to suggest to the new Prime Minister of Vanuatu, Walter Lini, on how he could overcome the constitutional problems caused by his nation having been a joint French British Colony for a long time.

He had a highly active and substantial brain, an incredible wit and a delightfully colourful means of expressing himself which I have tried to capture in this book. Some of the words I have attributed to him are ones that I heard directly from him at functions where he spoke. In particular, his comments about John Kerr were always highly colourful and scathingly uncomplimentary even on his most moderate days.

His debates in Parliament with Jim Killen are a joy to read as they are a combination of eloquence and humour that no one in today's Parliament comes anywhere near emulating, given the now inbred culture that honourable members have of disgustingly hurling abuse at one another.

What I admired most was the warmth of his relationship with his wife, Margaret, whom I met from time to time. It was warmingly awesome in its depth. She was quite a person, tall like him, to the extent that they had no trouble finding one another in crowded rooms. I hold the view that she had the talent and skill to become prime minister in her own right and to survive in the hotbed of politics much longer than Gough. She was the disciplined one in a great partnership.

Malcolm's Double

My contacts with Malcolm Fraser were fewer, mainly brief chats at political functions, but one was unforgettable.

By total accident of seat allocation, I sat next to him on a Trans Australia Airlines flight in a small Fokker Friendship aircraft travelling from Melbourne to Canberra on the very day that he had suddenly resigned as Defence Minister in the Gorton Government. His decision to do so was a decisive act in a series of events that subsequently caused John Gorton to lose his job as Prime Minister to a much lesser person in Billy McMahon. This controversial party room battle greatly accelerated the death throes of a conservative government that had ruled Australia for more than two decades.

I had the window seat, while Fraser occupied the aisle and we chatted occasionally about the state of the nation.

When we arrived at Canberra Airport in that happy era when there was no security, nor any enclosed airport gates, a horde of journalists and photographers ran across the tarmac and waited at the bottom of the steps of the plane, all ready to pounce on Fraser and accuse him of gross treachery.

Fraser, who at the best of times always managed to look like a Laird of the Manor looking with disdain at the peasants, had seen them coming and wore a face which was coldly expressionless. He did not move from his seat until all passengers, except he and I, had deplaned. Then, he quietly asked me if I would mind leaving just ahead of him, noting that we were of similar height and build, sufficient to create a moment of confusion.

I was pleased to cooperate with the great man. It seemed like a pleasant game to play.

The mob surged forward when I appeared at the door, cameras flashing widely as I held out my briefcase and coat to give Malcolm more cover. Capitalising on the moment, Fraser, who was slightly crouching right behind me as I slowly traversed the three short steps to the ground, tried to slip away around the other side of the plane. The media scrum soon realised their mistake and chased him across the tarmac, catching him just before he reached the terminal entrance. I followed and listened in from the sidelines while they gave him a torrid time, which I thought he handled quite well.

It is with more than a little regret that I report that I did not ever find out what happened to those plentiful photographs of me. Surely, they are now a treasure of history somewhere in the national archives.

Confession

You already are already aware that neither the dinner nor the luncheon ever took place.

In doing so, I express the hope that you have decided that, while both occasions are a figment of my imagination, they are quite plausible ones.

However, let me hasten to say that it is known that, on many occasions, the great souls who were the vanguard of Federation met to dine and wine in twos and threes at either the Melbourne Club or the Hotel Windsor to review what they had done and what they were planning to do.

Thus, all that I have done is put them together in the same place for one lengthy and splendid dinner.

The conversations that I have attributed to them are based on events that actually happened over the twelve years of Federation negotiations and during the first decade of the new Parliament where they had to strive diligently to make their Federation work.

As expressed earlier, they are based also around the personalities that are described in the biographies that have been written about them over the past century, making sure that I have not plagiarised any of those accounts.

I have a personal conviction that I have given a fair and balanced account of the epic saga that created a nation.

My decision to write this book as a novel, not a history, is based on my belief that few Australians spend time reading history, but they do read novels based on history.

90% of our population have not the slightest idea of how Australia became a nation, who were its founders and what is in the Constitution they wrote.

This means that it is important to reach as many of them as possible.

So, *Dinner with the Founding Fathers* has not been written for critical appraisal by political, academic and legal elites. It is to be enjoyed by genuine down to earth Aussies who would like to learn a bit about their heritage with a minimum of boredom.

When I began to write it, I debated whether to have five or ten Founders present at the dinner. I was concerned that people may find ten characters too many to relate to.

I started off with the most powerful five – Barton, Deakin, Griffith, Kingston and Forrest – but then decided that it would be an absolute tragedy to leave out Reid who was one of the great characters of Australian history. I also wanted Bird to be there because of his passion for a Preamble to the Constitution. And it really is impossible to leave out Lyne who went within a hair's breadth of becoming the first prime minister and almost caused the date of Federation to be postponed. The same applies to Watson who became the first prime minister in the world to directly represent the working class. Similarly, how could I leave out Fisher who rose from the coal mines of Scotland to join Deakin as the only prime ministers to be elected three times?

So, it became ten, and they are ten great men, giants of the folklore of Australia.

By a stroke of good fortune, they represent all six states, something which is most important in parochial Australia.

This will pose the question in your mind as to why, after choosing to have ten at the anniversary dinner, I chose to have only three at the Centenary Luncheon.

The fact is that there is no need to have more than three.

There were only three dominant players in the coup of 1975 – Whitlam Fraser and Kerr – and as Kerr had passed away, he was an obvious non-attendee.

So, I replaced him with his successor as Governor General – Cowen – who had to sort out the Kerr legacy and bring peace to the Parliament. He was the perfect person to make up the trio as he was by profession an eminent constitutional lawyer.

This brings me to the conclusion of my confession about two functions that really should have been held.

I leave with a fervent hope that those who read these pages will be moved to upgrade their sense of pride of what it really means to be an Australian and determine that the example of the Founding Fathers is a substantial foundation that we can build upon in a significant manner during the 21st century so that it will enhance the quality of life of all those who live here.

Memories

As you have already worked out, I did not ever meet any of the Founding Fathers as I was born exactly 30 years after they achieved their Federation miracle. Every one of them, except Chris Watson, had died by the time I began my life.

History and geography were the only subjects at which I excelled at school, solely due to the fact that I loved reading about both. I absorbed all that I could about Federation, avidly, then and ever since, admiring the Founding Fathers enormously. In truth, I was in awe of their wondrous achievement against all the odds that politics and prejudice can relentlessly throw up.

Being in the habit of visiting Parliament in Canberra, at least twice a year for the past sixty years on behalf of community projects and social policies with which I was involved, I came to understand how hard it is to motivate governments and parliaments to make decisions about even the simplest of things. Thus, it became glaringly obvious to me that all governments are an extraordinary haven of gross inertia. That the Founding Fathers put a new nation together in just twelve years is nothing short of a miracle. I doubt that there will ever be another achievement quite like it.

I have often wondered why no one had ever written an historical novel about the drama that surrounded it all. I have earlier noted that only a few people have written biographies about any of the Founding Fathers, and no one seems to have put together even a documentary that tells the full story.

So, I decided to make an attempt at it myself, and I live in hope that the tale I have written will give thousands of Australians an interesting insight into how their nation was born without having to struggle through reams of legal jargon in any precise legal fashion or having to put up with an immense array of historical trivia.

One of the factors that motivated me to take up my pen was the manner in which the nation celebrated the Centenary of Federation in 2001.

It was necessary for the official organising committee to take paid advertisements on press, radio and television to tell Australians who their first

Prime Minister and Governor General had been and who had been in the First Ministry. They even had to explain that Canberra had not been in existence then and that the first Federal Parliament had met in Melbourne. Polls showed that four out of five Australians had never heard the name Edmund Barton. I saw this as an enormous tragedy.

My distress was soothed somewhat when John Howard included me in the list of people to receive the Centenary Medal. He gave it to me for my service as the proponent of the Inland Railway and so I went with pride to Government House in Brisbane to the reception that the Governor gave in honour of all who received it. The discussion that evening centred on why we were all there and what had been the greatest achievements over the century that had passed.

Howard also invited Helen and me to go to the Centenary Celebrations in Melbourne of the Opening of the First Australian Parliament which had occurred on 1 May, 1901. It was held in the very building where the great event had occurred.

As I sat there that day, I tried to come to terms with the indifference of Australians to our national history and reminded myself that, whenever Americans celebrate independence, they do not have to receive any tuition whatsoever about who George Washington was.

One day, I hope to work out why it is that Australians do not try to generate national fervour. On Australia Day, we honour only the arrival of the first fleet of convicts, never the day when the colonial era ended and a nation was born.

Despite all of these concerns, we can and must find special ways and means to honour those splendid men who had been present at the creation of the Australian nation and, on whose shoulders, lay the burden of that creation.

They were broad shoulders, unbowed by the weight of responsibility, and proudly upright as they walked steadfastly towards 'the light on the hill' and the opportunities.

Everald's Preamble

These words are the opening lines of the Constitution of Australia.

Whereas the people of New South Wales, Victoria, South Australia, Queensland and Tasmania, hereby relying on the blessing of Almighty God, have agreed to unite in one indissoluble federal Commonwealth under the Crown....

Alfred Deakin and Bolton Stafford Bird were of the firm belief that there was a compelling need to upgrade those legalistic words by adding a Preamble to the Constitution which expressed the values by which Australians live. This seemed possible as Almighty God had already been mentioned.

They did not live to see their visions fulfilled, but, for today's Australians, it is never too late to attempt to reach for the stars and create the miracle that will embed it in history.

So, I have made a decision to attempt to revive, a century later, the issue of adding a Preamble to the Constitution so passionately advocated by Deakin and Bird.

I submit these words as a possible basis for community debate.

God is not mentioned, but the reference to him which is already in the opening words of the Constitution will be acceptable to Muslims, Jews and Christians

Almost certainly, greater minds than mine eventually will draft better words than I have recorded below so that they can be placed before the Australian people at a referendum, sooner rather than later.

For better or worse, here it is.

Australia is a democracy founded upon the heritage of indigenous people who were the first to enjoy life on our vast continent and its islands as well as on the traditions of settlers who more recently came from other lands.

Australians are free people who treasure honesty, decency, integrity and justice.

We reject greed in all its forms and we foster a sense of compassionate community which is based on family life and equality of opportunity.

It is our tradition to welcome to our shores migrant people of all cultures, whatever their religious and ethnic backgrounds may be.

We express the hope that they will become responsible citizens who ascribe to the Australian way of living in peace so that all achieve prosperity within a just society.

This includes an unqualified acceptance of our laws and respect for the institutions that administer those laws.

These are based on providing justice for all, particularly our freedom to practice a religion of our choice without ever being subjected to persecution for our beliefs.

However, no laws will ever be passed that are based on the religious beliefs ascribed to any faith or which discriminate against any person by way of their race, gender, disability or sexual preferences.

We live in peace with all who inhabit the world, but we will defend our nation and support others who are denied freedom or suffer oppression.

We regard it as essential that all who have the privilege of living in Australia will affirm under oath their wholehearted acceptance of our Constitution, especially the words contained in this Preamble.

EVERALD COMPTON
APRIL 2020

Constitution

The wording of the original Constitution of Australia which enabled the nation to be founded in 1901 can be found on the website of the Australian Parliament.

It is worth reading.

You will note that it provides for a change to be made to it at any time by conducting a referendum which must be approved by a majority of voters nationally, as well as a majority of voters in a majority of states.

Since the Day of Federation in 1901, there have been 44 proposals to amend the Constitution. They have been voted on in 17 referendums.

Only 8 have been approved.

The dates of the successful referendums, the subjects of each approval and the initiating Prime Ministers were –

1906 – Senate Elections – Deakin
1908 – State Debts – Deakin
1928 – State Debts – Bruce
1946 – Social Services – Chifley
1967 – Aboriginals – Holt
1977 – Senate casual vacancies – Fraser
1977 – Referendums for Territories – Fraser
1977 – Retirement of Judges – Fraser

Those proposals that were defeated at referendums covered subjects that are listed below. Many of them were worthy of approval, but were either badly presented or were destroyed by peripheral issues that were raised by opponents to divert debate into negative territory.

Finance, Legislative Powers (2), Monopolies, Trade and Commerce (2), Corporations, Industrial Relations (2), Trusts, Nationalisation of Monopolies (2), Railway Disputes, Essential Services, Aviation, Marketing (2), Post War Reconstruction, Rents and Prices (2), Communism, Parliament, Incomes, Simultaneous Elections (2), Alterations to Constitution, Terms of Senators, Interchange of Powers, Parliamentary Terms, Fair Elections, Local Government, Rights and Freedoms.

Of these losing referendums, five achieved a majority of votes nationally, but failed to achieve a majority of states. Nine failed by less than 1% of the vote required to attain a majority.

The vote in 1967 to affirm the right of aborigines to vote achieved a positive result of 90.77%, the highest YES vote ever in an Australian Referendum. It was led by Harold Holt and was a huge conscience vote to right a terrible injustice that was a blight on the character of the nation.

The worst defeat was in 1988 when Bob Hawke received only a 30.79% vote to change Rights and Freedoms.

The Prime Minister winning the most referendums was Malcolm Fraser who won three of them in 1977.

The one who suffered the most referendum defeats was Gough Whitlam who lost six mainly due to his presumption that voters would not question his advice.

Looking at the 36 proposals for changes that were lost, another reason for defeat may have simply been a case of voters wanting to tell politicians to leave them alone and stop annoying them with trivia.

It can be accepted as a certainty that there will be more attempts to change elements of the Constitution that clearly need repair.

There are several real possibilities in the short term.

The prime one should be to provide a Preamble to the Constitution that recognises Aborigines as the original occupants of the continent while including a statement of Australian values and ethics (similar to the one I have outlined).

A second will be to enable Australia to become a Republic, finally freeing itself from its colonial chains.

A third will be to make it easier to create many more states and change the powers of those states so as to eliminate the need for local governments. This can be achieved if Australia has 50 states, the figure that the United States of America has had for a long time in effectively governing a similar-sized land mass.

Yet another will be to reduce the size of the Senate, curb its powers and totally reform the manner in which it is elected. A reduction in the number of senators will require a change in the nexus provisions of the Constitution which requires the Senate to be half the size of the House of Representatives. It is currently quite ridiculous as Tasmania has twelve senators, but only five members of the House of Representatives.

At some time in the future, an addition can be made in the Constitution to expand the invitation that exists for New Zealand to unite Australia. This would provide for the inclusion of Papua New Guinea, Vanuatu, Solomon Islands, Fiji, Tonga, Samoa, the Cook Islands and East Timor if they choose to accept. This would create a huge nation in terms of its geography and make it the largest nation on the planet by size of land and sea mass other than Russia.

The combination of all of these will enable Australians to step into the future with confidence as Australia advances to become one of the top ten nations in the world, in quality of life, size of economy and growth of international influence.

Australia's finest and greatest days as a nation lie ahead as we tread a path of enormous opportunity that is there to enjoyed by the valiant, the visionary and the wise.